AMONG THE WALKING WOUNDED

ALSO BY JOHN CONRAD

Scarce Heard Amid the Guns:
An Inside Look at Canadian Peacekeeping

What the Thunder Said:
Reflections of a Canadian Officer in Kandahar

THE WALKING WOUNDED

SOLDIERS, SURVIVAL, AND PTSD

COLONEL JOHN CONRAD

DUNDURN
TORONTO

Cover image: Helmet: istock.com/Steve Zmina
Printer: Webcom

Library and Archives Canada Cataloguing in Publication

Conrad, John D., author
      Among the walking wounded : soldiers, survival, and PTSD / Colonel John Conrad.

Includes bibliographical references.
Issued in print and electronic formats.
ISBN 978-1-4597-3513-2 (softcover).--ISBN 978-1-4597-3514-9 (PDF).--ISBN 978-1-4597-3515-6 (EPUB)

      1. Conrad, John D. 2. Conrad, John D.--Mental health. 3. Post-traumatic stress disorder--Patients--Canada--Biography. 4. Post-traumatic stress disorder. 5. War neuroses--Patients--Canada--Biography. 6. War neuroses. 7. Soldiers--Mental health. I. Title.

RC552.P67C667 2017   616.85'210092   C2017-900159-0
                                                                   C2017-900160-4

1 2 3 4 5   21 20 19 18 17

We acknowledge the support of the **Canada Council for the Arts** and the **Ontario Arts Council** for our publishing program. We also acknowledge the financial support of the **Government of Ontario**, through the **Ontario Book Publishing Tax Credit** and the **Ontario Media Development Corporation**, and the **Government of Canada**.

VISIT US AT

 dundurn.com |  @dundurnpress | dundurnpress | dundurnpress

Dundurn
3 Church Street, Suite 500
Toronto, Ontario, Canada
M5E 1M2

CONTENTS

Acknowledgements   9

Terms and Abbreviations   11

Foreword by Martha Rutherford Conrad   17

Prologue   23

Introduction   25

PART 1: GROUPING   37

Chapter 1   Doppelgänger   39
Chapter 2   Remnants   49
Chapter 3   The Widening Gyre   77
Chapter 4   Andy's Song   102

PART 2: ZEROING   125

Chapter 5   A Funeral for Trooper Caswell   127
Chapter 6   Forward Momentum   156
Chapter 7   The Lonesome Death of Corporal Joshua Wood 165
Chapter 8   The Sun Also Rises   192

Epilogue   214

Notes   225

Image Credits   231

ACKNOWLEDGEMENTS

I want to thank Martha Rutherford Conrad for her support during the writing of the manuscript as well as for her advice and commentary on its early formulation. Thanks as well for the editing of the whole package prior to submission and for writing the foreword for this book on the walking wounded — a foreword that only she could write. Last, but most importantly, thank you, Martha, for your love and patience on this mutual journey.

I am very grateful to my friend Warrant Officer Andy Singh for agreeing to share his story, his early encouragement and support for the project, and for his patient review of early editions of several chapters. Thanks for your friendship, comradeship, and support over the past years.

Thanks as well to Bruce and Susan Wood, parents of Corporal Joshua Wood, who were very charitable with their time, despite the pain associated with covering such difficult ground once again. Joshua's loss is raw and difficult to deal with, so thank you to both of them for their courage in letting me tell a small part of his story and for reviewing the main Joshua Wood chapter. I, too, think often of your son and he will always have a place in my heart and my thoughts.

Thank you to my friend Darcia Arndt, who reviewed the parts of the book that pertained to her husband and our splendid convoy escort, commander Master Corporal Raymond Arndt. It is hard to believe I was so nervous about meeting you all those years ago. Thanks for your friendship and support and for helping us all to remember Ray.

Thanks go out as well to Shona Steven Neufeld of Vancouver, who provided valuable early comments and suggestion on the entire manuscript. Your insightful comments have made this a much better book. I am grateful for your support and friendship.

I want to thank Dr. Cody House of the Edmonton Operational Stress Injury Clinic and also Captain (Retired) Fred Doucette, formerly of the Royal Canadian Regiment. I have only met Fred through his books on PTSD, in which he relates own experiences. The work that Fred has done as a soldier, as a writer, and as a counsellor working inside an OSI clinic in New Brunswick has been extraordinary and is deserving of the highest recognition. Thank you for your service to Canada and to our soldiers, Fred, and for your courage in sharing your story.

Last, but by no means least, I wish to thank the good people of Dundurn for their support and advice on the front end and throughout the editing process of *Among the Walking Wounded:* Kirk Howard, Margaret Bryant, Kathryn Lane, Carrie Gleason, Kendra Martin, Jonathan Schmidt, Cheryl Hawley, and Dominic Farrell.

TERMS AND ABBREVIATIONS

ANA (Afghan National Army)
The main branch of the Afghan Armed Forces.

AO (Area of Operations)
The geographic areas (or portions thereof) assigned to specific land formations and units to conduct military operations.

APC (armoured personnel carrier)
A modified and reinforced combat vehicle that transports soldiers on the battlefield and affords some measure of protection.

ARVN (Army of the Republic of Vietnam)
The army of South Vietnam during the Vietnam War and the involvement of the United States.

AO (assisting officer)
The officer, usually a captain, assigned to assist the family of a fallen soldier. The Assisting Officer will help with myriad details of closure from burial through to settling the military entitlements of the deceased.

Bison (armoured personnel carrier)
The Bison was used heavily during the war in Afghanistan, primarily as a personnel carrier and for medevacs.

Cadpat (Canadian disruptive pattern combat uniform)
The digitized relish-coloured camouflage uniforms worn by Canadian soldiers. *Arid Cadpat* refers to the same uniform but in the brown-and-sand colour for use in desert climates like Southwest Asia.

CANEX (Canadian exchange)
The canteen store of the Canadian Armed Forces.

CanCon (Canadian content)
Most commonly used in reference to the mid-tour entertainment shows put on for deployed Canadian troops.

CFB (Canadian Forces Base)
The major garrison homes of the Canadian Armed Forces in Canada, such as CFB Edmonton (Army), CFB Trenton (Royal Canadian Air Force), or CFB Esquimalt (Navy).

CIDA (Canadian International Development Agency)
The federal agency responsible for strategic investment and economic development, in such a fashion that extends Canadian influence and helps to achieve foreign policy objectives.

CO (commanding officer)
The senior officer of a battalion or military unit. Normally a lieutenant colonel in the Canadian Army, although majors and captains can command smaller units.

CLP (combat logistics patrol)
This is the term for an escorted resupply convoy that was engrained in the doctrine of our U.S. Army allies in 2005. We came to adopt the term for our own Canadian convoys in southern Afghanistan. It suited the aggressive posture we wanted our columns to maintain.

DCO (deputy commanding officer)
The second in command of a military unit. Also known as an executive officer (XO) and by the short form 2IC.

DFAC (Dining Facilities Administration Center)
United States Army term for main dining facility on a base. KAF had numerous DFACs.

DFAIT (Department of Foreign Affairs and International Trade)
The Canadian foreign affairs ministry, now called Global Affairs Canada.

FOB (forward operating base)
A defended post or mini-base that affords a measure of protection to soldiers.

IED (improvised explosive device)
Refers to a wide variety of weapons used by insurgents that employ different combinations of explosive material, as well as detonating systems. Some IEDs are very crude, pressure-detonated devices; others can be remotely detonated with electronics.

ISAF (International Security Assistance Force to Afghanistan)
The NATO military force operating in Afghanistan in 2006. Sanctioned by U.N. Security Council Resolution 1386 on December 20, 2001, ISAF influence was extended in 2006 under the NATO ISAF expansion mandate, which sought to bring the mission in Afghanistan under one organization. Prior to this work, the U.S.-led Operation Enduring Freedom held sway in southern Afghanistan.

KAF (Kandahar Airfield)
The major NATO base in southern Afghanistan. KAF boasted some thirteen thousand soldiers in the 2006 period.

LAV III (light armoured vehicle III)
The LAV III was the principal fighting vehicle of the Canadian task force in 2006. Main armament consists of an M242 Bushmaster 25-millimetre cannon, as well as a coaxial 7.62 machine gun and 76-millimetre smoke grenade launchers.

Medevac (medical evacuation)
The extraction of casualties from the point of injury to a medical facility for treatment, usually by ground or air. (Most medevacs in my experience were by air, which saved many lives.)

NATO (North Atlantic Treaty Organization)
One of Canada's principal international defence commitments. Canada has been a NATO member since the founding of the alliance in 1949.

NCO (non-commissioned officer)
A military officer who does not carry a Queen's commission. The term generally refers to the leadership ranks of master corporal and sergeant in the modern Canadian Army.

Nine-liner
The radio request format used to call for medical evacuation on the battlefield.

NSE (National Support Element)
A well-established NATO term for the unit that provides nationally unique logistics support to a national military contingent. In 2006, the NSE provided close organic support to the Canadian battle group (1 PPCLI) as well as operational theatre level support to all Canadian units in Afghanistan.

OSI (operational stress injury)
Describes persistent psychological difficulties resulting from operational experiences while serving in the Canadian Armed Forces or as a member of the RCMP.

PMQ (private married quarters)
Housing provided to married couples in the services. The housing is usually provided at a competitive rate and in almost all cases is located on defence department real estate in close proximity to the major CFB (base).

PRT (provincial reconstruction team)
A new brand of joint military-civilian unit — such teams were used in the Afghanistan campaign to coordinate the elements of security, governance, and economic development in the provinces of Afghanistan.

PX (post exchange)
The American version of the CANEX. These commissaries come in different sizes and ranges of service depending on the size of the installation or post. The big FOBs in Afghanistan Bagram and Kandahar Airfields had sizeable PX operations.

RCAF (Royal Canadian Air Force)
The air component command of the Canadian Armed Forces.

RC South (Regional Command South)
In 2006, the military formation headquarters commanding Afghanistan's southeastern corner — the provinces of Kandahar, Uruzgan, Zabul, and Helmand. Regional Command South comprised the multinational division, which included the Canadian battle group, logistics battalion, and elements of the brigade headquarters.

Recce
Short-form for "reconnaissance." This crucial military function is conducted at all levels of conflict: operational, tactical, and strategic.

RIP (relief-in-place)
The replacement of an "in place" force with a fresh one. In the context of this book, RIP refers to theatre-wide replacements; however, RIP also can refer to a replacement that takes place during a tactical operation on the battlefield.

RSM (regimental sergeant major)
The senior soldier in an army battalion or unit — usually a chief warrant officer. The role is pivotal for the effective command and good governance of a unit.

SEAD (suppression of enemy air defence)
Protective fire and other measures to protect aircraft from enemy fire.

SVBIED (suicide vehicle-borne IED)
An IED that is delivered to its target by a vehicle.

TIC (troops in contact)
Soldiers are in contact with the enemy (firefight).

VAC (Veterans Affairs Canada)
The Canadian government ministry charged with supporting and delivering key services to Canadian veterans.

FOREWORD

I did not want my husband to write this book. I was tired of him opening a window into our family's private life. I was a reluctant participant in the writing of this book, just as I was initially a reluctant participant in his military life.

I met my husband when I was fifteen. It was young love; we were high-school sweethearts. I was devastated when he joined the army to go to university. In my mind, he had just thrown away all of his potential. We parted ways for many years but then came back together because we were in love and had always been in love.

My love of the army was much slower in blossoming. But eventually I came to love that family — and it truly is a family. Anyone who is in the army knows that it is not only the serving member who joins but also the wife, husband, partner, sons and daughters, fathers and mothers — all are enveloped into the army. It takes an entire family's support and love for their soldier to be a soldier. I have been witness to, as well as the target of, some appalling behaviour by the army. I have also been exposed to incredibly honourable behaviour by the army. The incidents of honourable behaviour greatly outnumber and overshadow the appalling, and my army family has grown to be a great comfort to me over the years.

As John wrote this book, I watched his interactions with the other families who chose to open their doors and their hearts to him for the telling of their stories. Their bravery and their kindness reminded me of all that was good about the army and it brought forward the deep, abiding familial connections that I feel toward my army family. I was wrong about my assumptions when John joined the army, just as I was wrong in my initial reluctance over his writing of this book about PTSD. I understand now that this book sheds a light on a story that needs to be told and that this story should galvanize policy makers to make the changes that need to be made in order to support the army family.

When John deployed to Afghanistan, we had a discussion about relocating our family back to Edmonton to be closer to his home base in the army and its support systems. We were living in an area east of Toronto in which we were the only Regular Force family, and certainly the only family with a member deployed in Afghanistan. We had amazing friends there and we decided that it was best to keep our children with their friends and their support system.

It was an interesting time. It was not our family's first deployment, so we knew about the long absence; but John's deployment to Afghanistan was a new experience for our family, since it involved John's first deployment to a war zone. We understood the dangers and the risks. However, at the time the community we lived in, just as most of the public in Canada, thought it was another peacekeeping mission. John was a member of the first of Canada's active tours in Afghanistan and the caskets had not yet started rolling home down the Highway of Heroes. I understood that they had not yet caught up to the plans of the political masters even as I listened to John having to decide how many flags to order for that deployment — flags for the caskets ... an estimation of our war dead.

My friends certainly attempted to understand and to support me, but they knew nothing of the long, long nights with the devastating feelings rolling around in my gut because I knew he was on a convoy. They knew nothing of hearing on the news that a convoy had been hit and just waiting and waiting and waiting for either the name on the TV, the telephone call about injuries, or the black car driving in the lane. But I know they wanted to understand, and I know that they sensed my loneliness.

I remember a group of wonderful friends who took me out to supper one night. Even now as I type this passage, I cannot recall that evening without crying. I thought it was going to be just an evening out at a restaurant, a welcome respite from single parenthood and dark thoughts. However, when I arrived at the restaurant, I found the wall behind our table was lined with coolers filled with meals that had been pre-cooked for our family. The love that night was overwhelming and comforting, and thoughts of it fill my heart even to this day.

There were other acts of kindness from friends — and there was support from strangers and from the community at large. Such support was endearing and lasting — from the wife of a Second World War veteran who quietly paid for the lunch of our family of six at the local diner to ongoing initiatives like the Coffee for Kandahar campaign that sought to buy Tim Hortons coffee for soldiers serving overseas.

Overlapping these experiences was the behaviour of some local politicians who had the opportunity to translate their support into meaningful policy. A local councillor used to park his truck in front of the museum where I worked. He was one of the first in the community to obtain a yellow magnet in the shape of a ribbon proclaiming support for our army. Every day he would park his truck in front of my workplace and say nothing to me, all the while knowing I was inside and knowing my husband was serving overseas. Then one day he suggested to my management board that a time clock should be installed in the museum and I should be required to clock into and out of work. He was concerned that I was not working my full hours in the office while my husband was away on deployment because he had noticed that my truck was not always parked at the museum when he would park his truck there.

Another time, I was due at a council meeting to present the budget for the museum. There had been a snowstorm overnight and the ground was covered in a deep layer of heavy, wet snow. Despite the fact that I was driving a four-by-four truck, I ended up suspended in the air in my lane, sitting on top of the heavy snow with the tires of the truck not even touching the ground.

I had called the clerk to advise her of my predicament and had been told to hasten along as it was the budget meeting and I had to be there.

So I sweated in the snow in my business suit, and dug with shovel and hands ... and cried as I dug because I had not slept that night at all knowing my husband was once again on a convoy.

I wondered if someone from town hall might send someone to help out. After all, they knew my husband was deployed. Most of them had the yellow magnets on their vehicles and the council had voted to put yellow magnets of support on all of their maintenance and snow-clearing vehicles to show their support for the Canadian Forces. No one showed. Eventually, I made it there, much dishevelled, and presented my plea for funds for the local museum.

Everyone thought it was quite funny. I laughed along with them outwardly, yet felt such sadness inside. It was a lost opportunity to learn and, as public officials, to move their support of the army from the display of a yellow magnet to more meaningful public policy. After all, this community did have a snow-clearing policy in place to assist the vulnerable in the community. To extend that to the very few serving army families in that area would have been such a small gesture for the council, and yet it would have been so meaningful to the families of those serving.

My husband came home and life seemingly went on ... seemingly. The war came home with my husband and it continued to rage inside of him. I was not particularly surprised by this; peacekeeping missions are not exactly peaceful and each time he had come home from a peacekeeping mission before there had been changes in him. But Afghanistan was bigger and sadder and deeper than all that came before. His experiences shaped him, as they do all of us, but the things he brought home this time resided deeply in his mind and in his heart. As he struggled with mental health wounds, our family struggled, our children struggled.

Then came the sad day when we learned of Darryl Caswell's death. By that time, our war dead had made their journey along the Highway of Heroes and the public was now very aware of the dangers in Afghanistan, but it was still shocking for this small community to lose one of their very own.

I had had a package for Darryl sitting on my desk at work. While we had never met Darryl, we knew he was deployed because our army family is small, after all. John was supposed to go over to Afghanistan for a meeting and Darryl's family had asked if he could take a parcel to Darryl. It sat on my desk for two weeks while John's trip stayed up in the air. One day the meeting was on and the next day it was off and then it was on again. Finally, the trip was officially cancelled. I returned the package to Darryl's family so they could send it on through the military mail system.

For a while afterward, Darryl disappeared from my thoughts, until one morning when news of his death came across the airwaves. I always listened closely for the name. I immediately called the town hall to let them know that the soldier was from our community. I recommended that the flag be lowered … immediately. They weren't sure if they could do that. They did not know who had the authority to make that decision. I remember being told, "I don't know how to make this happen." I responded that I was pretty sure that all they had to do was get the little key to unlock the compartment on the flag pole and then just pull down on the little rope inside the flagpole. They were not amused; I was not amused that public policy once again trumped overt support.

On the day of the funeral, I did not want to go. It was hard to be there with so many memories — memories of our many tours and then living with their aftereffects. Perhaps there was even a bit of survivor's guilt. There was certainly the fear of knowing that my husband still served and could be sent anywhere based on political decisions. I struggle with these occasions, just as I struggle with Remembrance Day every year. But as a fellow soldier, my husband especially needed to be there for Darryl. He told me that he needed me to be there with him.

The pain I felt in my heart for the family that day remains, but the most compelling memory for me from that day was when the army rolled in on their buses. We had been living in this community as one of the very few army families for several years by this time. I had not realized how alone I felt until the soldiers came pouring off the buses and encircled us. My husband was standing there in uniform and they naturally migrated to us and enveloped us in their warm embrace. Nobody asked any questions. I really do not remember people even talking. There was no need. I stood there with my army family in their warm comfort, knowing that they were with me and I was with them and I was so very proud to be with them. We swept into the church together and sat as a group through the service and then swept out of the church together as well. When they boarded the buses and left, I missed them immediately as one would miss any family member, but I held the comfort of their recent presence near to my heart … until a person who worked at the town hall wandered over and wondered why I had ended up sitting on the wrong side of the church. After all, this person said, you are not in the army.

I believe everyone has a message and everyone can be heard, no matter how small that voice. This book is my husband's message, and it is my hope that with this book people in positions of influence and with the ability to affect and mould public opinion and policy will do more than simply display symbols of support and send out short sound bites on social media. It is my hope that they will work to enact legislation that actively supports our soldiers with mental health injuries and that recognizes the needs of their families.

The army knows its family. It knows its mothers, fathers, wives, sons, and daughters. It is time for the politicians to recognize that supporting a soldier means supporting them, as well as their families, before and during deployment, and after they return home as well. If they want to send our soldiers to war, then they need to pay the price, the full price, just as our soldiers pay the price with their lives and their mental and physical injuries. Don't make them beg at the well, because they won't. They will quietly carry on as they always do and then sometimes they will quietly say goodbye.

Martha Rutherford Conrad

PROLOGUE

MAY 20, 2011

Toronto's workforce is fed by an ever-growing number of feeder communities. Nearly two million workers make the trip daily into the megacity to earn a living and the lucky ones tend to use the large GO train rail system that lies like a spider web overtop of the GTA, radiating out in all directions. I did the Toronto commute for five years after Kandahar. It is a hard operation, a job within a job. Weekends are highly prized by the Greater Toronto Area workforce, especially long weekends and especially this one. The long steel chain of white and green loiters on the rails in Union Station while the growing throng packs into it. Standing passengers abound in the stairwell to the second deck and in the aisles, the seats long since gone to the swift. Today, however, despite the crowding, there are happy faces everywhere. It has been a long hot week and anticipation for the first and very popular holiday weekend in Canada has peaked. Anyone lucky enough to have a seat is already nodding off. Shopping bags and briefcases slip from fingers and ease to the floor.

The train finally edges out of Union Station with a thousand commuters onboard bound for the outlying bedroom communities between

Toronto and Barrie. The run north is as straight as an arrow until it dips east at Aurora. Stop after stop, tired commuters stumble off eager to unpack their long weekend plans. By the time the train leaves King City, thirty minutes later, there are empty seats with only five more stops to go. At ten minutes after five the train suddenly comes to an abrupt halt well short of the Newmarket GO Station. There is no electronic voice announcing this stop.

There is a problem.

"Oh shit," a cry of despair emerges.

The minutes march past but the passenger cars remain still. Most passengers are fully awake. Besides, it's too hot to stay comfortable. Up and down the cars, some eight hundred stranded commuters check cell phones and watches. Impatience swells among them.

I just want to get home, for Christ's sake.

Whispers pass snaking down the aisle. "There has been an accident. A young man has been killed."

"Probably a suicide."

"Probably."

"That's awful. Surely not."

"Yeah. Hopefully just an accident."

After what seems like an eternity, buses appear, which spawns a collective groan from the hundreds of stranded passengers who have their worst fears confirmed: the train is out of service. Some people are angry; many are merely resigned. A lot are both. Everyone begins to file off the train. The train is not going to move for a long while, not until a full investigation has been completed. "Yeah. Hopefully just an accident."

It was no accident.

INTRODUCTION

The ranks opened covertly to avoid the corpse. The invulnerable dead man forced a way for himself. The youth looked keenly at the ashen face. The wind raised the tawny beard. It moved as if a hand were stroking it. He vaguely desired to walk around and around the body and stare; the impulse of the living to try and read in dead eyes the answer to the Question.

— Stephen Crane, *The Red Badge of Courage*

It upsets me that I do not even know their names. Canadian soldiers. No matter what form the dream takes, I can never recall who they were. I often wonder about that. Shouldn't I at least know who they were? I wonder too where they are today. Do they think about that far-away afternoon west of Kandahar as often as I do? A suicide attack has killed some of us and brought our column to a halt. Do they see our stricken convoy in the same near-perfect focus — a collection of discrete images rather than a fluid memory?

One of the nameless troops was a young woman, a medic. I can conjure her up perfectly and recall how slight she was inside the body armour and webbing. How her Kevlar helmet defied tightening and remained tilted at a sharp angle. She could not have been more than twenty years old, too young and too innocent to be involved with the bloody work that closed us in. This young soldier went about her task with efficiency, delicately exploring the wounds of our comrade, then checking for a pulse as lightly as if she were selecting an egg from a nesting box. The movement of her hands was deliberate yet infused with compassion. She gave a slight shake of her head, causing her helmet to wobble gently. Corporal Gomez was dead. This triage pantomime was out of step with the swirling chaos of choking dust and gunpowder around us.

"Let's lift him out," she instructed.

Spoken words came to us, as if down a long corridor; directions for the rest of us gathered clumsily around our dead. Again her instructions were firm and succinct — but never cold. Instead, there was a deep humanity in her language. I have the out-of-place notion that this is how angels behave. This is how all mankind should behave. There were two other soldiers with us. They were not medical corps; they resist full recollection, and most of the details of their faces are lost.

The pair wades into my thoughts as effortlessly as they did that day in July 2006. Eyes as round as pie plates, groping for instructions in the moment. Purpose-bent they forever remain. We are all hanging on every word the angel-medic gives us.

Shadows, Princess Patricia's Canadian Light Infantry (PPCLI) soldiers.

A second explosion erupted. Another suicide bomber. The second bomber was on foot. Ball bearings and metal bits from his mid-section ripped through the air, killing several innocent bystanders. Seconds turned into hours. The air was heavy. All the Canadians up and down the column hit the deck. There was blood on the highway, on the sides of white pickups, and on our brown Cadpat uniforms. There was blood in the air. A whole new stack of images runs its course in my mind.

In Kandahar, with one startling exception, I never had dreams — certainly none that I could reclaim after waking. Since my return to Canada in the fall of 2006, I dream all the time. My mind is alive with them. I have an enhanced capacity for the most vivid of nightmares. The human brain has a safety setting, a surge switch that will shield it from certain matters when you are engaged in them.[1] The workings of the brain will insulate you so you can carry on, but it will never let you completely forget. That is the deal: you get to keep moving and complete tactical tasks; however, you cannot ever un-see what you have seen.

For many of our soldiers, wars never really end. I am visited frequently in my dreams by the angel medic and this convoy ambush. A number of times over the years I have stolen glimpses of my angel medic at events, always on the margins. I have seen her in the edges of a thousand dreams; sometimes only the entwined serpent of her cap badge is recognizable. Sometimes it is her eyes, calm but arresting. Was that her on the periphery of Trooper Darryl Caswell's funeral service? Could that have been the angel medic leaving the Operational Stress Injury Clinic (OSIC) just ahead of me? She remains deeply imprinted on my subconscious.

During the worst years of my post-traumatic stress disorder (PTSD), I would find morning arrived and I would be exhausted with a few fragments of sleep. I would go about the workday in a quasi-daze. What energy I had was devoted to looking outwardly normal while my mind worked to process the endless slides of memory and the questions they inspired. What corner of Canada did these soldiers of mine return to after their tours? Will I see them again? When I have breathed my last breath, will the medic reappear from backstage and place those deliberate, compassionate fingers on my pulse and declare the race finally run? How are they doing today? Are their days and dreams like mine?

It bothers me that despite all of this frantic recollection I cannot recall the names of these soldiers. And yet this is quite typical for those who suffer with PTSD. The details get away from you. The internal landscape of the ailment is like a vast desert. The flat expanse of sand is dotted with numerous little oases of vivid, living-colour memories; these are divided, however, by wide tracts of memory loss, and by increased levels of paranoia and insecurity.

PTSD for soldiers has existed since the dawn of conflict and has had many faces prior to earning its current label in the early 1980s.

According to a report available from Veterans Affairs Canada (VAC), PTSD is defined as

> a psychological response to the experience of intense traumatic events, particularly those that threaten life. It can affect people of any age, culture or gender. Although we have started to hear a lot more about it in recent years, the condition has been known to exist at least since the times of ancient Greece and has been called by many different names. In the American Civil War it was referred to as "soldier's heart," in the First World War it was called "shell shock" and in the Second World War it was known as "war neurosis." Many soldiers were labelled as having "combat fatigue" when experiencing symptoms associated with PTSD during combat. In the Vietnam War this became known as a "combat stress reaction." Some of these people continued on to develop what became known in 1980 as Post-Traumatic Stress Disorder.[2]

There is an understated — and to my mind an unavoidable — cost for the treatment and support of thousands of veterans of Canada's wars and their families that needs to be better understood; it is crucial that we make informed choices when we send our men and women into harm's way. We also need to bear the cost of their wounds upon return. In the current situation, where the men and women of our military are sent to advance our foreign policy objectives, all of us need to know the true impacts of the decision. There is an old expression that the navy belongs to the king but the army belongs to the people. Today, Canadians do indeed own the entirety of the Canadian Armed Forces, including the field army, and they have every right to know about the full psychological cost of the army's use. The voting public ultimately decides how their military will be used. In a similar vein, the public has a say in the treatment of the veteran. And they have every right to know how shabbily a veteran can be treated by the current cabal at Veterans Affairs Canada. The Canadian government, through successive administrations, has placed little emphasis on the well-being of veterans. We should hold our government to account. The army — successes, failures, warts and all — is *of* the people. It belongs to all Canadians.

For the longest time after Kandahar, I could not accept that I was unwell. Part of it was embarrassment and part of it was denial. I was finally diagnosed with PTSD in 2011, five years after my tour in Afghanistan ended. I was pushed into a military clinic by a combination of my wife's frustration and a friend I found in the Reserves. Early on, I could not see the wound, and then, once I caught a glimpse of it, I would not readily accept it. I was concerned about the stigma and about being branded as a malingerer, especially as a senior logistics officer.[3]

I had many thoughts of ending my own life but I never fully subscribed to them. Something inside told me that I could still get my act together, that there was another way. Initially, I thought running away from the Regular Force was the only tonic required. As I kept running and becoming more unstable, however, I had to admit to myself that proximity to the full-time army was not the problem. The problem was me. I was unwell. I could not control my emotions, whether it was spontaneous crying or an unquenchable rage. A deep edgeless depression was upon me constantly. I found solace in alcohol. I noticed that hard-liquor bottles that had followed us on numerous postings across Canada over the years had started to empty at an alarming new rate. I would quickly replace them with others so my wife would not notice. It was much easier to self-medicate and adopt the view: *I can live this down.*

For many of our soldiers, the "universality of service" principle serves as one of the major reasons for avoiding addressing PTSD. The military strongly upholds the principle that a soldier must be physically and mentally able to deploy anywhere in the world with only minimal medical support. If a soldier cannot meet the requirements they must undergo a review of their medical state before a Career Review Board, and in many cases this means facing the reality that they could be chucked from the armed forces. The principle has been reaffirmed recently, even with high numbers of Afghanistan casualties. The fear of many soldiers is that if their mental wound is discovered they will be in violation of the universality-of-service principle and be out the door as a result. They wonder how they will pay a mortgage and feed a family. They may be two or three years from earning their pension. The support offered by Veterans Affairs is surprisingly not coordinated with that offered by the Canadian Armed Forces. Any financial support from VAC is well camouflaged by administrative barriers and outdated practices that ensure support is slow to reach a former soldier. Even worse than all of these practical considerations favouring non-disclosure is the fear of being excluded from the tribe. Many soldiers would do anything to stay with the service, a lifestyle that cannot be replicated — anywhere. It is a far better course of action to live it down.

I lived for four years with a thickening bundle of symptoms before I sought help. Even when I was diagnosed in 2011, it came as a shock. I had not recognized it. Of course, the disorder takes on so many forms. People easily forget that a large component of PTSD includes the healthy parts of the mind as well. The wound grafts so seamlessly to one's essence that self-detection is extremely difficult. We need the feedback of others to detect it and we owe this same kind of feedback to our fellow soldiers and veterans.

Whatever form the wound takes, PTSD arises from a set of external circumstances. As a result, this account must be understood within the historical context of my last operational tour in Kandahar in 2006 as a battalion commander. As we move further away from our Afghanistan experience, history will show that the character of the Canadian contribution changed dramatically after early 2007. The war in 2006 was uniquely wide in its scope. It was the most dangerous year to be a Canadian soldier in Afghanistan by the numbers, with thirty-two soldiers killed and 180 wounded.[4] In the early going, Canada's ground responsibility included all of Kandahar Province (some 225,000 square kilometres) at a time when the Taliban were gathering for a conventional-style comeback, a large offensive contrived by their leadership across the Pakistan border in Quetta. The whole idea in 2006 was to relieve the beleaguered United States Army. Having a Canadian contribution in Kandahar would lighten the load of our American allies who were also still heavily engaged in Iraq. The other intent was to bring all of Afghanistan under one strategic lead instead of two. NATO's International Security Assistance Force

(ISAF) mission only held sway in the north, and the United States–led Operation Enduring Freedom called the shots in the south. Under the auspices of ISAF expansion, Regional Command South, the bottom-right corner of Afghanistan, was to come under NATO command on July 31, 2006. Canada would play a large part in delivering this third phase of ISAF expansion — no small strategic feat.

As the war moved ahead from the winter of 2007, however, the focus of the Canadian Task Force became increasingly smaller, reducing with the NATO surge and the return of the Americans in 2010 to the point in which just one tactical district of Kandahar Province remained a Canadian responsibility. This reduction in responsibility corresponded to a sharp decline in combat fatalities. Between January 2011 and April 2014, only two soldiers were killed in combat in Afghanistan.[5] The magnitude of the task facing the Canadian Forces in the summer of 2006 was such that it posed a significant challenge to the battle groups of the period (1 PPCLI and 1 RCR) and my tiny logistics unit, the National Support Element.[6] We were one of a handful of nations that came forward with boots on the ground in support of the ISAF expansion into southern Afghanistan. It was the first planned combat mission for Canada since the end of the Korean War in 1953. The potential lessons of our first rotation of Canadians at the tip of the spear were plentiful. Conditions were ripe with such a large battlefield and so few combat forces for mental health casualties.

Setting aside historical context, the balance of this narrative describes PTSD from a number of perspectives. I share my own experiences, as well as those of soldiers I have known who also suffered and agreed to share their respective journeys. It was a confusing period in my life that can be described but is harder to explain; a period of constant anger that drove me to quit my job and drop out of the Regular Force to find solace with Reserve soldiers. When I look back on the period of untreated PTSD symptoms I am filled with embarrassment and regret. I see a wasteland of emotional carnage. Despite the wreckage, it was also a period in which I met some of our finest soldiers — each of whom contributed to my journey. You will meet Sergeant Andy Singh and Corporal Joshua Wood in these pages. In getting to know these excellent soldiers I learned a lot about the workings of modern warfare on the mind. In considering their stories, I could see my own challenges and experiences mirrored back to me. You will also meet Trooper Darryl Caswell of the Royal Canadian Dragoons, a soldier I came to know only after his death in Kandahar in 2007. Our stories shine a light both on the internal dynamics of PTSD and on how the disorder can characterize itself. In this vein, I hope the account provides some strength for others. I also hope the description can provide some measure of understanding for the men and women who love and suffer along with these walking wounded: their families, co-workers, and employers. PTSD is very unkind to loved ones and it furnishes deep impacts that will likely remain misunderstood and unacknowledged by the government of Canada and unaddressed by the military elite. Caring for the walking wounded and their families is expensive.

My own muddled journey follows my descent from being a senior army leader in Kandahar and very much on the inside of things to being on the outside, feeling attacked at every corner by those I once trusted. It was a strange time to be wounded because the war was not yet recognized by the entire institution in 2006–2007.[7] It takes time to immerse your body in a cold lake. Year by year, rotation by rotation, the Canadian Armed Forces slowly became acclimatized to the war that ensnared its soldiers. This acclimatization period made for trying times for members of the military at home. There were those who had seen the beast of a full-on counter insurgency and those who served at home unmolested by the tendrils of war working together, both side by side but using yesterday's rules. Against this backdrop of an army acclimating to modern warfare I bumbled ahead and tried to return to normalcy in Canada. I was numb and immobilized with an outrageous internal anger that grew like a cancer over the months.

Shortly after my tour in Kandahar, I resigned from the Regular Force and joined the Army Reserves — Canada's part-time soldiers. I did this because I needed distance from the full-time army but I could not bring myself to the point of a complete goodbye. As I began to recover my mental health in the Reserves I slowly came to appreciate two things: how ill I actually was and how little I really knew about part-time soldiers. I was amazed by how poorly the Reserve community is understood by the Regular Force.[8] In my slide away from the Regulars I got to appreciate first-hand how this ignorance added to my own PTSD struggles and the psychological suffering of the Reserve community. The Canadian Army Reserves are a national treasure that delivers a product in Canada far out of proportion to investment, attention, and reasonable expectation — a force that strengthens our country in a hundred impactful ways despite its relationship with the Regulars.

There is much for our military to absorb from the war in Afghanistan and the moral corrosion of PTSD. We always took sterling care of our men and women killed in theatre. Determined effort — quite appropriately — went into taking care of the fallen and their families from day one. However, adjustments and support for our walking wounded and mental health injuries in particular were unpacked very slowly. In an interview with *Globe and Mail* reporter Renata D'Aliesio, career army veteran Darrell McMullin explained:

> We spend a fortune training these soldiers to go over, and then we won't spend the money on them when they come back.... There has to be more money for the medical treatment when they come home. You have to be willing to put as much money into fixing them as you put into breaking them.[9]

At the core of the issue is an unspoken bias among our tribe, a spectre that whispers to our collective conscience and insinuates that wounds of the mind are not real, not really. There is a belief that these so-called disorders can be quelled with guts and resolve. I often wonder how many of the army's mental health wounds could be detected and addressed if we actually went beyond the simple question "How are you?" There is a viewpoint that still ardently believes that PTSD is all bullshit; that the whole army is given over to a bunch of babies and "softies." It is a position of absolute ignorance and it grinds against any institutional progress. The prejudice silently works against healing. PTSD-wounded are not "softies." They are not inept or weak — characteristics that the stigma feeds. These men and women are some of our finest soldiers; wounded but recoverable. Many of them, in fact, recover to redeploy on operations or to enjoy full civilian careers. We need to advocate for men and women with mental health wounds and for their families and caregivers. We believe whole-heartedly in the electron but as a society we accept so very little about wounds to the mind. In his book about PTSD titled *Better Off Dead*, veteran Fred Doucette notes the following exchange from a senior non-commissioned member: "When he raised the subject of PTSD with a captain in his unit, the captain commented, This is a bunch of bullshit. These guys are assholes. They are out there screwing the system and they have civilian jobs."[10]

The stigma of PTSD still exists in our society and the Canadian Armed Forces. However, the stories of the walking wounded get lost all too easily behind the television smiles and current habits of too many of our politicians. The contemporary political approach is to very quickly publish a thick deck of PowerPoint slides and declare early victory on things. Get the press release together, then find some "announceables" that a politician can let fly in front of a camera and some key media response lines prepared to support the PowerPoint deck. Take forty seconds to Twitter the hell out of it to show how pro-active you are. We live in an age of rhetorical leadership. Institutional problems such as post-deployment care of our soldiers and veterans cannot be solved in one "great" meeting, or in a flurry of Twitter outbursts from a Cabinet minister.

Meaningful change will require a fundamental cultural shift in the federal government with respect to mental health injuries. Very little time these days is spent on actually thinking about problems and attacking them in a meaningful way. It would have taken years of commitment to solidify the gains for which we paid so dearly in Afghanistan. Similarly, it will take some time before we have tackled the support challenge posed by a generation of soldiers who served in the most recent war in Afghanistan. In approaching this issue, we will have to decide for ourselves what kind of Canada we want to be. Are we a country that is only PowerPoint-deep? Are we a country that only serves up a thin gruel of rhetoric in the treatment of our veterans? Or a country that actually takes care of them? We are certainly a long way from the latter at present. The public has every right to challenge this and to demand complete answers and updates on the care afforded to their soldiers: their sons and daughters.

Finally, I hope you will not find this to be a dreary or depressing story, nor an "angry" book. I have no interest in projecting an image of self-pity or futility, nor of trashing one of our finest institutions. In my case, I have been helped by some pretty incredible individuals, friends, my family, as well as caring and dedicated professionals at the Operational Stress Injury Clinic. For the PTSD wounded, there are good days and bad, as well as the constant work to contain and diffuse it. I know, intellectually at least, that I am not lost. Through arrogance (and ignorance), I made things harder for myself than they had to be. I love the Canadian Armed Forces and I served with PTSD in the Canadian Army Reserve right up to 2017. Moreover, I am proud of the work accomplished by our armed forces and our nation in Kandahar. My point of contention is that we have to see the job all the way through and that means taking care of our soldiers and veterans who were wounded. We have not solved the support problem PTSD poses to our military and to our veterans, and we need to stop congratulating ourselves as if we have.

Current statistics in Canada suggest that one in five Canadians will suffer from mental illness each year — a full 20 percent of us. Mental wellness is something we all need to concern ourselves with, regardless of station, race, gender, or education. We all fight our personal battles daily, regardless of our chosen path. It is part of the human condition that binds us together. My intent here is to shine a light on mental health injuries and the PTSD fight as it affects the men and women I know and love best so their paths to better health might be shorter.

"You see all these fucking whiners now claiming to have PTSD," I remember a civilian colleague of mine almost snarling during a coffee-break conversation. He also had served in the Canadian infantry for many years before returning to civilian life, "It's all a bunch of bull. What's the issue? We never had this in my day. Goddamn sissies and malingerers."

"Uh, yes. Okay," I mutter, looking down at the grass. We had been having a good conversation about the war in Afghanistan and Canada's current challenges. I had been on the verge of telling him about my dreams and anxiety. Inches away from exposing myself as one of "them."[11]

GROUPING

The theory of the grouping is a subject that must be thoroughly understood by the [shooting] coach. The theory establishes that a series of not less than three shots fired from a rifle at the same point of aim, do seldom, if ever, pass through the same hole in the target. The pattern produced on the target is known as a grouping.... Finally, a soldier's grouping is a measure of his shooting ability.

— "Shoot to Live," Canadian Army Training Authority

The Second Coming

Turning and turning in the widening gyre
The falcon cannot hear the falconer;
Things fall apart; the centre cannot hold;
Mere anarchy is loosed upon the world,
The blood-dimmed tide is loosed, and everywhere
The ceremony of innocence is drowned;
The best lack all conviction, while the worst
Are full of passionate intensity.

Surely some revelation is at hand;
Surely the Second Coming is at hand.
The Second Coming! Hardly are those words out
When a vast image out of Spiritus Mundi
Troubles my sight: a waste of desert sand;
A shape with lion body and the head of a man,
A gaze blank and pitiless as the sun,
Is moving its slow thighs, while all about it
Wind shadows of the indignant desert birds.

The darkness drops again but now I know
That twenty centuries of stony sleep
Were vexed to nightmare by a rocking cradle,
And what rough beast, its hour come round at last,
Slouches towards Bethlehem to be born?

— William Butler Yeats

CHAPTER 1:
DOPPELGÄNGER

In Freudian psychoanalysis, the doppelgänger is often viewed as an aspect of an individual's self that he or she is struggling to control. The double usually has both similar and opposing characteristics to the original. In other words, the double will be recognizable as the individual, but will act differently, often in an extreme manner. Often, the repressed aspect of the psyche that the double represents must be confronted and ultimately defeated in order for it to go away.

— "What Is a Doppelgänger?" from the WiseGeek website

Kandahar's irony should not be lost on us. From the outset, it was always a war of the mind. After all, what is a good counter insurgency struggle without a play for the hearts and minds of a ravaged population? Without the drive to instill a belief across the land that things are improving? That the Western support that the Afghan government signed up for is making matters better for their children, providing better opportunities for work, providing education, and rule of law? We competed hard for Kandahar's population in the opening frame. All of these moral objectives we pushed for in Afghanistan. For a while

— especially early on — we even believed them ourselves. The problem any army faces in counter-insurgency is one of time. Time's passage works against the interloper.

Tick, tick, tick, tick, tick …

There is a tight window of opportunity for success in counter-insurgency and it always snaps shut against an incoherent approach. The Russians knew that. They learned that lesson on the same battlefields in the eighties. The other factor working against our campaign was inconsistency in approach. Different allies tackled the same set of problems in different ways. Nowhere was inconsistency more evident than in the fielding of the many provincial reconstruction teams in Afghanistan.

Nobody likes to hear that our approach in Afghanistan had a retro feel; that it was not that much different from that of the 40th Army of the Soviet Union over two decades before. However, if you look at the two stanzas in Afghanistan's history analytically, there are haunting similarities between Canada's approach as a member of a Western coalition in 2006 and the Red Army's during the Soviet War in Afghanistan from 1979 to 1989. Afghanistan's capital city was captured in the opening salvo of the Russian invasion. A Soviet-friendly puppet was installed to govern from Kabul and the die was cast. The next ten years of the Soviet Union's efforts pushed to extend the authority of the Kabul government to other corners of the country. It failed — spectacularly. The situation for Canada and NATO was not all that different in the recent Afghan War. The government of President Hamid Karzai once in place was strong in Kabul but the challenge remained the same — extending the Karzai government's authority to the far-flung corners of the country, across its different tribes, languages, and habits. What was markedly different in our time was the use of an unusual combined military and civilian unit known as the Provincial Reconstruction Team (PRT). When you boiled down the elements of our campaign, the combined civil and military approach embodied in the concept of the PRT was most of what separated the NATO plan for Afghanistan in 2006 from that of the Soviet Union in 1979.

I was present for the opening of the first Canadian PRT. We had taken over our very own PRT in southern Afghanistan relieving the Americans on August 16, 2005. But it was not my tour; not yet. We were in Kandahar that August on what was being called a strategic reconnaissance; in other words, a chance for Brigadier General David Fraser and his key officers to get a feel for the theatre and what would be needed for the imminent combat mission in the spring of 2006.

I can recall that change of command ceremony at the Kandahar PRT so clearly in my mind's eye even though it was over a decade ago. I wanted to preserve it. I recognized the historical convergence of the ceremony. It was a tactical moment fused with strategic significance. I watched along with city officials, NGOs, and allies with a sense of pride as the stars and stripes of our ally came down and the maple leaf of our country snapped crisply to attention over Camp Nathan Smith. The sinews of the Canadian campaign were unlike any other military mission before. The "whole of government" approach being extolled by Prime Minister Stephen Harper would entail efforts from the Department of Foreign Affairs and International Trade, the Canadian Investment and Development Agency, and the Canadian Forces. The "whole of government" approach referred to what was to be full inter-departmental co-operation of the Canadian government on the Afghan campaign — a joint effort defined by heightened integration that would see growth in Afghanistan in three key areas: defence, diplomacy, and development.

The timing of our arrival in 2005 had put Colonel Steven Bowes, the officer commanding Canada's initial unit in Kandahar, in a bad mood. Frustrated that the reconnaissance was occurring right on top of the assumption of command for the PRT, Bowes greeted us curtly and made it clear to Fraser that he was not happy: the "recce" could not have come at a worse time. Operations in theatres of war will work your mind in different ways, and friction on the battlefield between friends and neighbours is commonplace. Fraser and Bowes worked things out as best they could; the rest of us pretended not to notice.

Kandahar is a very off-putting place to be made unwelcome.

The soldier bursts out of the cottage-sized dwelling that was being used as a trumped-up briefing room by Colonel Bowes and his team on Camp Nathan Smith. We were headed into the small structure for an orientation briefing on this brand new Canadian PRT in Kandahar City. The soldier — a staff major — was agitated. His fists were clenched and he pounded the smooth adobe wall of the building, all the while looking up at the sky like it had all the answers. I was speechless. He just kept pounding on the baked-mud walls with his fists; his knuckles were skinned white and speckles of blood flecked the wall. I could not make out his mutterings; he was talking to himself; he was angry, however — that much I could tell. At first I thought he was upset at us, the interlopers here with General Fraser, upsetting the plans of the day inside an institution that worships the selection and maintenance of the aim. My next thought was, no, this is not about us.

Again and again the fists pounded the hard mud; more flecks of blood on the wall. We slipped into the briefing area one by one. We tried hard not to notice. He seemed oblivious to our presence and just kept muttering and pounding his fists. I never found out why he was so charged up. It was never explained — a crystal waypoint in a long hall of war memories. Only much later did I realize that externalization of turmoil had been a sign.

Your turn is coming.

Later that evening after we returned to the large airbase I met another Canadian soldier. He was stumbling more than walking across the compound. There was no mistaking the tight face of fear of this soldier on KAF. I waved at him and slowed my pace, stopping for a chat.

"Hi there. How is it going?"

"It goes, sir." After a long pause. "You're part of the Strat Recce, right?" he asked.

"Yes, that's correct. Out of Edmonton. Trying to learn the ropes here. You guys are doing great stuff."

"Sure," he replied, without inflection. A soft monosyllable that came across more like "fuck it." I felt a bit idiotic for my comment. I had not earned the right to bother the man. I am not yet of this place. I will be back in the other world by early next week.

"Everything okay?"

"Yeah. Had a close one earlier today. Just a few minutes sooner it would have been us." The young soldier was thoroughly exhausted. His rifle was slung loosely over his shoulder and it threatened to pull him over at any moment. He was truly running on vapour. Just maintaining a standing position seemed to absorb every ounce of strength he possessed.

It's dangerous here, his tired eyes told me.

At that point I had twenty-three years of service and two overseas tours and I had never met a Canadian soldier like that. I had seen the horribly disfigured and the dead in Cambodia. I had felt the hair stand up on the back of my neck in the Choeung Ek Killing Fields and had seen a freshly filled Balkan graveyard where every gravestone brandished the same date of death. I had never seen one of our own soldiers with a look like the one on this face; a vacuous, thousand-mile quality of a soldier worn down to the nibs. At forty-two years old, with over half of my life in the army, I realized my education in warfare was only just beginning.

It's dangerous here.

The PRTs were a mixing bowl of government departments such as foreign affairs, agriculture, and transportation. The very first PRT opened in Gardez in the Paktia Province of Afghanistan in January 2003. They also folded in development agencies and NGOs. The intent was for these PRTs to serve as military touchstones that would be secure sites but also dynamic portals to energize Afghanistan's economy and governance inside the various provinces. They were a good idea conceived by U.S. Army Lieutenant-General David Barno. Unfortunately, they were deployed in a very inconsistent fashion. Our allies staffed the various PRTs across Afghanistan. They all had slightly different priorities and separate interpretations of how to implement these crucial development portals — including the U.S. Marines in Zabul Province, who ran a very tight ship. I remember David Fraser nodding his head a lot as we were briefed and toured about the Zabul position by the Marines in command. General Fraser clearly liked the direct linkage of the PRT to the fighting unit. I think this model, which worked well in the sparsely populated province of Zabul, made a deep impression on my superior. It undoubtedly drove some of his thinking for the command relationship of the Canadian PRT in Kandahar City.

A reputed fourth-century B.C. Afghan fort photographed from inside the compound of the Zabul Provincial Reconstruction Team (PRT) in 2005. The Zabul PRT was commanded by the U.S. Marine Corps at that time and its organization made a good impression on the Canadians who had just taken command of the Kandahar PRT further south in August.

The Canadian campaign in Afghanistan always hinged on the success of the PRT and its ability to work with Afghanistan's Kabul-based government and breathe life into the fragile economy and governance of the Islamic Republic of Afghanistan. As soldiers, we were neck-deep in a war where the military was no longer the decisive component for victory. Bullets and brute force were important ingredients but not the decisive ones. To be ultimately successful, the sense that things were truly improving in Afghanistan had to trump the presence of our security forces. In the early going the Canadian Task Force placed the PRT directly under command of the battle group as a subordinate unit. The balancing act attempted between economic development and the security function was too difficult. Our PRT made very limited inroads in my time. Part of this was no doubt attributable to the loss of Glyn Berry, a diplomat with the Department of Foreign Affairs and International Trade (DFAIT) who had been killed by an explosive device on a treacherous stretch of roadway leading into Kandahar City known as IED Alley. This was in January 2006, a month before our arrival. It would be well into the winter of 2007, the following year, when the PRT would finally begin to get its feet underneath it. I had opportunity to express my opinion on this to General Fraser on a couple of occasions overseas in 2005 as we prepared for the mission. Although he liked me, and respected my abilities as his logistics commander, he made it clear that he wanted no input from his logistician on the sinews of the campaign.

"You stick to keeping us in beans and bullets, John." The comment was delivered with a kind-hearted smile. It was intended as an infantry compliment but it was also a firm warning to shut up.

Leave the campaign design to the Big Boys.

I kept my notions to myself but I never stopped thinking about the PRT. I wondered if this was not the beginning of where we slipped strategically. Notwithstanding military bluster and bravado, a counter-insurgency requires the steady hand of a surgeon. These sorts of wars cannot be won with an incoherent strategy. After ten years in Afghanistan, are we any better at helping the Afghans? Each Canadian rotation boasted a new battle group commander, with what was supposed a better idea for conducting the mission. Nearly all of these commanders harboured the need to make a mark instead of subscribing to a longer view and a consistent tactical approach. Each commanding officer rebooted the effort as we bounced between British, American, and Dutch senior military leadership in southern Afghanistan. It was hard for our respective armies to keep up between the different national styles possessed of strong military personalities. Just imagine how hard it was for Afghans who see us not as Canadian, British, or American, but as Westerners, as interlopers. Do we as Canadians have ten years of experience in assisting Afghanistan or has our own arrogance and cultural bias left us with nothing more than ten one-year experiences? Are we better poised to help another collapsed state as a trusted partner? I am not convinced.

It was a conversation on the PRT matter that provided my first sense of my poor mental health after the war. I had been back in Canada for two months and had only returned to duty for a week. Other than a short camping holiday on Lake Superior and a visit to St. Joseph Island in northern Lake Huron that seemed to dull my dreams, I was thinking constantly of Kandahar. I was working as an instructor at the Canadian Army Command and Staff College in Kingston, Ontario. I was edgy and uncomfortable in a brand-new unit, having left my battalion in western Canada. This particular day, I fell into a coffee-break discussion on the Canadian PRT in Kandahar City. Coffee breaks and beer calls are important rituals of the tribe at the Army Staff College officers' mess; they can be superb chances to share ideas and change gears between the demands of curriculum.

"The PRT concept is doomed to fail," a colleague predicted., I asked him why. "Not tight enough control by the Canadian Battle Group." I couldn't help but notice that he was well versed in the school of the loudest speaks best.

"It was not loose battle group control," I countered. "That was not the issue, quite the opposite, actually. In Kandahar City, economic development needed space, a healthy safe distance from the security side." I always felt that putting the PRT under the battle group commanded by Lieutenant Colonel Ian Hope was mixing church and state — too close to function properly as a centre of development and enterprise, as one capacity impairs the other. The officer I was talking to shook his head.

"Says you — but you're dead wrong. You don't get it."

I saw him just then as a buffoon in uniform; the sort of fool that does not listen to an opposing view but, rather, is waiting for you to stop talking so he can resume pontificating. His abrupt rejection of my entire perspective set my blood off. I felt a switch, under intense pressure, being flipped in my brain with an affirmative click.

"No, I do get it! Why would you say that? I was there. I saw the thing flounder." Under my combat shirt I could feel my heart tapping on my ribs. My voice rose with dark blood rage making other heads turn from their genteel coffee time conversations. "You are a fucking loggie." A "loggie" is widely used military slang for a logistics soldier. It is a benign term but in this instance it was used with negative connotation. In other words, I was a desk jockey and not a *real* soldier. "What would you know about it anyway?" In that moment I hated this Canadian officer, an opponent, not a colleague.

"How to campaign? How to read books?" I was literally shouting now. It was not my habit to get drawn out by an ignorant approach. But I could not help myself this time. Inside my head I was begging myself to stop. My heart continued to race with the emotion of the engagement. I was having the strangest sensation, like I was dividing inside. One half of me was enraged about the discussion and getting my point across and the other half was afraid of the spiralling poor behaviour; embarrassed by the mess I was making.

Stop. Stop. Stop. It does not matter.

I suddenly felt like I was out of my own body and looking down on myself. Watching myself become more and more emotional about the stupid PRT discussion; watching myself look like a bigger and then even bigger asshole. People around us looked confusedly at me. Who are you? I wanted to take back my words, to rewind the entire episode as if it was a badly written teleplay.

Whoa. Whoa!

Stop it, John, stop it. Dial it down.

It doesn't matter.

"What's going on with Conrad?" I heard someone ask. The demeanour of the officer I was talking to suddenly changed; it was as if he suddenly realized he was debating a madman. Clearly he wanted to get the hell away from me, and I couldn't blame him. I looked ridiculous. My behaviour was entirely out of proportion to the situation.

I finally ran out of words and energy. I was both sweating profusely and dimly aware of my colleague shutting down and seeking escape. I stepped away dazed, dizzy, and set the cup and saucer down, too heavily, on the crisp linen of the serving table. The room was fluid, swimming in my peripheral vision. Everything in an officers' mess is steeped in tradition, structured, and immaculate. The fucking pewter mugs hung in perfect order over the bar waiting for their owners' weekly return, the stuffed owl (the staff college symbol representing an institutional longing for wisdom) encased in oak, the medals of the Saskatchewan Campaign and Fenian Raids — all framed behind glass and metal with neatly engraved plaques that glossed over the blood, sweat, and fear of the operations they represented. Chaos cured, dried, and mounted for viewing.

The arrogance of the place smashed against the jumbled drawers of my mind. I was being culled from this herd and their rituals by an unseen force. I wanted to explain to people around me that it was all right; that I had just gone a bit offside; that none of it mattered anyway. I was deeply embarrassed but did not know what to do. The soldiers and officers here had no sense of who I was, having been freshly posted to the college from my Kandahar tour. This is not me. This is not how or who I am. I felt that they all knew now what a fraud I was and that they could see that I was nothing.

I could not meet anyone's eyes. I was shaking.

I simply wiped my sweaty brow with a quick forearm sweep, looked down and strode out as quickly as possible, leaving the doppelgänger to reap what it had sewn. There was no way to mitigate or qualify such an outburst. I was terrified at my loss of control and the strangeness of the experience. I was outside of time and context; standing apart from everything and everyone.

But what was worse than all of this was that I had flown from myself. I had torn in two. It was as if my fingers had brushed a large lump on my body, previously undetected. I sensed a deep wound in my mind.

Probably going to need stitches. No I don't need a doctor.

Inside my head was a Golgotha packed with wreathing bundles of vipers, black tornadoes underpinned by unbridled electricity — a centrifuge of palpable hatred and distrust.

My first doppelgänger moment. I fervently hoped it would be my last.

CHAPTER 2:
REMNANTS

When I think of it quickly, just seeing the name some-
where or being asked what it was like, I see a flat, dun
stretch of ground running out in an even plane until the
rim of the middle distance takes on the shapes and colors
of jungled hills. I had the strangest, most thrilling kind of
illusion there, looking at those hills and thinking about
the death and mystery that was in them. I would see the
thing that I actually saw: the base from the ground where
I stood, figures moving across it, choppers rising from the
pad by the strip and the hills above. But at the same time
I would see the other, too; the ground, the troops and even
myself, all from the vantage of the hills. It was a double
vision that came to me more than once there.

— Michael Herr, *Dispatches*, 1968

Kandahar Airfield (KAF), King of the Forward Operating Bases, was infinitely alive with the smell of modern warfare. The remnants of spent aviation fuel carried on the wind and gently blended with the choking dust of antique shit and sweet smell of fresh sewage: a curious cocktail.

All moments on the western side of KAF were framed by the pervading sweetness of an underperforming sewage treatment plant and its adjacent black lagoon. The "poo pond," as the soldiers called the sewage lagoon, cycled through different shades of green and brown and depths of foul smells depending on the time of the day. In the earlier time they burned feces here on KAF, from the point of the George W. Bush invasion right up until mid-2002. The burning practice spawns recollections of an earlier counter-insurgency and that granddaddy of all FOBs (forward operating bases) — the infamous Khe Sanh of the Vietnam War. By the time we arrived in Kandahar in 2005, a properly engineered waste-treatment plant had been established on the far western end of the camp. We harped repeatedly on the soldiers to clean their hands with the anti-bacterial goo. Unfortunately, with the high use of antibacterial solution in every portable toilet, every bed stand, and in every rucksack on the enormous base, the bacteria required for breaking down human waste could not hold serve. I did not long for a return to the Khe Sanh shit-burning days; instead, I grew to love the raw sewage smell. It informed on my sleep. It told my subconscious that I was on the King of the FOBs. You might die in your sleep but this was the least likely place in the entire south for that to happen.

This geopolitical cockpit is known as Southwest Asia, but there is little here to suggest Asia to the imagination. And yet there is something familiar about the place — something that echoes of déjà vu. The face of a long dead friend suggested in the cheekbones of a new acquaintance. Afghanistan is an antique place, as old as warfare itself, and Kandahar is one of the planet's oldest cities. Down the long corridor of military history, past the arrow cloud of Agincourt, the butchery of the Sommes and the Stalingrads, even past the shocking finality of Dien Bien Phu, Afghanistan stands unique. It is about as aesthetically different from the Vietnam War as one can possibly imagine. But Kandahar is, in many haunting ways, the Saigon of our generation. Folks at home live in the peacetime while soldiers here in Kandahar take a day-to-day approach to their world. The 205th Corps of the Afghan National Army (ANA), our allies in the fight, were evocative of the Army of South Vietnam (ARVN). I recall a U.S officer, well into his sixties, being re-engaged for Kandahar in 2006. He had been an adviser to the ARVN in the early seventies and was back in renewed American fatigues to ply his craft among the ANA. Even the contemporary bundle of buzz words and acronyms laden with certitude and might can be aligned with those of 1968. It seems that counter-insurgency warfare breeds familiar patterns in approach. Perhaps Afghanistan is more like Asia after all.

The passion for plywood is rampant throughout the giant FOB. The two-by-four maze of the Multinational Brigade Tactical Operations Centre (Brigade TOC) gives it the air of a low-budget movie set. Stand-easies,* canteens, and planning rooms were all decked out in fresh lumber and they harboured the optimism that accompanies fresh pine: renovation and progress. The similarity of form creates an endless plywood jungle, a series of midway funhouses with all of the mirrors torn out. There is the poignant loneliness that perpetually worked one's heart on the crowded air base. This sense of loneliness is so well entrenched that even the welfare flotsam of paperback stands, free Tim's coffee packets at the post office, stand-easies with thousands of letters from well-wishers in the United States and Canada — can only scratch at it. The letters probably come closest to making a connection in the wider head game. This correspondence came from all corners of Canada addressed to "Any Canadian Soldier" on Operation Athena. Some were actual letters, some came on government furnished cards, and still others were postcards depicting their points of origin.

Mrs. Deschant's Social 13 Class
Dear Soldier,

We are learning about World War 1 in my Social 13 Class, and I was wondering what life is like in Afghanistan? Is it hard to shoot at other people and watching your friends die and is it really hard being away from your family? I want to thank you for contributing in the war and taking the time to read this letter.

Sincerely Brandon (please write back)

---

* A stand-easy, in Canadian military parlance, is a small space to take a short break, have a smoke or a coffee, and mix with other soldiers.

Whatever glimpses of the war are offered by the history books, it will be difficult to retrieve Kandahar's perpetual assault on the mind: the churning electricity of that time and place; the omnipresence of death and violence tucked in nicely with contemporary pop culture; the incessant waiting. Fighting against the onslaught of boredom, which is the asymmetric battlefield's largest trap. The sun on your bones at a ramp ceremony while your mind filled with frozen thoughts — aluminum coffin visions of ice on flesh, melting slowly into horrible wounds. Getting up for still more ramp ceremonies for our allies in the middle of the night. Gazing at the maw of the C-177 Globemaster, the flying giant, its back deck like the jaw of a shark opened and ready to receive the fallen. Heading off on convoy at 0400 in order to be through Kandahar City before first light. The Dining Facilities Administration Centre (DFAC) with its ever-ready grits.[1] The large African-American cook who was part of the engineering company KBR[2] presiding over a grill of eggs the size of a Lincoln's hood. The cook's ancient face full of wisdom as he quarterbacked a wide swath of frying eggs. All of these experiences are tightly juxtaposed with Tim Hortons coffees, portable MP3 players and YouTube firefights with the Taliban. And all across the King of the FOBs, as silent and ethereal as the outlying dust tornadoes, lay the unspoken language of a shared tension.

I am constantly alive with the vegetative reality of that brown place, so vibrant even in the absence of colour. I can recover it all when I close my eyes, I can see it without any work. It's not a recollection like a high school graduation or one's first day with a driver's licence. These domestic memories — like graduations — require a gentle priming of the grey matter. The Kandahar motor is running all the time. It comes back to you, smells and all, in a micro-second. These memories need effort, not to conjure but to keep them packed up. The same way I imagine Danang or Hue lives with the previous generation of American soldiers. The same way Juno Beach and the Falaise Gap live with the Canadian veterans of the Second World War. For our children the time is fast approaching when Panjawaii and Musa Qaleh will not be wet and alive in the newspapers and news telecasts. These fights will soon sound as remote as Vimy Ridge and the Somme. But never for us. The King of the FOBs, he is always right here with you. Your own personal Vietnam. I want to share how these things felt before the current generation of veterans pass into shadow.

Come back to us. We have missed you.

You should never have left us. You won't mean shit back there.

The helicopter, a chubby CH-47 Chinook with the capacity to haul a platoon of soldiers, carves up the air. The bird is rolling with its side bay doors open to give the machine guns a wide swath. Afghanistan's panorama flows beneath us. We have been rattling along from KAF for about fifteen minutes staring across the cargo compartment at American Special Forces (ASF) soldiers and Marines who meet our faces with their own impassioned stares. We all sit stoically like a double row of Easter Island statues. There is no conversation; nor is there any desire for it. Even if we felt like chatting, the incessant beating of the rotors is too thick to permit an exchange. There is little to read in each other's expressions — helmeted faces with eyes hidden behind protective ballistic shades. My thoughts turn to the rattling metal of the Chinook around me, the CH-47 — ten thousand parts in close formation. That was the joke that we dubbed them with in the eighties. We used to own four of these gawky workhorses. Canada sold the Chinook fleet, all four, to the Netherlands in the early 1990s, eliminating the aerial logistics capacity of our tactical forces. Three of the former Canadian birds were operating in Afghanistan for the Dutch even in 2005. The fourth had been shot down by the insurgents earlier in the year — a gruesome thought as we sail on toward Zabul this morning. The heavy aircraft approaches an intersection of pie-crust hills beneath its belly. Suddenly the door gunner opens up an angry staccato with his machine gun that out-competes the Chinook's rotors. Hundreds of bullets are pounding down onto the summit of the hills below. Little tufts of dirt and rock confirm this.

Holy Christ! Shit on a stick!

This application of basic SEAD (suppression of enemy air defence) was a first for me and I find the door-gunner's work just a little off-putting. None of the other Easter Island visages to my front have changed, so I

Afghanistan from the rear of a Chinook medium-lift helicopter. Although the military purchased new Chinook helicopters during the Afghan War, all Canadian logistics convoys in 2006 were reliant on ground delivery.

do my best to take it all in stride. Is it 1970 out there beyond the hot muzzle of the machine gun? We could just as easily be cruising over the Mekong-fed jungle instead of the dry, dusty browns of Zabul Province. The violence of the machine gun's action contrasts with the neutral face of its gunner. Business is business and SEAD is definitely the key to survival. The dead Dutch Chinook helicopter proved that.

"Hey, man," a soldier yells, "it's just a little death from above; it'll wash out."

Jesus, anything that helps to keep this flying hippo in the air, I think to myself.

Thou shalt perish, ere I perish.

The physical line between war and peace is a clear one at least and it is drawn through the centre of the United Arab Emirates. Dubai, the capital of the United Arab Emirates, held Camp Mirage on its outskirts. Camp Mirage sat on the edge of peacetime, at the crossroads between the living normalcy of home and the war. It was the last port of call before Afghanistan. Here the ceramic plates for your blast vest were reissued, your rifle, your 150 rounds of 5.56 millimetre ammo. Here as well your civilian clothing discarded, crammed into the further reaches of your duffle pack.

Typically, the Canada flight got into Dubai in the wee hours of the morning, soldiers would be semi-stunned from eighteen hours of travel and connections in Central Europe and struggling to breathe under the oppressive heat of Arabia.

Weight of hours pressing behind your eyeballs.

Soldiers were stuffed into the transient quarters at Mirage for a short rest and then pumped over to the airfield where the hulking beasts of the Royal Canadian Air Force (RCAF) waited in silhouette. The C-130 Hercules line. On the surface a clean, efficient process of onward troop movement. Beneath the veneer of this outward simplicity was a tightening spring, a gathering of resolve. Behind the faces of soldiers a moral battle was joined — thousands of administrative concerns accompany a steeling of the mind: getting out of your civilian clothes and squaring away your luggage, not sleeping past the allotted ninety minutes, perhaps mailing one final letter home, a final phone call to Canada. The backdrop for this exercise was the "Moonbase Alpha" pallor across the dark little camp; a feeling of being in a strange final place at the edge of the war. Walking through stifling heat between air-conditioned cocoons. The bright-tangerine smell of the urinals; endless slide show images from the war in Afghanistan.

Finally the Hercules line where soldiers are stuffed into the hot fuselage groping to fasten the tiny webbing straps that hold you in. The big aircraft bakes until it gathers altitude. The Camp Mirage staff never referred to the final destination of the C-130s as Kandahar or Afghanistan, but rather the destination was merely "north." This was a matter of both discretion for the base's host nation and secrecy. Still the term "north" rang hollow in one's ear, given the true end point. The flight "north" was only four hours through a starlit Persian sky, but the trajectory was far deeper than a mere journey between points. The Hercules flight also had a metaphysical quotient that pierced the soul and honed the senses of all on board. When that rear ramp opened up on the King of the FOBs your concerns for mortgage rates, Montreal Canadiens trade-deadline moves, mutual funds, and the slings and arrows of a hundred peacetime concerns were stripped away. In Kandahar the focus was on the day at hand. One more day with no wounded, one more day with all my limbs, one more day with my courage still intact. In a war of the mind that is no small feat.

The journey to this modern battlefield requires a steeling of the mind, a gradual narrowing of focus until all that remains are the martial tasks at hand. The soldier's job in wartime — at its most fundamental level — is to absorb the never-ending stream of kinetic insults, hard little iron bits, inhuman realities, and bring an organic coherence to them, something actionable by flesh and blood. The first and the last of these drills belongs to the kingdom of the mind.

> I have travelled back to Afghanistan many more times over the subsequent years to keep track of the war, but for me nothing will ever match the drama and the violence of that long, hot, dangerous summer of 2006. It was a privilege to have been there to bear witness to the good, the bad, and the ugly.
>
> — Sean M. Maloney,
> *Fighting for Afghanistan: A Rogue Historian at War*

Operation Mountain Thrust (June–July 2006) is now over ten years ago. The military operation has become lost in the shadow of its more famous cousin, Operation Medusa of September 2006. Operation Mountain Thrust was the largest military operation against the enemy since the fall of 2001, an early attempt by our division to root out the Taliban command and support networks in southern Afghanistan before full NATO transition on July 31, 2006. Operation Mountain Thrust ran for six weeks through the summer of 2006, reducing the enemy's numbers even as they were concentrating for a late summer push. This September offensive conceived by the Taliban would be countered by Operation

Medusa, the better known of the two division operations involving Canadian soldiers in 2006. The two major operations against the enemy in 2006 are easy to distinguish. Mountain Thrust was characterized by wide dispersal of our division's forces, while Medusa was more about a concerted effort.

NATO's theme in Operation Mountain Thrust was simple: take the fight to the enemy. Operation Mountain Thrust would see us pushing deep into the various Taliban sanctuaries in southern Afghanistan and stomping the insurgents at the source, instead of waiting for them to attack. This meant focused operations inside the four provinces of Regional Command South: Kandahar, Helmand, Uruzgan, and Zabul. Our forces working in tandem with the ANA were to be proactive and not reactive to the insurgency. The operation was a challenge for logisticians as it sprawled across four Afghan provinces and involved some eleven thousand troops, including all of our Canadians.

In some ways the operation was congruent with the contemporary Canadian approach in Kandahar — to go out beyond the wire and to stay among the communities, among the enemy. This was Lieutenant Colonel Ian Hope's long-acknowledged approach with the 1 PPCLI battlegroup. Still, in other ways Mountain Thrust was an enormous distraction to Hope's inspired operating concept and our national interests. The higher NATO campaign design was diverse, covering many operational-level objectives for Afghanistan from the creation of a modern-style ANA through to serving domestic counter-narcotics interests. Of course, this wide swath of objectives was grounded on the political imperatives of our respective allies. This breadth and complexity made it difficult to graft NATO's desires with specific Canadian objectives in Kandahar. Mountain Thrust was hailed as the biggest coalition operation against the Taliban since the original invasion and regime removal in late 2001.

It will be interesting to see how history judges Mountain Thrust and Medusa. Most military pundits and academics write off Mountain Thrust as so much wind without rain. My own perspective of these divisional fights is raw, sorting through the experience only ten years on. However, Operation Mountain Thrust has left me with an enduring gift. It affords me the one division-sized battle of my career. It is an operation that I can look at academically as a footnote in the middle of the Afghanistan War. I can also recall many of its elements though the lens of experience. Tactically, Colonel Kevin Owens, commander of the 173rd U.S. Airborne Brigade, had briefed us on an increase in enemy activity throughout the latter portion of 2005. Colonel Owens had explained the "kill/capture mission" in which his forces were engaged. From the earliest briefings it was clear that there were head games. Enemy customs offered their own frustrations. The Taliban scrambled to remove their dead after a firefight. This Taliban practice had a moral element to it. Our own combat leaders felt the frustration of rumbling up to a captured objective only to find it vacated. The dead had not loitered to give testament but rather were dragged off with nothing more than bloody trails and spent bullet casings to speak of the blow they had been dealt. There would be no replicating the Viet Cong body count here. The numbers of destroyed enemy had to be estimated. Throughout the spring and into the early summer of 2006 the Taliban leadership was chatting from Pakistan with its charges in southern Afghanistan. The gist of their instruction was, "Knock them out, move the foreigners along, and take back Kandahar City." The Taliban expected both to be in control of Kandahar City by July 2006 and that Canada would have lost its will to continue with the coalition by the end of the same year.

For us, Operation Mountain Thrust comprised the realization of the tactical dream known as Forward Operating Base Martello. The FOB was intrinsic to taking the fight to the Taliban. An early visit to its construction site in April 2006 was like driving into the heart of Mars. The topography was reminiscent of the terrain along the Dempster Highway in Canada's Northwest Territory. Everywhere you looked there were the sharp-topped Afghan 'pie crust' hills defined by their broad sweeping bottoms and crimped summits. The location was a difficult one to establish a FOB, but it was well placed near a number of transit routes for the Taliban — what we called "ratlines" or enemy lines of logistic support. So good to intercept movement into the village of Elbac. Walking along the side of the hill led by Major Kirk Gallinger, the officer commanding 1 PPCLI's A Company, I was instantly out of breath with the crazy contours of the place. Five steps in any direction and I found myself confronted by deceiving elevation — bundles of tightly packed contour lines. I cannot believe how much I am sucking for breath just to keep a normal pace.

Who can fight here?

"Make sure your helmets stay on. We are being observed as we walk. They have eyes everywhere on this place," Major Gallinger tells us. "It's right in the middle of their ratlines."

While I sucked air and tromped along, I considered the term "ratline" and its loaded use to describe the Taliban logistic routes.

As FOB Martello inched toward completion with each load of Hesco bastion field fortification equipment and metal riveting, the Gumbad Safe House remained open for business. It had been established by Task Force Gun Devil, the American artillery regiment that preceded Ian Hope's battle group. Gumbad was supposed to be a short-term gig. Instead, soldiers from A Company, 1 PPCLI, held it down for over half the tour, a lonely outpost by the belly button range with only two highly visible and predictable road routes in. Gumbad fast became a hold-over from a thousand nightmares. The Haunted Hill House of the early Canadian deployment. Still the gritty little post stuck like a chicken bone into the throat of Taliban ratlines. This was not how our American allies had preferred to fight throughout 2005. Long-standing platoon- and company-sized sorties were rare. U.S. Task Force Gun Devil would surge out for kill/capture missions of three or four days' duration and then return to KAF to recharge. However, the situation was changing, building throughout the latter stages of 2005. The enemy was becoming more active, more concentrated. Presence, like that offered by the Gumbad platoon house, was fast becoming more important than short sorties. Task Force Orion like the wider fabric of Operation Mountain Thrust itself was all about being there and staying there. All of our soldiers took pride in the steel-edge resolve of our combat forces. We were playing our best hand with some of the best soldiers in the world.

Operation Mountain Thrust was also characterized by Canadian support and movement of Dutch forces into Uruzgan, the province to the immediate north of our own Kandahar Province. We sold the Dutch machine gun ammunition on agreement; we escorted their convoys with battle group LAVs. Canadian Hercules aircraft carried Dutch troops to their dusty new home. There was an element of the psychological here as well. The Dutch were down here with us as NATO allies in no small part because of a great friendship between our nations — a mutual affection with solid roots in shared experiences of the Second World War. There was the notion, I think, among Dutch leadership that if Canada was involved they wanted to be there too; the days and weeks of Mountain Thrust were all about supporting our allies and leaning into the wider operational goals of RC South. It is easy to forget, so many years on, that very few NATO members wanted anything to do with southern Afghanistan in 2006. We should never let this go.

We had an exceptional pair of barbers who had come over to work with the CANEX on KAF from Quebec City. Conversations with these two barbers were always spiced with the latest moves of the CFL Eskimos and Alouettes, or the NHL teams. We were largely a western Canadian task force, so the jabs between the Oilers and Montreal Canadiens' fans were frequently exchanged with a laugh, as were bits of news from home. They set up their sea container barbershop near the Canadian HQ off Enduring Freedom Way. These men were spectacular; in fact, all of the Canadian civilian CANEX workers were cut from the same cloth. They rolled with the punches of the odd rocket attack on the King of the FOBs. The attack on June 30 had critically wounded a Canadian artilleryman, and other rounds had fallen short of the brand new Tim Hortons on the boardwalk. They took this in stride, however, and went out of their way to make our soldiers laugh and relax. They gave shelter, however brief, from the storms beyond the wire. These great Canadians understood the moral battlefield, the endless play for the mind, and their contribution to force protection was not insignificant. When I tune into Quebec politics and the rhetoric of separatism that seems to wax and wane with the turning of the seasons, I always think back on these two Quebec City men cutting bushels of western Canadian hair.

There was no Quebec Bloc there, no talk of two different nations or of a separatist revival. We were one in the harness.

As Operation Mountain Thrust passed into the Taliban summer of 2006, the Dutch forces grew in number. By virtue of our support of U.K. operations in Helmand and an increase of IED attacks on the major communication routes, our forces became aware that an ominous concentration of the enemy was assembling west of Kandahar. This gathering of the enemy was the first significant concentration since the collapse of the Taliban in 2002. I left for Cyprus and decompression leave just as Operation Medusa was in its opening salvoes in late August. I hardly knew Medusa, seeing nothing more than its logistics fingerprints on our ammunition holdings. Operation Mountain Thrust, on the other hand, is with me always.

In so many ways, the goddamn terrorists have won early victories, and air travel is one of them. I don't think they had Nexus line-ups in those war days. Nexus amounted to this special little card one bought that shoots you to the front of an airport security line. We had patiently waited to get through the long line for security checks at Toronto's Pearson International Airport; Martha, my wife and best friend, and my four little kids. My home leave was over. Nichola Goddard, that most perfect of forward observation officers (FOO), was dead — killed in action during the first week of my leave. But it was time to go back to Kandahar and finish out the remainder.

I remember Martha and I sipped coffee at the open vendor area prior to saying our goodbye; we chatted about the kids and about plans for October when I would be home — little things — silly everyday parent stuff — that when in relaxed conversation seemed so light and inconsequential but under IED contact easily end up being the galvanizing final pieces of your life. We continued talking as I stood in line waiting to clear security. Suddenly I was next in line; I was instructed to place my metal belt, watch, and phone into the plastic bin. I was at the tearing point. I remember hugging my kids like I was drowning and they were the only thing that could keep me afloat.

"Boarding pass please, sir." My heart started pounding.

"Yes. Here you go."

I am going to a place where the Toronto Maple Leafs do not matter, where no one gives a shit about my tanking mutual funds.

I stepped through the scanner and turned to wave one last time to the kids. They were so small; so full of life unlived. I craved being back there with them just for one more hug. I had to force myself to move any further.

I only walked twenty feet at most when I was overwhelmed with the sense of how close they still were; I had to see them one last time. An irrational thought. I turned and sprinted to the security area, but they were long gone. My breath was coming in short choppy chunks and people were looking at me like I was crazy. I kept trying to lean this way and that as if that might help them appear. I had not fully anticipated the emotional immediacy of our parting. I was not ready to enter the other world. My reaction surprised me in its ferocity, way different from our Cambodia goodbyes, different still for the Balkan tours — both of which had held their terrors. This farewell had me hyperventilating, my face puffing.

What the hell kind of father am I? Why do I not know them better? Why am I always saying goodbye?

I retraced my steps and found a bar handy to the departure gate and ordered two scotches. And then two more to keep them company. By the time we were airborne for Frankfurt, both my heart and my brain were suitably numb.

Speed saves lives.

The business of logistics convoys in southern Afghanistan was a head game to begin with, a chess match with our opponent that moved pawns and rooks around on the game board of perception. We packed our columns with LAV IIIs for escort whenever we could — LAV II Coyotes and Bisons when we had to. Our logistics trucks bristled with weapons. No effort was spared to make the convoy look like a hard target to crack. For their part, our Taliban attackers zeroed in on our hardest targets, chiefly the LAV fighting vehicles. It was their part of the game, played in a manner that appealed to their sense of machismo. The amount of diesel tanker trucks we had in our aviation-starved army could have been counted on half of one hand. Knocking out the lumbering diesel haulers would have hurt us immediately. And yet the enemy never went after these juicy targets. We did everything we could to look the part of a tough nut. The convoys drove down the centre of the roads, avoiding the pavement edge where an IED could be more easily concealed and dug in. Years after the war soldiers find themselves avoiding walking on grass in a compound or a ditch and doing the five-and-twenty drills when they stop suddenly on a roadway. (Basically, a five-and-twenty drill means assessing your surroundings for explosives and enemy whenever your vehicle stopped in Kandahar. All soldiers were to look very closely at the ground up to five metres out all around the vehicle and then follow it up with the same scrutiny up to twenty metres out — a drill that forced us to be disciplined and look before we leapt.) It becomes a deeply ingrained habit. Maybe you hesitate only for a moment, but the reverberating psychological effects of combat linger on long after.

Is that an electric wire running out of that clump? Do you see that shit?

These old drills flash in the mind of all veterans for a second and then they evaporate.

But appearance alone was not enough. Initially in Kandahar the columns would move quickly. This provided us some small measure of protection with the belief that speed saves lives. It gave our soldiers more confidence against the attackers who owned the initiative. This practice was soon modified as it proved to be untrue in many cases. We used gentle force to compel vehicles to stay back from our columns. Soldiers would throw water bottles and rocks at vehicles that got too close to centre. Water bottles were the low end of the spectrum. Next came bullets.

"Move away, you stupid fucker!" air sentries and gunners would scream.

Warning shots went into radiators or ricocheted off of the engine blocks of any late model cargo trucks that did not give ground. Speed saves lives. These driving tactics seem insane now but they were eminently logical in Kandahar. The last ten metres of a military supply chain have to be closed with guts.

In an intricate war of the mind we fought to hide our Canadian frugalness from the enemy. We wanted to create the illusion that we had hundreds of LAV IIIs and that each of them was near indestructible. The workshop sweated buckets and worked around the clock to fix a damaged fighting vehicle. We never let on that a vehicle was irretrievably battle damaged. We never talked to our own reporters about the boneyard and the pile of equipment that had been damaged beyond repair in Afghanistan. Vulnerability and quantity are secrets in this psychological chess game.

These things are indestructible. We have thousands of them.
You cannot win.

OFFICIAL CANADIAN MEMO
ON THE CONVOY AMBUSH OF JULY 22, 2006

On July 22, 2006, at approximately 1730 hours local time, a Canadian convoy returning from operations in Lash Kar Gah region was proceeding to KAF when they were attacked west of Kandahar City. The attack was carried out by a suicide bomber using a vehicle-borne IED that detonated beside a Bison armoured vehicle. Two Canadians were killed and eight were wounded. This was followed up with a second suicide bomber who detonated a backpack device during the extrication procedure back to Camp Nathan Smith. Four local nationals were killed and thirty were injured.[3]

There are so many dreams that are stitched up from the remnants of memory. The worst of them is like a series of sharp-cornered hockey cards, fresh right out of the pack — a bundle of images that play in the mind, a series of discrete scenes. There is no clear beginning to the panorama. It is July 22, 2006. Operation Mountain Thrust, the big multinational division show, was nearing its end. The Canadian convoy had become strung out struggling with mechanical issues on the journey from west of Panjawaii. Now we comprised but a broken fragment of the original column struggling to get back to Kandahar before dark. It might start at any juncture, like inside the sweltering cab of the sixteen-ton HLVW (heavy logistics vehicle wheeled) with its air conditioning down, joking with Corporal Shawn Crowder about giving up our truck to swap out the crew who had suffered in this beast on the long hot trip out to Helmand. It might start with the little white Toyota truck making its slow path on the left of our column. The truck is a Toyota Hiacre, a tiny cab-over–style truck distributed almost

A view of a Kandahar street taken from inside an HLVW. Designed during the Cold War for the conventional battlefield, it was ill-suited for the guerilla tactics of counter-insurgency. Thick armour plating provided additional blast protection but significantly reduced visibility. This was my view during the opening moves of a double-suicide IED attack on July 22, 2016.

exclusively to the Asian market. It has the appearance of those weird little Tonka toys from the sixties. This Tonka toy was also harmless-appearing, but engorged with explosives.

Vehicle-borne suicide bomber.

The weapon of choice of our enemy on this contemporary battlefield.

It might start with the image of a tattered meat roast flying over the cab, twisted metal. Material, smoke, and flesh hurled toward the cab, the awful sounds of its contact. Canadian personal weapons scattered all over the highway like confetti. The blast itself and the ball of grey smoke. Regardless of entry point, the images are always as consistent and sharp as the emotions that accompany them.

"Shawn, get down!" I yell. Crowder is driving our HLVW and I am opposite. Despite rifle and bulky equipment it is astonishing how flat you can make yourself when you need to. I lived a lifetime in the span of seconds spent on the floor of the truck — waiting for the worst. Again, here, an object lesson: the mind is a complex machine. Designed for the Cold War, there wasn't enough protection on the HLVWs when they rolled off the assembly line. After-market armour had been welded to the floors and sides of our trucks in an effort to make them more blast resistant for counter-insurgency. A soldier wants to believe that the armour plate in their truck is thick and capable of protecting them. We cling to this small edge even though it was generally accepted that the ballistic and blast protection of the aging HLVW truck was pathetic. The metal plating was more for the mind than the body. The truck, manufactured in Kingston, Ontario, had been built for a different kind of war, a war with a "front" and a deep "rear area," a more structured battlefield that would have a well-identified enemy and need brute logistics, bulk supply. The windows in the prime workhorse of the Canadian fleet were large. They too had been covered in thick steel for this new type of game. The addition of armour plating to the windows reduced the large Cold War–sized view from the cab down to slits. There had been cases, though, where the armour plating had fallen out of the window area onto the laps of occupants. And so, naturally, the eternity between the explosion and the final arresting of debris, metal and flesh are filled with questions. Would the armour save us this time? Have we earned that luck?

I am running. I can now see the stricken Bison that vanished somewhere in between the detonation and scurrying for the floor of my truck. There is a Canadian soldier, Corporal Jason Warren, laid out behind the vehicle. His wounds tell me immediately that he is gone. A strong sense of responsibility meets me over Jason's body.

We will get you out of here. And soon.

I move on. A scrawny female medic makes her entrance. She goes about the carnage unfettered, checking for vitals, triaging the casualties. The angel medic.

Suddenly, two other soldiers are beside me. Like Warren, they are infantrymen from the battle group headquarters. They nod as I bark out a couple words of reassurance. We all look to the little medic for her next instruction.

"Let's lift him out," the medic says softly.

I glance into the tight driver's hatch and cannot find enough torso remaining to grab on to.

"Just a sec. I need to grab a hold yet." I finally find a swatch of material to gain purchase. I recoil inwardly from the puncture wound where the shrapnel has pierced his skull and exited with bits of grey matter. It is only a tiny hole.

You can't be dead, I think. *You can't be dead!*

Such a slight wound cannot possibly kill a man. Sometimes I yell at him, urging him to get up.

"Stand up, man. We need your help!"

Most of the time the dream stays congruent with the reality and we redo our morbid task. The four of us work as one as we pull our fallen soldier, Corporal Francisco Gomez, 1 PPCLI, up and out of the driver's compartment of the Bison. Once Gomez is out we turn our attention to the back of the personnel carrier. A poor man's hell had been reborn inside the machine. Captain Tony Ross lies in a crumpled heap, blood oozing from a wound to his head.

"Is it his ear?"

I think it's his ear. Please God let it be ear and not skull.

The vague reminiscence of a butcher shop flowers inside my nostrils. The carrier scene is the opposite of the subtle wounds to Gomez where death's fingerprints had been so gently left. These unnerving contrasts make the skin crawl and the earth bounce like jelly beneath my boots. I freeze for a second then take Tony Ross's hand in mine.

"Tony? I am here, Tony. You're going to be okay." Something dark and pulpy had affixed itself to my boot. The awkwardness and weight of the dead soldier, the blood, puke, and granola-bar wrapper swill around the survivors of the Bison. Both of these scenes present obscene vignettes lived over and over again in dreams: the quick and the dead — a feature part of a slide show that plays routinely in my mind. Remnants of actions taken and others left undone. In all cases a dream so real that whether I am having it at night or in the form of a daydream I have trouble interacting with people for a long while.

It was not the first explosion. That initial blast had taken two Canadian lives but it left me unscathed and still functioning. In my adrenalin-fed state I could easily remember the drills and the checklists: touching base with the sergeant convoy commander; confirming reports for contact and medevac (medical evacuation) had gone in; checking the Bison for the wounded and removing the dead. Being present and trying to make the right decisions against an inorganic vertigo. After the exertion of the medevac and the recovery of the vehicles it seemed like we were getting close to moving on. The first signs of sunset were upon us and the sooner we could move the better. The Quick Reaction Force (QRF), our rescuers out of the Canadian PRT Camp in the city, were leaving our protective cordon.

Good. We will be moving ourselves momentarily.

Ka-boom! A loud explosion at the front of the convoy. Another suicide bomber attacked the departing QRF. The human body rigged as a weapon. This attacker had packed himself with ball bearings, metal bits, and shards. The cheap electronics required to detonate might power a child's train set or a garage door opener back home. One had only to pack the detonating device down with the plastic explosives. Extreme simplicity; a marriage of elegance and evil. The image of flying meat hits my senses once more. Some part of the suicide bomber. The chaos was rekindled. Bodies and blood seemed to be instantly everywhere. Afghan civilians stumbling in the smoke in a daze. The head of the attacker being hauled away in a green garbage bag by an Afghan responder.

The head always survives.

It was the second explosion that cracked something fundamental inside me. It snapped like an over-wound rubber band. My mind unhinged for the moment. I stumbled, heard the explosion and the screams.

Somehow, I was outside myself, looking down on this hopeless combat. I could imagine the doubt in my own eyes.

This is out of control. You might lose this whole column.

My heart was racing and I could taste the salt at the edges of my mouth. And yet I was apart from myself.

Christ alive, I am thirsty.

Afghan civilians and Canadian soldiers were stumbling about dazed in a smoky dreamscape. My mind maintained a healthy distance, a firm disbelief of the dead. These are just actors in a low-cost production. Body parts from the murdered civilians are being loaded into the back of a white pickup truck like firewood. The clunking sounds of bits of human beings landing in the truck box are awful. I try not to hear them. Children being picked up like broken dolls with a solemn, perverse acceptance by their parents. Blood has started streaming out the back of the civilian pickup onto its rusted bumper. As I focused on sharp image after image, something inside my head tore away from its mooring. I felt an enormous weight breaching the fortress of my belief. An Angus bull crashed into the fabric of reality and crumpled it such that all around the edges I could see a white-hot enlightenment. An Afghan civilian approached me, fresh blood stains on his Old Testament garb. His lips are moving without sound. Finally his words reach me through an intense ringing in my ears. He is asking for my help, indicating the carnage with a sweep of his arm, as if I might not have noticed the deep tear in the fabric of reality. I explain to the man that we cannot help him; that we could barely take care of ourselves right now. My eyes then glimpsed beyond the present tactical circumstances into a timeless reality.

We shouldn't be here. We have no business being here.

A deep cowardice wafted into my conscience. I was startled and ashamed of these thoughts but I could not stem them. We have no place in this country. We have got to get out of here.

I have got to get out of here.

In that crystalline revelation on Highway 1, a moment within a moment, I was left with a cold thought.

I might be a coward.

The sky suddenly broke into loud clap-clap-clapping as two Apache gunships descend onto the chaos. The ferocious-looking helicopters had the effect of panicking the guilty and scattering the innocent further back from our stricken convoy. I was heartened by the appearance of these gunships, and looked on them gratefully as they loitered above us. Guardian angels.[4] The arrival of the Apaches closed out my hot epiphany. I am stirred out of the moment and the edges of sheer light fade to leave only Kandahar's browns. Reality coalesced once again in my field of vision.

I have got things to do here. Do your goddamned job!

I stumbled forward and spoke to the convoy commander, an armoured corps sergeant.

"Can we get this vehicle on an A-frame and tow it?

"Pretty sure we can, sir," he yelled back. His eyes were round behind his yellow tinted blast goggles — a Canadian sergeant in battle mode.

"If not let's destroy it right here. I can have Master Corporal C.J. Price rig something up, I'm sure. We have got to get moving again," I heard myself bark. The goggled helmet of the convoy escort commander was nodding aggressively. The second explosion had not killed any more of us although a number of Afghan civilians were murdered in the secondary attack by the cheapest of contraptions. Most of our vehicles were okay to move. We were set. Finally, as darkness descended with authority, we began to move deeper in to the streets of Kandahar. There I sat in the blackness of the sixteen-ton cab, thinking about my kids, about the images that flashed through my head while we lay on the steel floor of a Cold War–era truck and waited those fractions of seconds for the metal and bone to make contact. I thought back on that white truth I had glimpsed for a few seconds back on the highway as I stumbled about in the aftermath of the secondary attack. *What the hell was that?* I could not un-see what I had seen.

I could not unlearn the things I had learned about myself.

The morning of July 23, 2006, our convoy reassembled in the PRT in Kandahar City where we had sought refuge the night before. We headed out again on a short junket for KAF. Although I packed down the events of July 22, 2006, and locked them away in my mind, every convoy after that date was harder. Every move beyond the wire required more steeling of the mind to look the part. It was like playing in a rugby match with an ever-deepening bruise.

What you can do about Combat Stress Reaction

- Make yourself look calm and controlled
- Focus on the task at hand
- Expect to carry on: concentrate on your supervisor's instruction

- Think of yourself succeeding
- If Combat Stress Reaction Signs don't begin to improve, tell your supervisor

> — Canadian Army self-help booklet on
> combat stress reaction, July 1992

You can never tell me it was an accident. Not in a thousand years. Master Corporal Ray Arndt, an escort leader in our Reserve Defence and Security (D&S) Platoon, was killed on August 5, 2006, when a large cattle truck slammed into his vehicle on the Spin Boldak Highway. In the early going the task force had called it an accident. However, the likelihood of a large civilian truck accidently drilling itself into a NATO convoy never seemed to add up. Not completely. Everywhere in the south, the activity of the Taliban continued to grow toward the September crescendo of Operation Medusa. August 4, 2006, the previous day, we had sent four Canadian fallen back to Trenton after a clash with the Taliban in Pashmul, west of Kandahar. Today Ray was co-driving in a G-Wagon with a column headed for the Pakistan border. Our tour was now deep into the rotation, our relief-in-place (RIP). A task force RIP is among the busiest and most vulnerable parts of any operational tour. The RIP comprises a brittle period, a steady flow of soldiers and box lunches, orientation briefings, long days, and multiple time zone changes. The energy of the RCAF is thrown onto the RIP period as a shuttle system of Airbus jetliners moves soldiers across the planet. Major Scott Mackenzie, my deputy commanding officer, was with the column along with Major Glen MacNeil and Sergeant Major Miles, both of the Royal Canadian Regiment — members of the incoming rotation from Petawawa. Scott was going to show these two senior soldiers the layout in Spin Boldak as part of the handover. This would be one of Mackenzie's last convoys beyond the wire. He was due to return home soon owing to a medical matter with his spouse.

No one fought harder than Ray Arndt to join the army. He had been born with one foot a full three sizes smaller than the other. This peculiarity had made it challenging to join the Loyal Edmonton Regiment, one of two Reserve infantry regiments in Alberta. However, Arndt, who had grown up in Edson, Alberta, loved the army and once he set his mind to something, as those closest to him knew, he would not be dissuaded. Ray persisted and was ultimately successful. Ray Arndt had missed out on a tour in Bosnia earlier in his career and he was determined not to miss the opportunity to deploy to Afghanistan as part of a Defence and Security Platoon (D&S) of the National Support Element (NSE). He had only been married for nine months to his wife, Darcia, whom he had met at a regimental function in Edmonton. They had plans to start a family as soon as possible but this would have to wait until after Afghanistan.

My emotional bank account was pretty low by this point of the tour. Within a period of less than two weeks, we had lived through the double IED attack on the way back from Helmand Province, lost four superb

Me with Darcia Arndt, December 2015. Darcia's husband, Master Corporal Ray Arndt, served with the 2006 NSE until he was killed in a convoy in August 2006.

battle group soldiers in the Pashmul battle, and the full-on thrust of an artillery ammunition shortage had only just recently presented itself. Given the shortage of certain natures of 155-millimetre ammunition for our new titanium M-777 artillery pieces, General Fraser had reason to be concerned. For a host of reasons, we had fallen behind in maintaining proper stock levels. Fraser had blasted me hard on this.

"You told me we were never going to run out of ammunition!" I had believed it too until combat operations heated up in the month of July and began to chew up large stocks of munitions. The consumption rate had snaked invisible though our fighting force like a ghost. This new burn rate positively shocked us and made a mockery of the false metric we had used to confirm our holdings earlier in the tour. The math was wrong. Even worse was the ability to communicate with Ian Hope and his company quartermasters. This dialogue was eroded with the velocity of the summer. Every soldier, regardless of stripe or cap badge, knew how serious our tactical situation stood in that Taliban summer. Logistical briefings between my NSE and the battle group — all manner of technical discussions — were paralyzed by extreme distances and the need to hold on, to keep going. Ammunition dominated my every waking thought.

I listened intently in the NSE command post on KAF the morning of August 5 as the contact report came in. Scant detail came across the radio. The transmissions we received were rushed, the soldier's efforts extreme against the event. I imagined the worst. Staff from NSE Operations was organizing a road recovery party to recover what was gelling up as one destroyed vehicle: a G-Wagon escort truck. I nodded acknowledgement of the imminent departure of the recovery team and then bolted for my battle rattle and rifle. (A "battle rattle" is the soldier's term for the fighting order — helmet, load-carrying vest, fragmentation vest, and full complement of ammunition — worn by a Canadian soldier when operating beyond a FOB [beyond the wire].) I had arrived at a decision, and a poor one at that. I was going to them.

"Hold that column a second. The RSM [regimental sergeant major] and I are going along," I blurted. Pat "Paddy" Earles, the RSM, already had his fighting order in his hands and was checking his rifle bolt. Earles and I loaded up with the recovery team and deployed out to the incident site on Highway 4.

The scene at the incident site made my stomach lurch to attention. It seemed as if this section of our D&S platoon had been scattered like broken mannequins along the halted convoy. Major Mackenzie had the unbroken soldiers in an all-round defence. A section of infantry from Major Bill Fletcher's C Company had that task bolted down. I noticed that Afghan civilians, a dazed slowness to their movement, circulated beyond the cordon, picking up the remnants of the collision. Bawling cattle provided background music to make the nightmare complete: a stockyard and butcher shop rolled into one. Corporals Ash van Leuween and Jared Gagnon were both badly wounded and needed immediate medevac. They had been in the truck commanded by Master Corporal Arndt. A ballistic blanket covered one of the soldiers with the exception of his boots.

Two different sizes of combat boots.

Corporal van Leuween was touch and go. Corporal Gagnon was not expected to survive the night. Raymond Arndt was already dead. Killed instantly. He was thirty-two years old.

> I wish I could tell you about the South Pacific. The way it actually was. The endless ocean. The infinite specks of coral we called islands. Coconut palms nodding grace-fully toward the ocean. Reefs upon which waves broke into spray, and inner lagoons, lovely beyond description. I wish I could tell you about the sweating jungle, the full moon rising behind the volcanoes, and the waiting. The waiting. The timeless repetitive waiting.
>
> — James Michener, *Tales of the South Pacific*

My dreams and memories of Kandahar and its eternal airfield are iron-clad. But what shape will the King of the FOBs take in our collective memory in fifty years, when Panjawaii will be as odd a term as Saint Julien or Beaumont Hamel? What context will southern Afghanistan garner next to a Hill 70, a Verrières Ridge or a Juno Beach? Will history be able to document the pressing omnipresence of the non-linear battlefield as well as it has preserved "going over the top" into no man's land of 1916? What will the next generation of Canadians see in their mind's eye when they read about the war on terror and specifically our war in Kandahar? Perhaps they will see those groovy seventies-era arches at the original Kandahar Airport terminal building, so suggestive of an alien McDonald's restaurant? The antique machinery of the Soviet Empire scattered around the battlefield will no doubt be prominent for some. There were fragments of the Red Army and Cold War imagery threaded in and around our contemporary fights. The MiG Gate* that marked where the ANA assumed responsibility for KAF's outer security perimeter was decorated with a Soviet-era MiG fighter jet. Additionally, the interior perimeter of KAF was the responsibility of a former Warsaw Pact member. A scrappy Romanian battalion guarded the towers of the FOB's inner wall with (again) highly evocative retro-Soviet equipment.[5] These are but a few of the waypoints along the hall of memory, raw remnants for the historian's harvest.

I will see the shining light of truth I glimpsed for mere seconds standing on Highway 1, at the centre of my collapsing universe. The one instant that saw my known world turned upside down, shaken like a soda can, and then abruptly righted.

It was only for a moment, but it was enough.

We are on our way home. I am lying flat on the tarmac enjoying the oily heat of the Arabian runway on my limbs for an additional moment. With a grunt, I struggle to stand up in just my socks and underwear. The others around me are doing the same. A ghostly platoon of underwear-clad soldiers. My sweaty Cadpat (Canadian pattern combat uniform) is off and I am now grabbing my civilian clothes. We are back on the little camp at the edge of the war — Camp Mirage. In the morning we will be on an Airbus bound for decompression in Larnaka, Cyprus. This whole scene is not what the Bible meant by Judgment Day,

---

* MiG is the short form for the Russian aerospace design bureau that was a major producer of fighter jets for the Soviet Union.

not entirely. I would wager, however, that Judgment Day is going to feel a lot like this. I pulled on my civilian slacks and looked north out across the starscape where four hours away lay the holy city of Kandahar with all of its angels and demons — the only place in the world where I felt the presence of the beast. Kandahar smoulders in my mind as the high-water mark of the Canadian Army I grew up with. I have never been back.

I have never stopped thinking about it.

Some of the walking wounded cannot bear to hear another word expressed about Afghanistan and will go to great lengths to avoid hearing about it or being reminded of their time there. Some go the other way and become Afghanistan junkies who are eager to snort any fragment of news, any sign of positive change or increased stability in Southwest Asia. I am definitely in the latter camp. I came home from Afghanistan thirsty for the latest details of the war and obsessed with the notion that time had not yet run out for success. After so much bloodshed, the possibility that it had been spent badly became unthinkable.

CHAPTER 3:

THE WIDENING GYRE

I was naïve to think that the top brass and the medical branch of the CAF would start to deal with stigma of mental illness when faced with the Ombudsman's reports and the attention of the media. Mental Health education and awareness is still nonexistent. What training there is, is usually left to a few briefings presented prior to an operational deployment.

— Fred Doucette, *Better Off Dead: Post-Traumatic Stress Disorder and the Canadian Armed Forces*

I am in my sea container office on Kandahar Airfield. It is late July 2006, near the height of that Taliban summer. KAF at night is owned by voices. Remnants of conversation from ten thousand faceless soldiers lumbering from one point to the other. Groundhog days ending or opening depending on the duty roster. Uninvited words carry through endless canvas walls or steal along plywood corridors. These fragments of conversation are generally succinct and focused. It is dangerous here and there is little room for embellishment of language. Soldier words have the hard edges of coins and they fall into place like exact change. Clarity and economy are all one need understand about military communication.

My voices had long since left for their canvas shire and the sweet comfort of the sewage lake — the infamous poo pond where my part of the Canadian Contingent is bedded. The unit orderly room was vacant; the last of the clerks had finished their Canada calls almost a full hour ago. All was quiet in my sea container headquarters save for the hum of the air conditioners. Everything is refrigerated in this theatre: your canvas quarters, the stand-easy where you grab a chocolate bar, the little shitcan post office where you get a Canadian magazine or a pouch of Timmies coffee, even your vehicle for beyond the wire. This is a war we try to fight in air-conditioned cocoons, avoiding the searing heat, entirely if possible or at least until the last possible moment. The infantry job here is leviathan. The combination of weapons, extra ammunition, protective gear, and the marrow-sucking heat makes fighting excruciatingly tough.

I was sweating despite the artificial cold, waiting for the set time to call General Bouchard back in Ottawa. General Charles Bouchard was a deeply respected and elegant man; he was also the top logistician in the Canadian Armed Forces. Fluent in English and French, Bouchard spoke both languages with precision, selecting his English words carefully. His aide had managed to get me a window of his time for a personal call. The horrors of July were slowly giving way to even greater stressors on our theatre ammunition holdings. My heart was black with anxiety; I wanted to stay with my troops for an additional year when we went home. There had been an unexpected change with my replacement in my battalion in Canada. The lieutenant colonel earmarked to take my job at home was abruptly moved to another billet and this had created a fresh vacancy in the posting assignments. I immediately thought that perhaps I could stay on. This is not the usual way of things inside the peacetime army. Two-year hitches are all you get in key command billets. The Canadian Forces personnel system and my own corps were both resisting. I had some hope that this phone call would be one final opportunity to plead my case and solicit some influential aid in staying in Edmonton.

Please, God, let me stay with my battalion and my soldiers when we come home.

Finally, the hour arrived. It was late in Afghanistan but early in Ottawa. One deep breath, a glance at a couple of scripted notes, and I punched in the numbers. The general's aide picked up a few moments later and ushered my call through.

"You have about ten minutes, Lieutenant Colonel," his aide informed me. "He has a busy morning." There were a series of satellite clicks and I heard Bouchard pick up the receiver.

"Good morning, John; or I guess I should say, good evening. What time is it over there anyway?"

"It's twenty-one hundred hours here, sir. General, sir, thank you for taking my call. I heard the new commanding officer back in Edmonton has left the role somewhat unexpectedly."

"Well, yes ..."

"I would love to keep my battalion one more year when we get out of here," I blurted. So much for the pleasantries and professional discourse.

"Yes, John, I understand that emotion. All of us feel that way when we come out of battalion command," he explained, somewhat pedantically. He was in the other world. He could not know how dried out and brittle my resolve had become. I decided to play my lone ace.

"As you know, General, I have not had the full two years of command normally allotted to battalion commanders." My tour in Kandahar had resulted in a slightly truncated turn as the commanding officer of the battalion in Canada. "With what my folks have been through, I think it just makes sense to leave the Afghanistan commanding officer in place. I know what these men and women have been through. I think the case is strong."

"No, it is not. You have punched your ticket. Others need that opportunity and you need to move on as well. We have already found the next replacement. He needs that job."

"Sir, I understand the system and I can only imagine the challenges you have to face getting the postings sorted, but the war has been hard on the soldiers in this unit. I think an exception might be justified, given the lay of the land. I can move on the following year once we have fully reconstituted in Canada. There are merits to this, believe me."

Silence. Only the robot clicks of connecting satellites fed my ears. The business of national defence in Ottawa is a different game entirely than in the field. I was not good at the Ottawa stuff. Even worse, I had used the word "war." The word was corrosive to Ottawa-ears in 2006. Our grandchildren will look back on this time and miss the fact that the army was not immersed in war all at once. Rather, the Canadian Forces was exposed to its new war incrementally — like a child dipping her toe into a chilly wading pool. Very few senior leaders in the Canadian Forces had been exposed to the southern Afghanistan experience. Calling the mission "a war" was considered bad form, even melodramatic — right up to that fateful Operation Medusa Thanksgiving of 2006.

"Stability is what this group needs, sir. In a way it's fortunate that this opportunity has come around." More silence greeted that sentence. "Is there no possibility of changing your mind, sir?"

"Is that all, John?" His tone was the perfect mix of boredom and impatience. Could the call really be ending before the minute hand moved twice on my watch? I should not have come to the point so quickly. I was in that space where the longer I extended the conversation the worse it was going to go. Put down your sword.

"Is that all, John?"

"Yes, sir."

"Good luck with the rest of the tour."

His word *luck* nearly made me laugh aloud. I was in hell with current ammunition shortages. The ammunition situation in the middle of increased combat activity in July posed a wide and highly visible problem. It could not be solved quickly.

Good luck.

I felt suddenly desperate as I replaced the phone on its cradle.

I had lost. Hell, there hadn't even been a contest. Now what? I had no idea how my battalion was going to fit back into peacetime. I did not want to even contemplate moving on to other work myself.

I was going to be moved to the Army Staff College in Kingston, Ontario, when I returned to Alberta. Away from the men and women I have been with in Kandahar — the people I had grown to admire and love — and into a demanding job instructing the army's top captains. I could not imagine moving on from this battalion so soon. Who will understand what we did here? Who will understand what happened to us? I glanced at my fighting order and Kevlar helmet draped on its wooden storage rack; my battle rattle awaiting its next trip outside the wire — a scarecrow soldier.

In the deepening darkness the protective equipment looked like another person silently condemning my mental descent.

You are a pathetic piece of shit.

I felt as scooped out as this webbing on a stick — a burned-out shell holding up a uniform. Over the signature din of Kandahar Airfield and its sea of voices and miles of plywood corridor I heard the sound of one of our Nyala gun-trucks firing up. I tucked my disappointment into a deep recess and stepped back out into the twilight heat, determined to hone my thoughts back to the here and now. The counter-insurgency was a perpetual war of the mind. Mine against yours, you hard little bastards. Packing soft, distracting thoughts away and locking them down in your mind is a necessary task in any war. We still had several weeks to live through, including the worst of the Taliban summer. Peacetime problems of new job posting and career could be unpacked later.

Master Corporal Shawn Crowder in full fighting order (battle rattle) at Camp Nathan Smith — the Canadian PRT, July 2006, the height of our Taliban summer.

- Within the HQ Compound headdress not required
- Do not wear individual combat equipment in the PX, DFAC, MWR centres or chapel unless the alert level dictates
- Must have your weapon with you. Loaded only (Round not in chamber)
- Weapons will be exposed and visible
- Do not enter a building that has not been cleared and proofed for mines
- Use your Permethrin-treated mosquito net to reduce threats from mosquitos and sand flies. (Malaria has been a factor on both KAF and in Kandahar)

— Rules extracted from camp briefing,
Kandahar Airfield, 2006

I recall some discussion circulating around the Department of National Defence in the winter of 2008 with respect to post-traumatic stress and the Afghan War. Officials inside the federal government, including National Defence, wondered aloud about the difficulties imposed by the peacetime posting process of the military. Was there value in terms of mental stability and PTSD in keeping units together for a longer period after the tour? Hell, yes! I felt deep in my bones that this was the case and I waited for a policy change with respect to the expensive peacetime posting process. Perhaps others coming home could be spared this additional stress. Soldiers suffered because of the immediate break-up of the NSE, our 2006 logistics battalion. The short week in Cyprus to decompress did not cover the requirement. Several of my soldiers drifted out of the service and into ill health after that tour. I have spent ten years now listening to some of their stories about their rocky paths. An additional year together, with leadership that knew and understood their soldiers and their context — where they had come from and where they might be headed without the right help — would both have avoided a lot of suffering and curbed attrition. A unit's cohesion needs to be respected if it is to be truly made whole again. It is a shame that the old posting game continued throughout the Afghan War and that the 2008 conversation never blossomed into a policy change of any sort. A lot of our people felt abandoned as a result. Our institution was too rigid or perhaps too small to profit from the lessons of war that were right under its nose.[1]

To look at me you would be able to tell that I am dreaming, so shallow is my sleep.

The general is leaning in closely now so he can be assured of receiving every detail of my response. "Why have you not cleaned it out? This is the third time you have been told to do it. It will be the last — pure insubordination." His anger is palpable and I am fully sympathetic to it. I have fucked up. I cannot believe I forgot to clean out my locker. His simple order comes back to me now emerging from a dense fog. Days ago General Fraser had approached me about cleaning out my locker on the airfield. He had been very emphatic about it. How could I have forgotten?

"It is starting to reek. It's a health hazard. You know better, John! Make sure whatever is in there is properly cleansed by the Preventive Medicine Techs — including the locker." In the next moment the fog shifts and I am standing in front of my high school locker from grade twelve, its vibrant yellow enamel paint like an unmistakable porcelain sign. My C-7 rifle leans against the front of the neighbouring locker. "Better make sure I secure that after this." The smell of the locker is beyond description. Like a large dead snake, or perhaps a bunch of rats have passed away inside. I am agitated, concerned that I might not remember the locker combination. I might need the technical quartermaster sergeant to come with the bolt cutters. I touch the locker and it flips open with ease revealing a small bulging garbage bag speckled with chunks of gore on the outside. A pulp that can never be removed. I know this bag. I know its contents. I screw up my nose and gingerly lift the remains of the suicide bomber with my right hand, keeping the disgusting load at full arm's length. The bottom tears and out with a liquid sound and out rolls his head, bloody, but remarkably intact after the blast. The skin colour is light. The head is Persian but not of Afghanistan. He is not an Afghan. Can you see, he is not an Afghan. The hall begins to shake; there is a large convoy en route.

A jolt of clear air turbulence shakes me from the dream. My knuckles are white, tightly engaged on the arms of my seat. I look down the aisle of the Airbus 320 and blink a couple times to ensure I am not still dreaming. The Airbus is empty. What the hell is going on? Gradually, reality returns to me; I am the sole passenger making the trip from Edmonton back to Trenton, Ontario. The soldiers I parted with yesterday were western Canadians. I am five days out of Kandahar and officially have been culled from the herd, heading for some leave and then the new assignment in Kingston. The sensation of an empty airplane augmented the intense *Twilight Zone* feeling from my dream. The last thirty hours have been full of exciting pieces.

Only yesterday a CF-18 out of Cold Lake, home of the 427 Squadron in Alberta, met our military Airbus on approach to Edmonton. There were 150 soldiers on this flight with me coming home from Afghanistan. The fighter pilot's voice was piped into our passenger jet broadcast system for all to hear.

"Congratulations, members of task force one oh six, and welcome home." There was loud applause from the sea of Cadpat uniforms around me. It felt good to see our own fast air alongside and to hear the acknowledgement of the fighter pilot. We had grown so fond of the Hawker Harriers on KAF and their impact on a tricky ground situation. Fighter jets and helicopters had taken on a jewel-like lustre in my mind. Precious assets. I could sense the growth of the entire Canadian Army, so ground focused before this war, beginning to embrace joint air-ground co-operation. The day before — when we touched down in Edmonton — we were led from the gate to the baggage area by a young movement captain to one last surprise. When we exited the secure area we were greeted by two rows of Canadian veterans of the Second World War and Korea. I shook as many of their hands as I could, glimpsing the various campaign stars, service medals, and jump wings on their blue blazers — the heroes of the Greatest Generation. On my way to the luggage lounge for my rucksack and barrack box, I listened to my young soldiers joking and laughing with the Canadian veterans. My thoughts were crowded with a curious sense of comfort. In the faces of those veterans, all smiling and congratulatory, there had been a much deeper message.

I know where you have been.

I closed my mind to yesterday's reception in Edmonton and focused on seeing my own family at Trenton.

Canadian Forces Base Trenton is one of the last remaining "superbases" in Canada and the other great airfield of the Afghan War. Trenton was the counterpoint to the King of the FOBs and it inspires many memories. CFB Trenton was the kingdom of the dead, the last military stop for the fallen where they were reunited with families and ushered out onto the so-called Highway of Heroes and the trip to the Ontario coroner. But Trenton for me meant home as well. The base was so close to my family and to our farm. When I saw the word "Trenton" handwritten on my boarding pass that morning I had to acknowledge that I was going to see them again. I braced for being reunited. I was a bit frightened. It had been over four months since we parted — not a huge amount of time for most people. For me, however, that day was on the other side of a deep mental chasm. Back then, my boys had been somewhat taken aback by the shaggy-haired, bearded Special Forces soldiers they encountered who were reading graphic novels and fiddling with MP3 players in the passenger lounge. "Dad, they look like the ZZ Top guys from the music videos," one of my sons said. "What's up with them? They look different."

"They have a different sort of job in Afghanistan, an important one — one so important that they get to dress down and relax. That's why they look like that."

"Oh!" He was impressed.

This time — today — there were no members of ZZ Top. The theatre relief-in-place was nearly completed and few soldiers remained in the airflow.* The CFB Trenton passenger terminal was nearly as empty as the Airbus. Only a few soldiers in combat uniforms were waiting to get on the plane and flow forward to the war. I turned my eyes away, not wanting to chance recognition. I gave Martha a big hug and a kiss and clutched

---

* Airflow refers to the series of flights that bring fresh soldiers into the mission area and take home those who have completed their tour. The entire operation takes a number of days of dedicated flights to support a military relief-in-place.

at each of the children in turn. Our family unit had been through this before many times — the endless series of long absences, noisy hellos, and solemn sulky goodbyes. There was no way of telling them that for me this one felt very different. On this redeployment I could not get things to level out in my head. I was agitated — bothered by the artillery ammunition shortages in Kandahar; bothered by criticisms I had heard about our team's handling of the matter. I was alive with my experiences inside the double IED attack in July. I felt like I had fried my circuit board and was not sure how to move forward in life. I felt exhausted, empty, like I could not move on. A hundred frightening impulses flashed in my head. But I could not even begin to say this to my wife who had suffered alone and had faced her own demons throughout the long tour. She was exhausted too. A family bears the weight of war together.

I cannot move on.

But I did, like the physically battered soldier in Stephen Crane's *The Red Badge of Courage* who — though mortally wounded — stumbles on with his comrades in the column. I elected to keep up and keep my thoughts and problems to myself. I threw my barrack box and gear into the back of the pickup, watching the duffle bag hit the truck with a last little puff of Afghanistan's emery powder. In a matter of minutes we were driving west on what would soon be dubbed the Highway of Heroes toward home. The truck was full of peacetime banter: school updates and stories about friends and of the kids' most recent activities. I couldn't digest all of the news, though. Maintaining appearances was about as much as I could manage; the content of our conversation was overwhelming. I looked at my family. They all seemed older and different in tiny ways. After months of shared loneliness on the tour, the moment seemed too rich to digest. I felt unequal to the task of being the dad.

"We just need some milk and a few items," Martha mentioned at one point. "Are you okay if we stop at the IGA? You can stay in the truck with the kids." *So normal.*

"Yeah, for sure. No problem."

Orono is the little town closest to our farm. Martha turned in and parked. I was still in my arid Cadpat uniform, and I was only too happy to stay in the truck with the kids. I remember being struck by how luxurious it felt to be stopping for groceries. *So simple.* Suddenly, a face appears at my window. Lori Osborne, a neighbour. She has a big friendly grin on her face. Our kids are in the same grades.

"John! Hi! Oh my God! Are you home for good now?"

"Hi there yourself. Yes, Lori. I just landed in Trenton. I am home. Have not even been to the farm yet to change — that's how fresh my return is."

"Oh, that's great; that is great," Lori says and leans into the window a bit further and directs her comments to my children in the back seat. "I bet you guys are pretty happy to have your dad home now. Isn't it great?" They nod and agree. All of us nod. How do you explain to a neighbour that it is indeed great but a little bit scary at the same time? We are a veteran army family. We paste up good, defensive grins.

Behind my grin I am marvelling at how well the human head tends to survive a suicide detonation. I am mulling on the fact that my suicide bomber, a man met only in death, was not an Afghan.

"See you around, eh, Lori?" I say.

> I am sick and tired and hearing this shit from the guys on Roto 1. Afghanistan this, Afghanistan that. I mean, wake up and smell the coffee, right? Afghanistan is not *the* mission; it is *a* mission. Get over yourselves....
>
> — coffee-break banter, officers' mess,
> Canadian Army Command and Staff College,
> Kingston, Ontario, October 2006

Fort Frontenac in downtown Kingston broods at the confluence of the Cataraqui and St. Lawrence Rivers. A formidable player in the wars of Canada as far back as the Sun King's infamous ancien régime, the old fort today stands as a blend of early-French and late-British construction and it houses the Canadian Army Command and Staff College. The elite program designed for army captains comprises a rite of passage, a demarcation line between promising beginners and wizened professionals. Known affectionately as Foxhole U, the Army Staff College in Kingston is a plumb posting for the lieutenant colonels providing instruction inside its walls. The college had been a dream job of mine before the Afghan War.

I reported to my new job on October 30, 2006, with more dread than I have ever felt on a posting. Intellectually, I understood my posting was logical. I had just returned from Afghanistan, and the Army Staff College is where we expose our captains both to the age-old secrets of the profession of arms as well as to the latest doctrines and tactics from the field. This logic, however, reflected the rules of peacetime. I was on fire with anxiety over what I knew would be a tough and demanding assignment. The Army Operations Course that I would be teaching was difficult, especially as it was based on a constant assessment system. Students are scrutinized for performance from breakfast to last-light on a wide range of leadership criteria: deportment, professionalism, and tactical acumen. Every day of the six-month course students are hit with tactical-assignment presentations to study, to discuss, and to pull apart with their instructors. The students work hard, but the instructors, who always need to be at least one or two steps ahead of them, work even harder. My dream posting was far from ideal in my present condition. The entire time I taught there — and I only lasted six months — was a deepening nightmare. I could not concentrate enough to even read. I could not control my emotions; I could not focus on anything but the news from southern Afghanistan. I was dead tired all the time, despite going to bed most nights right after supper.

The army provided me rent-free married quarters (PMQ) on CFB Kingston Base. Our farm in Orono was only two hours west from the college and we did not want to sell. Martha enjoyed her job and the kids were in school; life was stable.

Stable for them.

I wanted to support her and the kids but I was nursing a subconscious — even campy —desire to escape to the farm and earn a living on the land. It was in this vacuous little PMQ that the worst of my dreams found me. I was on what is called "imposed restriction" — an evil-sounding term for a military member who moves to his or her new post without moving family or effects. It is surprising how many of our senior men and women use IR to balance careers and marriages. Unfortunately, IR is also an administrative tool that preys on the mental well-being of our people. My IR to Kingston was the exactly wrong step to take given my state of health in

2006. My PMQ was wartime-vintage and I decorated it with barrack-box end tables and a rented TV. A great-looking novel that I had purchased in Dubai sat on my barrack-box end table the entire time I lived in the PMQ. I had read the first paragraph umpteen times but was never able to turn to the second page. The descriptive opening salvoes of the book would not take hold. Each time I read the paragraph the words disappeared and images of Kandahar suddenly unfurled inside my head. Over and over. And I would start to think about artillery ammunition consumption and imagine what the holdings would be like now at KAF two months later.

I sat at my desk, coming further and further unhinged while I waited for the phone to ring. I was expecting a call from the army's chief of logistics, my military career manager in Ottawa. The call was twenty minutes past due. The Canadian Forces has long boasted a robust system of career management that sees the files of its soldiers reviewed, vetted, and utilized by a centralized personnel organization in the Ottawa headquarters. It was an inexcusably plodding system for this new time: too slow to adjust to the ramped-up tempo of a faraway war. In 2006, with the war in Afghanistan heating up and with Canadian involvement growing inside the worst parts of Southwest Asia, the career management system had little to offer its returning veterans. The disparity between home and away was at its height at this critical juncture. Ottawa continued to play the game by the old rules even as Canadian soldiers were being killed and wounded. The career shops talked about career courses, second language profiles, and increased exposure to the right generals, the right levels. All *I wanted* was to be left alone.

I bolted upright in response to the phone's clamour.

"How are you this evening, John?" the colonel at the end of the line asked.

"Sir, you have got to get me out of here! I cannot do this job; not right now," I blurted.

"What? Now wait a minute. Think about it, *mon ami.* You always wanted to be an instructor at the college. This is an enormous compliment; a handpicked assignment. Take it in stride."

"Goddamn it! Listen to me! It's the night before my teaching assignment begins, and my desk looks like a war zone. I am staring at a stack of books, papers, and shit that make no sense to me. I … I don't know what to say, sir. I don't know how to explain this but I just cannot do the job. Not right now. Fuck! I am freaking out." My voice found a level that I did not recognize. I was in an unfamiliar place. All around me lay material and lesson plans in a dishevelled heap. I would look at a document and be able to read only the opening paragraphs. "Look, my French language profile is set to expire. Maybe some individual French training for a few months?"

"No. That is not how the system works, John, and you know it. The second language training is merit-loaded and you are not competitive for promotion; won't be for a couple years. Listen, do your two to three years at the fort and —"

"That's not good enough," I broke in. "The logistics branch has got to help me. Look at Ian Hope. The infantry is supporting his posting outside of Canada and he is working on finishing his Ph.D. Don't tell me the system cannot give me a garden variety French course."

"Hey, man. You are locked in now. It's late in the game. What's more, you're not special."

"Loud and clear. I get that. I am not asking for the moon, I just … I just … I need time. I am just asking for some time."

"I will make some inquiries up here but don't hold your breath. You had better get your shit together for tomorrow."

"Thank you, sir." I looked out the window on the sunlight retreating slowly west from the fort's inner walls. Despite the army G4's promise to look in on my situation, I was panicking, tears were running down my face. After sunrise I would have ten smart young captains with me eight hours a day. The mere thought of it tightened the invisible vise one more notch. The workload was hopeless. The tactical shorthand that had been ingrained in me since my days as a lieutenant was damaged. The military symbols of battalions, brigades, and divisions suddenly looked like hieroglyphics. I glanced at my car in the courtyard and wished dearly that I was driving home. I had the overwhelming urge to be away from the unachievable task in front of me.

I'm bolting. The hell with this.

I retrieved my keys from my jacket and heading for the door when something quite extraordinary happened. In a college infused with the culture of strength and competition — competition between students, between different corps of the army, and between directing staff — a good Samaritan appeared in order to save me.

I didn't ask him for help. Even if the thought had occurred to me, I would have dismissed it in order to maintain the façade — the illusion of taking it all in stride. Lieutenant Colonel Roger Cotton, an armoured officer (tanks) of the Royal Canadian Dragoons, was suddenly standing at my office door. Cotton, who had been at the college for nearly two years, is that rare blend of social intelligence and tactical excellence. Somehow he knew I was in trouble. Unlike the other overworked instructors who went about the day with their own heavy load of preparation, Roger took the extra time to zero in on me. He rapped his knuckles on the door frame.

"Hey, John. How are your preps coming? All set?" I suddenly realized with embarrassment that my door was wide open. *How much of my telephone conversation had he just heard?*

"I am just setting down to it, Roger," I lied. "I am behind, but making progress." He came uninvited into my small office and began walking me through the maze of paperwork.

"These forms are filled in by each student. One copy goes to the Registrar and the other will go on each student file."

"Oh," I said, doing my best to appear engaged. Cotton continued unfazed.

"These are your folders to build your student file right here, these heavy grey ones. Go up to your Syndicate Room tonight and lay them out at each desk. I usually have the students fill them in because it saves me time and generally guarantees accuracy, right?"

"Okay. Makes sense. Thanks for the tip," I mumbled, keeping up what I hoped was a competent front. Inside my head, my brain was screaming, *can't do this, I can't fucking do this.*

Cotton, however, was just warming up.

"You will need to read this publication on manoeuvre tonight, or at least this week. Maybe you already have? It is the latest approach to the function of manoeuvre and the commandant is really keen on it. It's a must read, 'cause he will grill you and your students on it."

"Okay. I haven't read it, but I will."

I looked unhappily at the publication, knowing full well it would probably take all night for me to read — especially at my diminished rate. My ability to focus and absorb reading material had evaporated somewhere between the waging of a disjointed Operation Mountain Thrust and the opening salvoes of Operation Medusa in Afghanistan. I had found myself fighting to digest operation orders and documents since the back half of the tour. These days, it took me an hour to read a three-page memo. I had not read a complete book since 2005 — not so much as a Stephen King yarn.

"This reading you will want to assign tomorrow, even though the exercise is two weeks away, because they will need the time to form sub-syndicates and prepare. I usually take the syndicate to the mess on the first Thursday and assign the lead roles. It's a good way to break the ice with them and get the work moving in a relaxed setting."

I tried to hold the details as on and on Lieutenant Colonel Cotton talked. It must have been about forty minutes. Quite a lecture, but not in an arrogant, show-off way; rather, in an empathetic manner: detail after detail of pointers, most of which bounced off of my uncomprehending but grinning face. Some of the work he just did himself while he talked. It was not so much the content of his message that reached me as much as the soft and soothing Maritime-flow of his words, his sincere concern for my situation. He was not going to let me sink, nor my students. With each word of his I could feel my heart rate slow down a bit; feel thawing the icy grip of panic on my heart.

I am and will be forever grateful to Roger Cotton, who today is a senior colonel in the army. He deserves to be. He had plenty of the right stuff that makes our army successful above the rhetoric and the relentless pursuit of credit so commonplace in a competitive institution. As the next dozen months marched by and I slowly took steps to regain my head, I found myself looking back on that desperate night in Kingston and the way Roger had made me feel. He was a good Samaritan who steered me away from an invisible menace.

A week later I heard back from the head of army logistics, the G4. The news was not good.

"Hi, John, it's the G4 again. I am sorry, *mon ami*, I talked to the army commander; he wants Afghan veterans teaching his captains. You are going to stay put whether you like it or not. After two more years there, we will get you up to Ottawa to round out your education on the strategic level. You will be competitive for promotion then."

"Competitive for promotion in two years' time. Oh my God! What about Ian Hope? What did the army commander say about that? Why can I not get some special consideration? I need help!"

"Listen to yourself — 'special consideration'! Can you hear yourself, man? Listen, neither he nor I have any visibility on Ian's doctorate program. That is an infantry, regimental matter. Ian Hope is in a much different space than you are. And I might add he is doing his job."

"You mean his corps is taking care of him — as they should." I could feel my doppelgänger winding up for another emotional flight. "What about *my* regiment? What about the fucking Logistics Branch?" My voice raised two octaves.

"Hey, John, I gotta go right now, but I will be in Kingston next week with General Leslie. Why don't you and I have dinner together and have a nice long talk." He recognized the urgency in my voice and was working hard to keep a safe distance — an experienced Ottawa staff officer! "We can maybe explore some of this special consideration you are talking about."

"Wait, sir —"

The call was over. I sat there with the receiver in my hand and an ocean of rage inside me and no outlet. I pounded my desk and swore. At the same time, I felt numb and helpless. Defeated. I sat staring at the harbour and the Wolfe Island Ferry for a thousand years.

It wasn't the first time I had flown off the handle. The day before I had unloaded on that smug colleague during a coffee break. Bits of that outburst played out in my mind. I had the weird sensation of being outside of my own mind again.

"The PRT concept is doomed to fail. Not tight enough control by the Canadian Battle Group."

It was not loose battle group control. That was not the issue — quite the opposite, actually. In Kandahar City economic development needed space, proximity from the security side. I always felt that putting the PRT under Ian Hope's battle group was mixing church and state: too close to function properly as a centre of development and enterprise.

He — the smug bastard — shook his head. Like he knew it all and I knew zilch.

"Says you — but you're dead wrong. You don't get it."

You don't get it.

I felt like my head was about to explode. The pent-up rage and anger had blinded me. "God damn the army G4! God damn the whole fucking army HQ!"

Why do I need to hold these things? Why do I need people to understand that I am right? Does any of it matter anyway? I am out of the war. I am home, a staff college teacher.

Slowly my breathing evened out as my thoughts returned to the present. I typed out an email to the army G4: "Sorry I raised my voice. Dinner sounds great next Thursday. Pilot House okay?"

His response was back to me in a few moments: "Sounds like a plan."

The ensuing Thursday took forever to arrive. Lieutenant General Andrew Leslie, the army commander, was with us for a portion of the day, talking to our captains as we put them through their paces at the Simulation Centre. Andrew Leslie is an electric sort of leader, a gifted orator with the power to inspire. The young captains are awestruck by his celebrity and availability.

"Walk with me for a moment, John."

I was glad to. I too admired the man.

"How are things?"

"Things are good, sir," I lied cautiously, knowing better than to engage a lieutenant general in my problems.

These matters of pain and administration were better solved at lower levels, and if absolutely necessary, they could be brought to him by his own staff. I was convinced that it was much better to have the G4 advocate for me.

"I mean, I am having an important meeting with your G4 tonight in the city. I am hoping that we can get things ironed out."

I was deeply torn. I was not well; I was confused, paranoid, and nervous. At the same time, I had an overpowering desire to not let him down, feeling his intense charisma at work on the last remnants of my pride. As desperate as I felt, I did not want him to know how much I felt like a fraud. General Leslie nodded, a gesture I imagined to be his acknowledgement of the meeting. We talked for a few more moments on the state of the army, about the war in southern Afghanistan, and then he was pulled away by a group of simulation contractors, men who had served with him and were keen to say hello. I hurried home to change into my civvies for dinner at a pub in Kingston.

A short time later I began a slow descent into hell.

"Ya want anything else?" the waiter asked.

"Maybe one more draft."

It was getting late and it was a cold, wet night. My belly was uncomfortably tight with beer. I had been waiting for an hour and a half, initially nursing the time with one drink but then several. I eventually gave in to hunger and ordered a meal. That had been ages ago. I had sent a number of emails to the G4 — my career manager, my supposed friend. There had been no responses. It was clear to me now that he was not coming.

I brooded and drank. Could he have mistaken my need? my desperation? Did he miss the fact that my entire life was fixed on this meeting and its outcome? Did he think I was being selfish with my nagging? To this day I do not understand. Too many pints of beer later, I stumbled home, fighting the wind up Fort Henry Hill past the remains of long-ago wars and eventually into the "modern part" of the base and my PMQ patch. Strangers watching me stagger along Johnson Street downtown would have assumed I was an escaped convict, barking to myself, crying, trying to suppress a deep, untapped rage.

As I passed out in the empty tomb of my PMQ, between my barrack-box end tables, I drew a thick, black line across his name in my mind.

I am apart from them.

The ship is one of those glamorous superliners with an enormous stack and several decks lifting to the sky from the main superstructure. My wife and children are departing on vacation. I am watching from the jetty and wishing I was with them on the luxury ship, one of the hundreds of souls soaking up the sun on holiday. I can imagine the kids spending most of their time at the pool, my wife reading one of those impossibly thick paperbacks and relaxing as she keeps watch over their antics. The vessel is so beautiful and so large, its movement nearly imperceptible. To the right of my field of vision a large black mass is moving, much faster than the graceful ship. It takes a moment for me to process the image: a rogue-wave double the height of the ship. The sun-baked dots on the decks of the superliner do not see it. They continue to walk the decks with daiquiris and umbrella-festooned cocktails.

No, no, no. My heart tightens.

The wave hits the ship head on, coming down with its full force on the bow of the giant vessel. The noise is terrible. Crashing china, shrieking metal, and thousands of voices raised in unified horror. The mammoth ship follows its nose into the sea, fully capsizing as I watch helpless from shore.

Suddenly I am underwater and face to face with a porthole. I can make out the image of the angel medic peeping out from the capsized ship. Her compassionate eyes are probing my face. I am powerless to assist her. The dream shifts again and I am looking down on her pulverized corpse among the melting ice of an aluminum casket. Her broken body starts to scream.

I wake up in my hollow Kingston house to find that I too am screaming.

Kingston under a rain shower smells of the slow passage of time. Something about the wet limestone and the mist of Lake Ontario inspires a sense of the ages. In the midst of my struggles with work at the Army Staff College came devastating news out of Kandahar. On November 27, 2006, the Canadian Battle Group in Kandahar lost Chief Warrant Officer Robert Girouard, its regimental sergeant major. Girouard was killed on convoy in Kandahar moments after leaving the heavily defended wire perimeter of the airfield. Lieutenant Colonel Omer Lavoie's RSM was dead. Unbelievable. Just a few weeks ago Bob Girouard and Omer Lavoie were attending our ramp ceremonies on KAF. Now they were paying a horrible butcher's bill and I was at home in full-fledged peacetime. This simple fact tortured me. The flat-out combat effort of our Canadian Task Force existed in the same dimensions as our peacetime work-a-day world. This two-world phenomenon fed my PTSD and my sense of guilt. I lined up at lunch across from the big simulation centre at CFB Kingston with everybody else but my mind was a long way away. Flags across the base and indeed the centre of the limestone city were already at half-mast. Everyone was talking about the day's casualties. Despite the realities of the modern battlefield it is still shocking that a senior soldier in the Canadian Battle Group could be killed. The friggin RSM, the principal disciplinary adviser to the commanding officer, a full-fledged member of the task force executive, was gone. I remember watching him and Omer at Raymond Arndt's ramp ceremony on KAF. My impressions of Bob were those of a kind man who, although soft spoken, exuded strong leadership and cool infantry competence. The sort of soldier you would want to follow and never let down. Bob was such a great fit with Omer Lavoie at the head of the task force.

More and more people in Canada were beginning to understand the nature of the war in Afghanistan. My colleagues at the college were rattled. The news was unsettling. I listened to the banter at lunch. I could imagine with ease where the IED had been detonated. It was a long-established ambush alley and unfortunately known too well to Canadian soldiers by the fall of 2006. I kept my mouth shut. Inside, all I could feel was a hot shame. I was hyper-agitated, disgusted at myself for being home and comfortable in Canada.

There is a war on. I should not be eating in a pristine cafeteria, working on pointless electronic battles with my students. It's all wrong. I should be there too.

In my mind's eye I see a yellowing photograph in a simple, dated wood frame from Woolworth's. It has hung on the wall in the living room of this

Hanna, Alberta, farmhouse through multiple hay and wheat harvests, decades of different Eaton's catalogues and pronouncement of Stanley Cup champions over radio and television air waves. The grinning, youthful face behind the glass is not at all dated like its trappings. The soldier is strong and full of vitality, and his face could be any one of our Kandahar soldiers from Task Force 1-06.

One Friday, shortly after RSM Girouard's death in Kandahar, we were nearing the end of the simulated phoney war on the venerable Kingston Base. No time for the cafeteria today as there would be an early hot wash after lunch and then we would be standing our captains down for the weekend. I grabbed a coffee and a granola bar in a small coffee room in the simulation building. Lieutenant Colonel John McNair, whom I had come to appreciate as a highly intelligent, cerebral officer, was leafing through the *Globe and Mail*, checking for updates from southern Afghanistan. Lieutenant Colonel David Holt, our British exchange instructor, was working on a strong tea. David was an infantry officer from the King's Own Scottish Borderers (the Jocks). I loved his dry sense of humour, which was largely expressed through epic understatement. I imagined him at Agincourt with Henry V as one of his men-at-arms — Sir David — with his thin, tough frame, fighting overwhelming odds and winning — ever-bent on carrying the day. As a logistician, I often got paired with Holt for student exercises. David's rapier wit, his "stiff upper lip" foreignness and lack of Canadian context helped me to relax. I found parts of my old "me" rallying when I worked with David. Despite my struggles as the new instructor I had begun to grow fond of our little pack; fond of the little Hogwarts in combat uniforms that old Fort Frontenac resembled.

Lieutenant Colonel David Patterson, our artillery guru, came in to the coffee area to complain about the atrociously inadequate fire plan (artillery plan) that the student gunner had formulated. It lacked coordination, synchronicity, and a hundred other things that only Patterson completely understood. My eyes suddenly fell on McNair's *Globe and Mail*. The prominent story was not yet another Kandahar piece, but rather a front-page write-up on a Canadian soldier of the First World War. His remains had just been identified after having been unearthed in France by a utility construction crew in 2003. The soldier's bones had been entwined with the remains of another Canadian soldier who had not been identified. The brass badges, .303-millimetre rifle ammunition, and accoutrements eventually confirmed their identities as Canadians. Because of the dedication and heroic efforts of the researchers and DNA technicians, they were actually able to make a positive identification of the remains using the DNA of the soldier's nephew. Private Herbert Peterson, 49th Battalion, Canadian Expeditionary Force, had originally hailed from Hannah, Alberta. He had been saved from eternity's grasp by his nephew and namesake Herbert Peterson, who lived in Lethbridge, Alberta, just a few hundred kilometres south of Hannah.

"I wish my dad was still alive. He never got over the fact that his brother never returned," Peterson told the *Globe* reporter. Glen Peterson had only been eighteen years old when his brother Herbert had gone off to France. There is something compelling about the redemption of — the reclamation of — a family member from the previous generation by a relative.

A series of images invaded my thoughts. My mind was a thousand miles away from the little staff room. The expansive sandscape and pie crust–shaped hills of Kandahar Province immediately swam to the front of my brain. I recalled how small and insignificant I felt on convoys earlier in the year as I looked up through the air sentry hatch of a LAV III at a vast and empty vista of bright blue and brown nuances. It would be so easy to be vaporized and lost forever in that antique place. The soldier's ultimate fear of being lost without a trace, loved ones never knowing. No final goodbye for the unrecognizable corpse. No one wants to be sent home in that aluminum casket that cannot be opened. I remembered the heavy, metallic sound of a casket being set on the cargo deck of the C-130 Hercules, a mournful sound. My next thought was of my children mere hours away from me by car up Highway 401 and the notion that this Canadian soldier had been brought home by family: by his brother's son, a relative that he had never met. My thoughts skipped to the truck ride in our smashed convoy of July 2006 heading into the PRT with my mind a mass of pudding, trying to focus on the tactically necessary but dwelling on my children. My boys were just starting to come of age and the girls were babies still in my mind. But for the grace of God, I might have missed getting to know them at all. Who is going to love them, be as curious about their achievements and supportive of their failures as their own father?

I am not here in Afghanistan because I am not interested in you, because I don't care about you. Good Christ, quite the opposite.

I remembered how I did not want to call Canada that night of July 22. The IED event had left my mind raw, freshly bruised. I wanted to avoid fresh stimuli. I certainly did not want to tell my wife what had happened. Lieutenant Colonel Simon Hetherington, the post commander and one of my dearest army friends, forced me to call her. In that rough infantry post battened down from rocket attack and frontal assaults, I was guided by angels....

I came back with a jolt to the present. My throat felt tight. I was suddenly aware that I was still in the staff room at the simulation centre sitting over the open *Globe and Mail*. I was startled to discover that heavy tears were sliding down my face. One of my tears had actually hit the newsprint with a soft "thwonk." I choked back a spontaneous whimper and became hot with panic. I dropped the newspaper on the table and without a word spun away from my colleagues and bolted for the door, leaving Patterson in the middle of his impassioned rant on the student fire plan.

I went out to the parking lot and found my old Volvo station wagon, clawing at the lock with my keys. I sat in that car sobbing and gulping for air until the lunch break was well past. I dried my face with old paper napkins, oblivious to the gritty glaze and residue of an unhealthy breakfast. I pushed back against the emotional tide of my thoughts and tried to return my focus to the tactical exercise we were running. The further I travelled from Kandahar, the harder it was becoming to suppress my emotions or to force thoughts and feeling into airtight little boxes. They would no longer stay locked; their walls were permeable.

Suck it up. Everything is leaking; people will see what a jackass you are.

Despite my distraction, I had managed to retain the main critical points Dave Patterson had been making on the shoddy student effort for indirect fire. Artillery is the most mathematical of combat arms, trigonometry and vectors — something logical and safe to hold onto. I took a very deep breath and edged my way back in to the simulation centre, hoping my face would not look puffy.

People know what a jackass you are.

It was only during the latter part of my time in Kingston, at the staff college, that I realized there was a fundamental shift in my mental state. I had to confess that my doppelgänger moment was not a singular event. I was out of balance in the way I looked out at the world and down at myself. Hobbies, pastimes, and simple pleasures were of no interest. I could not relax; I could not concentrate. My mind raced on any one of a number of different fronts. Most of my colleagues were threats, enemies. Kind words were spoken with ulterior motive and manipulation in mind. My own branch of the army had turned its back on me and offered me no assistance. My world, in the span of a few weeks, had turned into an ugly battlefield. Despite years of training and sessions on PTSD, taking care of soldiers and their families, I did not recognize my own wounds. PTSD is a beast with a thousand faces, and when it grows inside you it becomes so ensnared with your sense of self that it is nearly imperceptible.

You can unwittingly harbour the disorder for years, oblivious to the harm it is raining upon you and your loved ones. So silent is its work: the devil touching you on the sleeve.

Later that afternoon when everyone had left for their respective weekends I stopped by the staff room in the simulation centre and grabbed the *Globe and Mail* about the recovered soldier from the First World War. I still have it.

I needed to remember his name.

CHAPTER 4:

ANDY'S SONG

I can tell the difference of soldiers that have been there over two weeks, versus two days. The difference is simple and complex at the same time: mortars, ambushes, IEDs, and a transportation platoon's worst nightmare: SVBIEDs (suicide vehicle–borne IED). Within three weeks of being on ground, most soldiers in the platoon had experienced contact with the enemy. We were now functioning as equivalent to a seasoned transportation platoon, just in time for Op Medusa.

— Master Corporal Andy Singh[1]

Major General Malcolm Smith Mercer, commander of the 3rd Canadian Division in 1916, would be as surprised as hell to know his notoriety today. Smith Mercer went down in the annals of Canadian military history as being the highest-ranking soldier killed in battle. He would understand, however, the moral blow of his loss on the spirit of the soldiers. Even in the bloodbath of the Somme, where the cynical might view the general's loss as just one more assault to the numbed senses of the war-weary Canadian Expeditionary Force, his loss would have been dislocating to his command. Losing a senior soldier brings an extra level of shock to a military unit, even to a country; it's a special affront to the kingdom of the mind. One only needs to look to the loss of Major General John Reynolds, a prominent Pennsylvanian, in the opening salvoes of Gettysburg in 1863. Reynolds had the recognized potential to be a future U.S. president and his death was a blow to the Union at the time of the pivotal confrontation at Gettysburg. Losing a senior soldier emphasizes, more abruptly than anything else, the random nature of battle. Violence inside of battle and a combat death do not possess the quasi-rationale or structure of a traffic fatality or a farm accident. Combat deaths have an immediacy and tenor all to themselves.

The day after Chief Warrant Officer Bob Girouard was killed on IED Alley outside of Kandahar City on November 27, 2006, the large Canadian Battle Group was understandably rattled. Their Battle Group RSM was dead. The five-and-twenty drills were discussed with reinvigorated emphasis. In the predawn light of November 28, the set-pattern of the convoy brief already was being chanted with refreshed determination by the congregation of soldiers about to depart. Points of posture, individual jobs in an ambush, and convoy discipline were prevalent. Master Corporal Andy Singh remembered to me that he took in the charged mood in the convoy assembly area at FOB Masum Gar and inhaled a deep breath. He checked his watch one more time then climbed into his Bison carrier for the convoy to KAF. The show had to go on.

Andy Singh and I overlapped for a short time in Kandahar. It seems funny now to think that we were there together; that the man that would help me so much was on KAF at the worst of the bad time. He landed on KAF two days before our own master corporal Raymond Arndt was killed and three of my infantrymen were badly wounded on Highway 4 between Kandahar and Spin Boldak on the Pakistan frontier. I did not know Andy Singh at that point in my life and even if I had, it would have been hard to connect on KAF given the ebb and flow of soldiers during a rotation or RIP (relief-in-place), as they were called in those days. Synchronicity is crucial during the RIP. Some of the soldiers in place need to remain to help settle the new troops into their mission. My

Master Corporal Andy Singh on top of his LAV II Bison, October 2006. Andy Singh and I overlapped in Kandahar for three weeks in August 2006, but we did not meet until four years later when I joined the Army Reserve and found him recovering from his wounds in my Reserve battalion.

soldiers were flowing outward toward Cyprus for their decompression week before heading home. I was focused on getting my troops home and away from the buzz saw, seeking out long-deployed faces for a final "thank you" before they disappeared from my life. My immediate posting to Ontario would see me only overnight in Edmonton. On any given day of the tour, logistics soldiers were spread across Kandahar Province with the infantry battle group Task Force Orion. We were so dispersed it took three parades on KAF to award all of the tour medals to the unit; such is the ethereal nature of a logistics battalion at war. Tracking down specific soldiers during the RIP is nearly impossible. The new men and women were coming from Petawawa, Ontario — Andy Singh among them. They were keen to get acclimatized and learn as much as they could from the departing troops from western Canada, the "in-place" force. Meeting Andy Singh would have to wait until some four years later when we would serve together in 32 Service Battalion.

His arrival was not without incident. The C-130 Hercules bringing him to Kandahar was held off as it approached the King of the FOBs at 0300 hours on the morning of August 3, 2006. The aircraft had begun topsy-turvy Khe Sanh–style battle entry to the airfield that made so many of our visitors motion sick. Plenty of our own troops as well. Up and down, back and forth the aircraft would pitch, offering a difficult target to ground rocket attack. The motion of the aircraft made stomachs lurch beneath the body armour. The Canadian Armed Forces stuck with the dramatic tactical landing approach long after other nations abandoned it in the south.

The morning of August 3 was interrupted by another Taliban rocket attack and the Hercules was warned off until the all-clear was given on the ground. It was the opening gambit of our worst day of the tour. Later that morning, Task Force Orion would be engaged in a full-on fight in the small town of Pashmul, in Panjawaii District, some twenty-five kilometres west of the city. The last serious fist fight between our infantry and the Taliban before the RIP ended. Preliminary moves by the soldiers of 1 PPCLI toward Pashmul were underway as the C-130 finally got the clearance to land.

In the back of the noisy Hercules, Singh remembers checking his body armour straps and feeling a surge of adrenaline for the delay: *Ha! Okay!* He braced himself. *Bring it on.*

He said he looked up and down the fuselage at the soldiers filling the belly of the aircraft, and remembers feeling ready and proud, simply because everyone else portrayed that same confidence. They would need this sort of resolve. All summer the Taliban had been concentrating west of Kandahar City, building for a conventional fight with the NATO forces. The Canadian Task Force would be mightily tested before 2006 was over.

Andy Singh had been a soldier since he was a little boy. He started out in North York, Ontario, as an army cadet going through the early paces of drill, uniform preparation, fitness, and fieldcraft training. And he loved it. He joined the Army Reserve when he came of age, not even having to change armouries from where his Cadet Squadron continued to parade. Singh worked his way up the ranks, making master corporal in record time in the Reserves. He was already starting to think about making the army his full-time career with a transfer into the Regular Force — and why not? He had a young family and he was continuing to enjoy the challenges of soldiering. Around the time of the strategic move of the Canadian Forces Task Force in Afghanistan from Kabul down into Kandahar in the fall of 2005, Master Corporal Andy Singh got distracted from his Regular Force ambitions. There was something unusual brewing in Afghanistan. I think that all of our soldiers felt it. It was whispered in the corner of canteens and mess halls across the land, moving like a silent, unseen wildfire through the rank and file — a relentless, deliberate message: *our country is going into the fight.*

Canada was not only going to remain committed in the country but it had upped the ante by agreeing to move its ground forces south into Kandahar Province, where the fighting with the remnants of the Taliban remained at its worst. By Andy Singh's calculation it was clear that Canada was going to be involved in Afghanistan for the foreseeable future, and the army was going to need to draw on Reserve support if it was to meet the combat demands of Kandahar. There would be overseas jobs for Reservists, he recalled thinking. He was right. There is something a little "August 1914" about the Reserve call-out system in Canada. The Army Reserve is different from the Regular Force in that soldiers need to volunteer to go on overseas missions. In the full-time army, you go where and when you are told. In the Reserves you put up your hand and volunteer to augment where the Regular Forces are going. It is an age-old system and one that worked well for supporting Canada's Afghanistan mission. The army could not have survived Afghanistan without leaning heavily on its tiny Reserve component. Singh was concerned about getting his name on the volunteer list first. The Regular Army transfer could wait; this was an unusual opportunity that might not knock again for an age.

> Corporal Dissanayake and I both paced around when we heard this news (about Reservists being accepted for the Afghanistan mission in Kandahar). I could tell exactly what he was thinking, and I'm sure he knew

what I was thinking. After about ten minutes of this pacing, he asked, "Well, are we going?"

I laughed. "We had better get our names on the list before anyone else!"

A short time later we submitted our names to the Operations Cell in Toronto: we were Petawawa bound. Like everyone else involved, we had no idea what we were about to endure.[2]

Task Force 1-06, (based on 1 PPCLI and the logistics elements from 1 Service Battalion), my own unit, was in Kandahar on operations by the time Singh and Dissanayake's names were called to head to Petawawa to begin their training with the next battle group. This battle group was based on the first battalion of the Royal Canadian Regiment (1 RCR).

Our platoon was made up of unseasoned and untested soldiers. Within our ranks, we had seventeen privates. All of us, including our chain of command, had to learn quickly within a very short time frame. Tremendous efforts were put in place to prepare us for our Mission Specific Tasks, especially in Wainwright, Alberta. However, it didn't prepare us for the physicality of urban warfare that we were about to experience.

The war in 2006 was still somewhat veiled from the wider Canadian Forces community. The realities of combat in southern Afghanistan had not fully permeated the invisible telegraph of soldier talk. Southern Afghanistan would prove a shocker for many soldiers, especially long-serving members of our force better accustomed to the structure of the Cold War–era battlefield and mature peacekeeping theatres. This new battlefield was akin to a lava lamp, with no clear-cut front line, no discernible rear area as there was in the Second World War and in Korea. The absence of structure — like the need to be prepared for combat at any moment along any point of a journey — gave Kandahar much more of a Vietnam-feel. Such tactical realities demand a lot of mental toughness.

Singh found many of his Toronto soldiers needed additional coaching to get fully acclimatized.

> I had just arrived at FOB Wilson. I lowered the ramp on my Bison and I hear, "Master Corporal! Master Corporal! I'm a trucker, an MSE Op, I did not sign up for this! I'm a trucker! The enemy is right there, three hundred metres away in the tree line! Can you please get me back to KAF?"
>
> After attempting to calm Private Phil Agar down, I explained that even though we were combat service support (CSS) soldiers, we were soldiers first and this was just another part of our job. I told Private Agar that I would make no promises, but I would ask the platoon commander to consider his request to be reassigned to KAF.
>
> A few days later, I returned on a resupply convoy, better known in the Afghan theatre as a combat logistics patrol (CLP). Phil Agar calmly walked up to me and asked to remain in FOB Wilson; he didn't want to return to KAF anymore. He had, in short order, developed into a seasoned CSS soldier.

Convoys adhere to a warped mathematics. The normal function of distance and time are perverted. A glance at a map might tell you that a certain distance could be covered in three or perhaps four hours, but in reality it will take a Kandahar convoy the better part of sixteen. Similarly, a trip that might be completed in six hours, say the simple run from KAF to FOB Wilson, can quickly become a prolonged combat operation. Andy Singh remembers how one combat logistics patrol (CLP) lasted over twenty-six hours:

> In this particular "Convoy from Hell," the column struck an IED, executed a vehicle recovery, was engaged by an SVBIED, and we were — to cap it all off — ambushed.

Master Corporal Rich McLeod, the logistics commander on that CLP, was the first of us to engage the
enemy, killing and injuring a number of insurgents. A
master corporal from Maintenance Platoon was shot in
the shoulder but stayed in the fight. Later he was given
the choice to return to Canada; he said, "No!" He would
remain in Afghanistan with his military family.

I came back to our farm in Orono from Kingston to be with my family for the 2006 Remembrance Day service. It was my first Remembrance
Day since returning home, and as I was driving up Highway 401 toward
home my mind was focused on our own fallen: Nichola Goddard,
Raymond Arndt, the soldiers I had been with on July 22, 2006, the
numerous fallen from Task Force Orion. A municipal election was being
held, and red, orange, and blue candidate signs for town council and
mayoral races dotted the landscape. I picked up Martha and the kids
and we drove downtown the ceremony. I was in full uniform with all
the medals and buttons in more or less the right place. We parked and I
fell in with the other uniforms to march to the town's historic cenotaph.
Among us was a small contingent of Royal Canadian Legion members
out of Bowmanville and a handful of veterans from the Second World
War. As we ambled along the picturesque main street, a combination
of Legionnaire pipes and drums and an energetic Air Cadet band gave
us our cadence. We came to a halt in front of the cenotaph, a regal slab
of stone that had been dedicated by Major John Weir Foote, a Dieppe
veteran and Victoria Cross–winner, who hailed from Cobourg, further
east on the 401.

There was a short service from a clergyman and then a litany of speak-
ers. The first was the local councillor, who was careful to acknowledge
the acting mayor and the local members of the provincial legislature and
federal Parliament. The next was the regional councillor acting for the
mayor of Bowmanville. He brought greetings from all of town council
and took the time to acknowledge certain fellow councillors in the small
crowd, who would need votes in the coming days. The ceremony had little to do with remembering; rather, it was all about local politicians and

the election. My blood began to boil as I realized the entire proceeding was being leveraged as a platform to advance individual campaigns. I barely listened to the words of the federal and provincial representatives while they prattled on. I was seeing red; my heart was pounding. I could not rationalize the Kandahar I had left behind two months ago and the vibrant faces of the fallen with this peacetime sham.

When the service ended, the master of ceremonies made the announcement that he was not going to run "these things" anymore. He had done so for a number of years and he was tired of doing it. If anyone wanted to volunteer he asked that they please step forward.

No takers today.

Warfare and the true responsibility for peace were as remote from this gathering as the moon. I had had it with the whole pack of assholes. I broke out of the little phalanx in front of the cenotaph and found Martha and the kids. They were standing with Marg Zwart, editor of the *Orono Weekly Times* — the town newspaper — and a few of our friends from the old town.

"Nice service," someone said. It sounded like an awkward ice-breaker.

I looked away, unable to form words. My anger was near the doppelgänger level and I was feeling a bit dizzy. Martha came to my rescue.

"That was not a Remembrance ceremony; that was a crock of shit! Could we get more campaign signs any closer to the cenotaph?" she said with disgust.

The exact words I wanted to say.

I kept my mouth shut, afraid of what might come out of it. I let my wife, a savvy veteran of our many trials in military-service life, take a few more swings at the botched service. Inside my head, black thoughts were snapping and flailing about like a rogue electrical cable. I could see Marg Zwart looking at me. *Really looking.* There was nothing I could do to mask how upset I was. I was so angry about the ceremony that I physically hurt. Nothing to do about it. I just let it lay there, warts and all. Marg, however, is a razor-sharp person and an insightful journalist. She knew exactly how perverse the whole event had been.

"We are leaving. See you all later," Martha finally spat out and spun on her heels. I tracked along, full of boiling emotion.

I am not in favour of over the top soldier-worship and the deification of the veteran; too many well-intentioned organizations overdo it. All of us have the duty to remember and the same responsibility for the attainment of peace and protection of our country, our fellow man. That said, politicians of all levels and types should talk less at Remembrance Day — unless it is to say a brief, "Thank you."

Marg Zwart put her critical pen right into the heart of the sham ceremony with her editorial in the next edition. I loved her for it.

The night I decided to quit the army was yet another doppelgänger experience; an embarrassing departure that I seemed to watch from outside myself.

We received the invitation over email and I was positively surprised. General David Fraser was being awarded the prestigious Conference of Defence Associations Institute 2006 Vimy Award in Ottawa-Hull at the Museum of Civilization. He was allowed to invite a set number of guests, and Martha and I had been among them. It was so good to be back with recognizable faces, people I respected and admired, like Major Bill Fletcher, the spectacular C Company commander, Lieutenant Colonel Ian Hope, and members of the Multi-National Brigade Staff — people who understood all too well our shared experiences. For one night, at least, I could be away from my new staff college post and back with some of the key personalities who understood the context of what had happened overseas.

Near the end of the formal dinner there was a speech from the master of ceremonies and then a short acceptance speech from General Fraser. Next would be an introduction of General Fraser's special guests.

"Ladies and gentlemen," announced the emcee, "General Fraser has invited a small group of people who were a big part of his time in Regional Command South in Afghanistan. It gives me great pleasure to introduce to you these individuals, and I would ask each one to stand when your name is called. Lieutenant Colonel Ian Hope." The emcee provided a brief synopsis of Ian's role overseas. The room explodes with applause and cheers for the battle group commander. Hope stands and draws himself slowly to height. He is wearing a civilian tuxedo instead of the proper military mess kit; it turns out his personal effects are still in storage somewhere between Alberta and his new assignment in the United States. This breach of protocol has put a number of our superiors on edge, wondering, I imagine, if this is some sort of "message." Ian Hope flashes his wry Maritimer grin and nods to the wide expanse of Canadian military and political elites around us. The introductions continue: Major Bill Fletcher, Colonel Tom Putt, and on and on. My brothers-in-arms take turns standing up around me. I am awash with pride and camaraderie, the feeling that it is so good to be back with them — I drink in and absorb the applause cannonading around the darkened museum and warm to the smiling faces gleaming in candlelight of the formal dinner. Abruptly, however, the introductions are over.

"Finally," concludes the emcee, "I would like to introduce Mr. Rick Smith." My heart turned to a lump of ice. "Rick is an employee with ATCO Frontec and one of the lead planners for the contracting capability that we will soon be installing on Kandahar airfield to help with the logistics burden. He has been over to Kandahar on a number of planning visits during General Fraser's command."

One last round of polite applause from the tribe as Rick Smith stands up and acknowledges the applause with a curt bow. The emcee looks down at his cue card and moves the agenda along. From across the opulently appointed table I can feel embarrassed, inquisitive candle-lit faces upon me. I cringe with a hot wash of emotion. I cannot believe it. *What the hell?* I was upset and embarrassed to an exponential level. I can never describe the rage and the pain that was pulsing through my veins any more than I can explain why in the hell it mattered in the first place. I was ignored but they managed to announce *the name of the contractor* who was working on a deployment for his company on subsequent tours?

The fucking contractor?

Martha was holding my hand under the table. She knew I had been hit hard. She gave my hand a hard reassuring squeeze. Her support was immediate even though her understanding of my anguish was not. Her eyes met mine.

"Stay calm," her eyes told me. " None of this matters." I was anything but calm, however; I was angry at how much I cared, angry that a simple error could burn so much; angry that even here, with fellow veterans of my own tour, I still did not belong. Sure, it had been a simple oversight, an administrative error. Big deal. In my mind, however, I took it as a clear message: I was not good enough — not even here among my fellow Task Force 1-06 companions. I was apart — a pariah. I had to get out. I couldn't breathe. I leaned in to Martha and gasped: "Fucking — clowns — done — talking — leave this fucking place."

"Okay." She was accustomed to my emotional shorthand.

I stood abruptly and headed to the bathroom. I had to catch my breath.

"Hey, John, good to see you again." It was the contractor, fresh from his announcement as a special guest of the general. He was a retired army officer from the Royal Mechanical and Electrical Engineers.

I nodded. "You too," I lied. He was not a bad fellow, but I wasn't interested.

"How are you?" he asked.

"I am fucking done is how I am."

"How's that? Done?" His look in the mirror was the picture of confusion and I could feel his eyes searching my face as we both dried our hands. I was vibrating; looking down on the scene. My out of body sensation was complete.

Fuck, fuck, fuck.

"Yes. Done. I am leaving the army as fast as I possibly can. I am going to set the land speed record for quitting this fucking gong show. Goodbye."

The following Monday I went into work and submitted my release request. After nearly twenty-five years of service it took less than twenty-four hours to decide to quit the Regular Force.

In the treatment of PTSD, clinicians use a number of approaches to help deal with the ailment. One of these techniques is called cognitive processing therapy. It takes a soldier back to revisit what are referred to as "stuck-points." A stuck-point comprises a bundle of thoughts that may not be 100 percent accurate but are derived from an individual's assessment of why a traumatic event happened. When these stuck-points are activated by an event — be it a dream, a song, a newscast — a series of negative feelings and thoughts come pouring out. In a nutshell, stuck-points are conflicting beliefs that create intensely unpleasant emotions and unhealthy behaviours when they are set in flight. But when you can recognize them and boil these stuck-points down to their essential elements they can become like traffic signals, signs, and triggers your mind can pick up when activated. This gives someone with PTSD the nanosecond to acknowledge the traffic signal and take additional steps to manage or rationalize the flow of negativity. Quite amazing. When they are clarified it is like drawing the monsters that have been under your bed all your life out into the light of full recognition. Stuck-points are as varied and unique as people are themselves. I only came to grips with my own stuck-points eight years after coming back from Kandahar.

The Staff College commandant is a tall, lean, Armoured Corps officer by the name of Brigadier General John Collin. All I really know about Collin is that he is a water polo fan by virtue of the fact that we were all playing water polo as part of the college sports curriculum now. I am also aware that he had served a tour at the U.S. base in Bagram in northern Afghanistan at the same time as my Cambodia-tour buddy, Paul MacDonald.

"What's this document all about, John?" he asks me in an accusing tone, briskly brandishing my request for release from the Canadian Forces.

"I am done, sir."

"Are you fucking nuts? *Are you fucking nuts?*" he thunders. I realize he might be having his own doppelgänger moment.

Someone else for a change.

"Every general officer in the Canadian Forces knows who you are. Do you now that? You can't throw this away!"

I have nothing to say.

"Are you fucking nuts?" he repeats.

"Yes," I admit. "I am afraid I might be."

The army G4 is very busy in the spring of 2007 supporting the fight in Afghanistan from the Ottawa headquarters, and he is extremely irked at having to circle back from pressing duties to make this phone call to a quitter. That is the way of the army, however — no loose ends, however distasteful. I have the impression that I am supposed to be grateful for his time lost to have this final conversation.

"What are you going to do with yourself?" he probes.

"Well, I have the Class B job. I am going to write a little bit and I am going to get the farm going full bore." A naive urge to make a living with our antique farm is pulling me like a Siren's song. Through the line, I imagine his confusion and see him looking at the receiver like a pig looking at a watch. No clue what — or who — he is dealing with or what I have become. My hopes and aspirations must have sounded completely alien to his ears, which strikes me as odd as once we had been friends. Not any more.

"Write?" he snorted. "What about? You're a logistics officer and you're stale-dated."

"Army officer," I corrected, "and so what? Churchill was an army officer first. I have a lot I want to write down — for my own sake if nothing else. As you know, I have been giving some talks on the Afghanistan War already."

"Yes, as for your talks," he snarled, "long before you know it you will be yesterday's man." His tone was threatening, not remorseful. "Well, I've got to get back at it here. Just mark my words. You will be time-expired before you know it."

Look at my wounds, you arrogant bastard. I am already time-expired. I am gone, baby, gone.

And just like that it's over.

I sat and looked at the phone on its receiver. I was overflowing with hatred but I could not pinpoint the source. It was everyone. It was everything. I was at war with the outside world and needed to be sharp against attack. All my energy went into keeping the outer facade looking competent. I needed to get away from these assholes and things would normalize.

I had been so sure it would be that easy.

The sun was shining brightly in Ottawa, making the newly laid copper roof of the Parliament Buildings sparkle. I was oblivious to this beautiful image as I sat tensely in the office of a senior officer in the main National Defence headquarters tower. The office's owner looked me over like he was assessing an errant child.

"You are quitting? Your mind made up?"

"Yes, sir."

"Well, let me tell you a little something about those who leave. None of us is indispensable. We can all be replaced. You can be replaced. Yes, even you."

I could tell that he savoured saying it a second time.

"Yes, I realize that, sir," I replied.

"You know, John, when a soldier leaves the army, it's kind of like a fist being taken out of a bucket of water. When the fist is in the bucket, the water comes up to a certain point. Here's the thing, though," he said, leaning toward me for emphasis. "When that fist is removed from that bucket the water settles. It finds its own level."

I knew what he meant. The institution has got to carry on, and in a good one like the Canadian Armed Forces, there are plenty of able people to replace you. The thing about the "fist in the bucket of water" analogy is that it devalues the individual over the needs of the machine. For a soldier with PTSD the words and needs of the wider system can be particularly painful. Depending on your own stuck-point, it might be the very worst thing another person can say to you.

TRAINING AREA, CANADIAN FORCES BASE BORDEN, OCTOBER 2010

The response to the night attack was going very poorly. In truth, the "enemy" probe we had launched upon our troops was probably a bit too much at that point in the training year. Logistics units in combat cannot repel much more than a handful of dismounted enemy probing. If there is too much enemy interference we call the cavalry or move out to protect scant combat supplies. Tonight's nuisance attack on my Reserve battalion consists of three soldiers whom we detailed to play the enemy — they are plucked from our own headquarters staff serving double duty on the task. Despite the small size of the mock enemy force their efforts have sent the platoon-sized location completely haywire. There was little centralized control as the keen but young Toronto soldiers scrambled to do their best. I sat outside the command post (CP) hunched over a cold coffee and looked to the stars, feeling every bit the "grand old man" of the battalion and appreciating how good this earthy tactical experience felt. It was like riding a favourite old bicycle once again. Andy Singh, recently promoted to sergeant, is here beside me, looking as cool and collected as if waiting for his wife Natasha to come out of a clothing store at the Eaton Centre. Business is business. At this point I had only been the commanding officer of this Reserve unit for a little over a month. I had met Sergeant Singh on parade nights in the Toronto Garrison but I did not really know him well yet.

"Maybe a little too much love for the gang tonight, Sarge?" I surmise.

"Maybe, sir, but good lessons are coming out of it." He began to enumerate the corrective lessons we could cover in the "hot wash."* I nodded, impressed with his professional depth and articulation. *One hell of a talented soldier,* I thought. *Glad he is on our side.*

"You had a tour in Kandahar? A rough one, I understand." I could see his head nod slowly in the ambient light.

"You were there too, sir. Task Force one-oh-six. Your NSE was the one right before mine. Kind of a rough-go as well," he replied.

"Omer Lavoie was your commanding officer, yes?" A hot-trigger click sounded off in my head; puzzle pieces melting in perfect union. *We had overlapped on KAF on that horrible August of 2006.*

I cannot recall how the conversation started. Whether it was something Singh offered of himself or something I said about mistakes and learning. It was clear to me that he had been suffering from mental wounds. I proceeded cautiously, not wanting to go offside with him. Mistakes were all I had been making since my own war had ended. All I can recall is that at some point I found myself telling this sergeant about my biggest PTSD stuck-point: ineptitude — a deep sense of shame and paranoia, the firm conviction that I was not a good officer.

---

* Army jargon for a review session; a sharing of lessons observed and how to better ingrain them into habit and formal operating procedures.

"I wish I had learned my lessons at a younger age," I suddenly found myself saying. "Most of what carried me through my tours was the result of mistakes or just-in-time learning."

Crack! Crack! A pair of rifle reports, harmless blank rounds, sounded on the far eastern edge of our perimeter.

"Let's give 'em another thirty minutes before we shut it down, eh, sir?"

"Yeah. Sure." Suddenly I was ready and willing to unburden. "I wonder if I might not be a hypocrite," I blurted. "I had these thoughts during that double suicide attack in 2006 that came out of nowhere. I felt like our army, our country had no business being there. That none of it was worth dying for. And yet we, the men and women of my own unit, were immersed in the fight every single day." My words surprised me a bit as they tumbled forth. Andy did not leave them unchecked. He came back immediately.

"For me it is that black Toyota Corolla. I see it in my dreams. The eyes of the suicide bomber meeting mine. Understanding too late what was about to happen before he detonated … being powerless to stop it."

He went on to describe the events of November 28, 2006, and his stricken convoy out of Masum Gar, the wounds he received and the pain it still caused him. Across the blackness of the bivouac I offered him some of the details of July 22, 2006, and the attacks that our long convoy endured that endless day. I even told him about my daydream visions of the interior of the smashed Bison LAV and the frequent glimpses I had of the angel medic.

"It was the day after RSM Girouard was killed, November 28," Singh began. "We were running combat logistics patrol thirty-two from FOB Masum Gar back up to KAF. My Bison was targeted by a SVBIED. A single occupant driving a black Toyota Corolla station wagon detonated approximately three metres away from my vehicle. I was the ninth of ten vehicles in the convoy's order of march."

Our convoys owned the middle of every Afghan highway, forcing civilian traffic to the edges of the road, the most likely part of the road for IEDs to be emplaced. It was an aggressive stance, a moral salvo to our enemies.

"Our lead vehicle," Andy continued, "informed us all that there was a single-occupant vehicle on the left side of the road, so we all pushed

Master Corporal Andy Singh on convoy operations in Kandahar in fall 2006. Convoy tactics represented a cat-and-mouse game with the Taliban in the kingdom of the mind. Our columns would drive down the middle of the road, bristling with weapons, and moving at speeds designed to enhance our own force protection. The enemy would let heavy logistic vehicles pass unmolested, targeting the LAVs and Bison instead (a tactic that appealed to a clear sense of swagger).

right to get maximum standoff. I pushed my C6 machine gun to the left and pointed my C8 rifle toward the driver of the vehicle. No movement was observed from the occupant, until I noticed the young man slowly raising his eyes to catch a glimpse at me. Those goddamned eyes. It immediately set off alarms for me."

The language of the battlefield speaks volumes to the fine-tuned ear: a normally crowded street at prime market-time void of shoppers, evidence of fresh digging on a culvert or at the edge of a road. Innocent Afghans would normally have their heads raised up to gawk at our massive trucks and armoured carriers. The Bison LAV II is a squat, mean-looking beast and, if nothing else, most Afghans would give it a look to ensure that they were not in its way. Not this time, however. The driver of the black car had his eyes bent down, intent on his mission, running an internal targeting calculus until the last possible moment when he stole a glance to confirm the right point of detonation.

"Within half a second," Andy recalled, "I heard a crack, saw an orange ball of flame, slammed into the hatch, and was on fire." I nodded in the glow of the naphtha lantern making sure I met his eyes. I could feel the emotion of the man, extrapolating my own convoy experiences, thousands of fragments of memory, to what he was describing.

"I thought I had lost my right arm at first. I ended up in the belly of the Bison. I remember screaming out 'Contact! Contact!'" These are the simple words we use in our radio communications that indicate we have made contact with an enemy. The word is intended to keep other less-pressing chatter off the radio net as the entire effort dials into the event. Our language was always evolving in the field. The most recent euphemism for the dead, for instance, was VSA (vital signs absent). A new term for engagement with the enemy was TIC (troops in contact). TIC wore itself out during the summer of 2006, but has wormed its way deep into the Canadian Army's lexicon.

Andy said he woke up "to a medic slicing my clothing off" with "particles of burnt flesh all over me." The he passed out again. Luckily, he recalled, his driver, Private Ryan Ricketts, "had instinctively carried out the drills that we had practised so many times before to manoeuvre us out of the kill zone. The convoy made its way back to KAF with haste, escorting me directly to the ROLE 3 (emergency hospital). Master Corporal Kellie Smith and her husband Master Corporal Jeremy Blair, an infantry soldier, were the first people I saw after being patched up by the medics."

"Kellie had tears in her eyes," he remembers, and that was when he realized what had taken place. "My platoon was waiting outside the hospital. Despite the situation as I came around the corner, we all started laughing. We had nine SVBIEDs that week." Singh recalls:

> What mattered most in the end was that we all took care of each other. Our chain of command, like concerned parents, stayed awake until we got back from convoys, made sure we ate, called home, slept, laughed, or cried, and had

enough ammo when we went back out. They also gave us a kick in the ass when we needed it. The tremendous display of courage, selflessness, grit, and leadership was simply "Second to None." We were stronger than ever.

It was my turn to share.

"It was the convoy in July 2006," I said, "that was the tipping point in my head. After that day I could not get the workings of the clock to go back together. You know when you take something apart and go to reassemble it and there are all these parts left over? That's how I feel. I went from being who I was to playing the person I once was."

I could see a deep nod of recognition in the ambient starlight of the bivouac. Rank and judgment were long banished from our circle. The bivouac took on an otherworld feeling. I felt the weight of ages in our midst, as if thousands of wounded soldiers from a hundred different armies sat among us. There was a distinguishable lightening in my mind.

A broken windshield on a Canadian G-Wagon, May 2006, the result of a rocket-propelled grenade inside Kandahar City.

I was thinking about Ray Arndt. "When Ray was killed on August 5, I took it personally," I offered. "His death came just at the beginning of our ammunition crisis — a shortage of just about every nature of 155-millimetre artillery ammunition. I blamed myself for the ammo shortfall and things got fucking ugly, really ugly." It was like everybody from the new Petawawa headquarters people through to Ottawa staff officers were telling the world how I had fucked it up," I said, "scurrying to be the fixer without pausing to understand. God," I said, "it was … like being crushed under a bus." He nodded. I continued. "Looking at Ray's smashed remains under the ballistic blanket on Highway 4 and feeling the spark of doubt in my heart — and in our mission — filled me with a bottomless sense of guilt; guilt and cowardice."

He nodded again.

The funny thing, I recalled, was that the ammunition failures were worse than the double suicide attack. "The Taliban at least are pretty direct and transparent in what they are trying to do to you." Some of the Canadians that had arrived to replace us had not seemed so transparent. Some of the criticism I heard first hand. Other remnants I caught from secondary sources, people from my tour that had not yet ripped out. Most of the attacks I am pretty sure I imagined. "But my mind was packed with paranoia," I said. "I really lost my confidence, like I could not absorb any more bad news. But you cannot say those things, not if you want to keep working here, right? You cannot show that the cheese has slipped off the cracker. Christ. I lost it, Sergeant, and now I am here."

It was the first time I was able to tell anyone anything truthful about my experiences in Kandahar. Anything about how unglued I felt and how ashamed I was. Major General Stuart Beare, one of Canada's most personable general officers, had pushed me on the matter for nearly two hours when my release request in Kingston hit his desk, but without success. Talking with Andy Singh had been different. I felt numb in the cool October darkness, wide-open vulnerable but lighter.

"You can, you know."

"Can what?" I asked.

"You can get help and keep it low."

"Hmm," I acknowledged with a grunt.

I reached behind me and rapped my knuckles on the side of the command-post van and presently heard the stirring of the duty watch inside. The door cracked open spilling blood-red light from the CP onto us.

"Let's shut 'er down and bring all the troops here to centre ice for the debrief," I instructed the watchkeeper. He moved to his radio set to issue the orders.

Sergeant Andy Singh led the tactical debrief by the light of a naphtha Coleman. I sat on the periphery of the lantern's warmth and slightly behind the semicircle of young soldiers being debriefed. Singh led them through the positive and negative points of their defence with the eloquence and sensitivity of a poet.

I mulled on this strange new lightness that I suddenly felt.

In October 2007, nearly a year after RSM Girourad was killed and Sergeant Andy Singh was wounded, I attended a medal presentation ceremony at Rideau Hall in Ottawa. Bob Girouard's widow was there to receive her husband's Meritorious Service Cross posthumously. Omer Lavoie, Bob's commanding officer, was in attendance to receive the same decoration. Lavoie has always been a man of few words. Today he had none at all. His eyes seemed to be focused on some far-away point miles from Rideau Hall. It was not a day for small talk, but I still wanted some. What monstrous thoughts must be rolling beneath his calm exterior? The emotion of the event was electric. Jacqueline Girouard was barely able to function when her turn came to stand up and receive Bob's medal. I had no sense for how this would go and what could be done to comfort her. I was helpless in this moment. I would have done anything to reduce her pain and suffering but this was not my place. Bob was Omer's RSM. I need not have worried. When she stepped gingerly forward to receive RSM Girouard's medal, Governor General Michaëlle Jean stepped forward and held her up, throwing protocol to the wind. Here was our governor general binding our wounded family in a walloping embrace. This told me just about everything I would ever need to know about Michaëlle Jean.

ZEROING

The purpose of zeroing is to "superimpose the Mean Point of Impact [as defined in your grouping] onto the Correct Zero Position" so that the grouping will form centrally at all ranges.... It is essential that each soldier zeroes his rifle. Zeroing is the individual's responsibility. It is unusual for two persons to have the exact same zero with the same weapon....

— "Shoot To Live," Canadian Army Training Authority

Ozymandias

I met a traveller from an antique land
Who said: Two vast and trunkless legs of stone
Stand in the desert…. Near them, on the sand,
Half sunk, a shattered visage lies, whose frown,
And wrinkled lip, and sneer of cold command,
Tell that its sculptor well those passions read
Which yet survive, stamped on these lifeless things,
The hand that mocked them, and the heart that fed:
And on the pedestal these words appear:
"My name is Ozymandias, king of kings:
Look upon my works ye Mighty, and despair!"
Nothing beside remains. Round the decay
Of that colossal wreck, boundless and bare
The lone and level sands stretch far away.

— Percy Bysshe Shelley

CHAPTER 5:
A FUNERAL FOR TROOPER CASWELL

Glad to have these Canadians along with us
But all they seem to do is turn food into shit
And make a T-shirt about it.

— U.S. Army scrawl, portable toilet,
Kandahar Airfield, 2005

Our long-ago KAF community boasted heroic names like Screaming Eagle Boulevard, Enduring Freedom Way, and Mountain Way. Additional bricks in the moral wall. Screaming Eagle Boulevard was the main artery that ran parallel to the airfield in front of the little Canadian headquarters compound. It eventually intersected with the equally glorious Mountain Way (after the U.S. 10th Mountain Division) right in front of the old Afghan structure known as the Taliban Last Stand (or TLS). The kinetic imagery inspired by names of streets and buildings helped assure us that the positive outcome of this mess was inevitable. The whole of KAF was festooned with the labels of might and certainty — all the way from Chinook Road to Enduring Freedom Way. Is there not something of Shelley's "Ozymandias" in these names? an echo of the romantic poet's poignant reflection on the physical remains of Ramses II's conquests?

"Look upon my works ye Mighty, and despair."[1]

The brazen names probably did bring familiarity and comfort to the contemporary Kandahar battlefield but they tend to ring like a bad punch line with the march of time.[2] Screaming Eagle Boulevard will be as gone from Afghanistan as Alexander the Great's army at some near point. Armies keep coming to this enigmatic place and yet they may be no more successful than was Ramses II in making a permanent mark. The ageless character of Afghanistan's horizon still stretches past the limit of the invader's reach.

"Climb to glory, sir!"

"All the way!" blasts the 10th U.S. Mountain Division response.

"Huuaaahhh!"

The majority of my soldiers made their home in the modestly named Canadian quarter — the Weatherhaven tents very close to the poo pond. Our little canvas subdivision sprawled westward away from the larger carpet and plywood cathedral known as Canada House — the main Canadian stand-easy in those long-ago days. Canada House was a social centre — the "old time" general store of the Canadian village on KAF where you could catch up on Stanley Cup playoff scores and cheat the pressing heat by purchasing frozen chocolate bars and energy drinks. This shabby beatnik canteen was intended as the bastion of our mental strength. The telephone trailer for calls home was adjacent to it. A small deck with stand-up tables for smokers bracketed its north side. VIP visitors from the Cancon (Canadian content) shows, NHL hockey legends, celebrities, and Cabinet ministers would congregate at this rug-lined fortress.

If I die before I wake … throw me in the fucking poo pond, for Jesus' sake.

The hippy-style hangout would be expanded shortly after the 2006 tour, swelling like NATO itself in southern Afghanistan. A shame, I think — the smaller the house, the more love that is in it. And this earlier house inspires many memories. Canada House was one of the bingo centres — the rendezvous point for roll call after a rocket attack. The soldiers would huddle in and around the canteen to ensure their name was ticked on the bingo sheet by the grease pencil — I am still here! In the blackness, troops would wait for the "all clear" while reading novels by penlight or watching episodes of *Corner Gas* on miniature video players. Canada House factored into my own Saturday-night routine. I would try and purchase a Coke and a chocolate bar from the canteen on my way to the tent. It was a simple indulgence to commemorate the passing of another week. Nothing like a fix of sugar before crashing. I would sleep the dreamless sleep of the dead on that airfield. While a frozen candy bar disintegrated in my tummy, a new layer of Kandahar's dust would be refreshed over my sticky Cadpat uniform and boots. Midpoint in our tour, our Weatherhaven tents had been reinforced with a series of portable concrete abutments. The heavy protective barrier dotted the circumference of each air-conditioned Canadian tent to shield bones from rocket explosions while you slept. We would lie down on the fresh dust, inside our modern rock of ages, knowing the cement wall was just a few inches beyond through the canvas and let the comforting smell of liquid KAF shit carry us off to a dreamless sleep.

Green Beans Coffee outlets, resplendent with their cheap cigars, barista-crafted product, and high coffee prices were outside the Canadian sphere. The most expensive item at Green Beans was their MOAC (Mother of all Coffees). The caffeine content in this large paper cup could shock a horse. There was no small change on KAF. You could buy your expensive MOAC coffee with the U.S. paper coins, which were distributed in droves to make change. They were for use on the big U.S. FOBs, and as the war continued in Iraq and Afghanistan, you could find U.S. Iraqi Freedom currency surfacing in your Enduring Freedom change in Afghanistan. Karl Marx would have been pleased at this demonstration of economics moving right along with history. Green Bean's motto was Honor First, Coffee Second, and it was a meeting place for quiet conversations or to simply relax after hours and enjoy superb coffee. The conversations that echoed inside its plywood walls and out along the boardwalk were laden with the weight of a shared experience.

On one side of the counter, a splash of colour on the unfinished wooden wall is a signed eight-by-ten photo of the Royal Air Force pack of Harrier jet fighters — a parting gift from an earlier rotation of British pilots. There were six Hawker Harriers on KAF in 2006 that were a god-send. They were the only fast air we had back then. The Harrier is the sort of jet fighter that can launch itself vertically before it roars off into horizontal flight. The state of the Kandahar runway in early 2006 was such that other types of jet fighters, what ground forces call "close air support," were not able to operate from the tarmac. We all loved the Harriers, and their pilots were rock stars. The Taliban, like any opponent, were not of uniform quality as a fighting force. However, some of the enemy were very shrewd. The pack of Harriers had a ramp-up time of sixteen or seventeen minutes from when they were hailed from a TIC until they could be over-head. Within a twenty-minute span they would be with Coalition ground troops to lay down aerial munitions on the enemy. Any Taliban fighter worth his salt knew that they had about twenty minutes of free fighting time before they need be concerned about punishment from the air.

This convoy is not going to make it to Spin Boldak today. Rather, we are in full retreat. The sun is slowly setting on Kandahar, a giant red ball easing toward the horizon and pulling darkness down around us. The level sand around us has a red hue. The crumpled G-Wagon in front of mine is hoisted up by its maw onto the SMP (Standard Military Pattern wrecker). My eyes are not focused on the Registan Desert, nor are they really trained on the destroyed vehicle. Even the various nuances of browns and reds painted by the lowering sun are but backdrop to my focus. My eyes are on the camel-back canteen that skitters along behind the G-Wagon.

Was it Ray's? Should we stop and pick up the expensive piece of kit? No. Stopping is bad. Keep the column moving.

Up and down the camelback bounces and gyrates like a perverse kite that cannot gain enough altitude for sustained flight. It is full of life unto itself. A remnant left behind by the fallen. My Ray Arndt nightmares tend to start with this stupid camelback.

Corporal Ash van Leuween was crying as I walked beside his stretcher. He had stabilized and made it through. He was now on his way out to Lahnstuhl, Germany, the theatre support hospital.

"Sir, I am sorry I let you down," he grimaces through his tears. Solid iron in his words.

I was just thinking the same thing, Corporal van Leuween.

Our Army Reserve troops were magnificent men and women and they took a massive physical pounding on the tour. I found their energy to have a bracing effect. I wanted to do well by these smart, tough young men and women because I would have been screwed without the courage and stamina of my thirty Reserve infanteers in the NSE D&S Platoon. As the war continued through to 2011, thousands of Reservists cycled through Afghanistan because the tiny Canadian Army needed them. We could not have sustained ourselves in Afghanistan for so long without the folksy, oft-neglected, and quickly forgotten Army Reserve.[3] The challenge of the Reserve Army continued after the Afghan War. Keeping track of the wounded is hard enough in the Regular Force, but more so for the Reservist. Consider the case of Afghanistan-related suicides. According to Renata D'Aliesio writing in the *Globe and Mail*, "The exact count [of war-related suicides] is uncertain; the federal government doesn't regularly track suicides of veterans and has incomplete records on Reservists, who made up more than one-quarter of Canadian troops in Afghanistan."[4]

Nowhere was the measure of the Reserves better punctuated than in the treatment of those Reservists who served on full-time Class B contracts. During the war in Afghanistan, the army swelled its Class B Reserve Force (Reservists on full-time contracts). The level of Class B employment was the highest it had been in many years. As the war began to wind down in 2010 and 2011, and the defence budget was ever tightened, the approach to its enlarged Reserve workforce took on an element of the sinister. There were financial pressures as the defence budget realigned and senior leaders could not ignore them. However, some of the generals saw inside the Reserve-workforce problem a career opportunity for themselves and leaned forward to cut more Class B contracts even sooner than the army required. In leaning forward the senior officers hoped to get a star in their notebook. Let's cut these troops sooner to help the bottom line. It was during this period that I heard that one general officer referred to the Class B workforce in his formation (some of whom had been serving loyally on Class B for many years) as "crack cocaine addicts." Most of the contracts in his formation were terminated early, at Christmas time. These were our own soldiers and they were discarded, in some cases, like trash. Forget that this myopic approach to a business problem was far from emblematic of a quality employer in an institution that prides itself on taking care of its own. Forget as well that the decisions were made with only money and professional advantage in mind. The treatment of the Class B workforce was caustic on the entire Reserve community. The approach told all of us that we were dispensable and that we could — in fact *should* — be discarded. No one disputed that the army's employment levels had swelled with the war and had to be readjusted. That fact was irrefutable. How the problem was dealt with, however, was chilling — chucking soldiers like junk. When your own leadership takes this sort of approach it collapses a wounded soldier's low self-esteem.

"How much for this framed Afghanistan brochure?" I ask the lady behind the counter. I am poking around one of my favourite Sparks Street haunts in Ottawa where old prints and posters of Canadiana are sold.

"That one is $125 but it's not original; that's a reproduction. You can probably appreciate how few originals remain with what Afghanistan has been through."

I smile in spite of myself. I have two of them — real ones — that I bought in a Kandahar market for about the equivalent of $3 Canadian.

"What would a real one be worth, for argument's sake?"

"Oh my gosh. That is an old brochure. Pretty hard to put a price on it. The originals are nearly non-existent now — probably no more than a handful on the planet."

"Oh."

"That country is probably never coming back. It's a goner. That is one old, old document, and even good reproductions are getting tough to find."

I withdraw from the shop shortly after. I am upset with the vendor's comments about Afghanistan. It cannot be gone.

The price has been too high for that.

The day after my release from the Regular Force, Colonel David Erickson became my boss. He worked out of Petawawa, but I reported to him from my Toronto location. In those days you could leave the Regular Force and transfer directly into the part-time army. There were two options available: part-time Class A service where you worked only one evening a week and one weekend a month on average; or full-time Class B Reserve service. I opted for Class B and I quickly discovered that working in the Reserves was not going to be a cakewalk. I knew little about the Reserve system and had to begin from scratch. The first thing I learned was that a Class B officer was hired to do a very specific job, essentially like a military contractor. My responsibilities were minor and focused on drumming up training opportunities for Reserve logistics soldiers. Before my PTSD, I would have been bored with such a small responsibility; however, my life had taken on a grey monotone. Every day was an effort to make the long commute from the farm into the North York headquarters of Land Forces Central Area. As the dreary weeks ground on one past another, I was given additional responsibility to oversee the formation's outreach program, a small cell that worked on opportunities to highlight Canadian Forces' members at events and connect our institution with the public. Operation Connection was the brainchild of General Rick Hillier, a brilliant idea to keep the public in touch with its military. Through this cell I waded ever deeper into the netherworld of the career Reservist.

On Operation Connection I picked up three Reserve captains who were serving on long-term Class B contracts. Two of them had been in the headquarters through many rotations of Regular Force commanders and staffs. They really knew where the bodies were buried in Toronto and their level of connectivity and influence was much different from a captain in the Regular Force. From the perspective of the Canadian Army, they amounted to contractors in uniform, full-time Reservists that merited minimal career management. One captain, Mike Wiesenfeld, was well connected with the commandant at Canadian Forces College in Toronto (my former Kandahar Brigade commander), Brigadier General Fraser. Mike had served on Operation Athena in Kabul during General Peter Devlin's tour in 2003. Operation Athena was the Canadian contribution to NATO's ISAF in the City of Kabul from 2003 to late 2005. The Canadian Area of Operations under Athena was completely based in Kabul. Mike Wiesenfeld was on the Operation Athena G2 (Intelligence) staff back then and had been able to make a number of connections on the tour.

A charismatic storyteller, Wiesenfeld agreed immediately that I had been left for dead by the Regular Force Logistics Branch. With his never-ending stream of army news and innuendo, he kept hope alive in me that an unnamed senior officer was going to kick some ass and have me vindicated in front of some faceless throng of senior logisticians. It was a fool's notion but my self-esteem was so feeble — and Wiesenfeld so flattering and convincing — that I ate it up. His entertaining rants fed my deep sense of paranoia. I was living my life like I was still embroiled in combat. Everything had a tactical imperative; everyone from the bank manager to my former career manager was out to harm me, my livelihood, and my family. I subscribed to too many of Mike's theories. I was in such a pathetic state that I truly could not wait to hear his next yarn. I cherished sitting in the smoking area at the big Toronto headquarters with Mike and listening to the clandestine moves of powerful officers. I was not yet at rock bottom, but as I sat smoking the first cigarettes of my life the good parts of my brain began to sense that I was close.

The head of my Op Connection cell was an old warhorse named Wayne Johnson. Johnson had served in a number of combat arms and combat logistics regiments largely in the Ontario army throughout his long career. He had recently come through a very trying assignment as the repatriation officer for the large Ontario headquarters. Given the location of the Ontario coroner's office, the established coroner for Canadian Armed Forces casualties overseas, this meant Wayne was the repatriation officer for the whole of the army. This also meant that Wayne Johnson had spent more time than anyone else in the army with the fallen and their families. Wayne's service to our fallen was insightful, articulate, and deeply compassionate, service for which he was never properly recognized. The moral pressure on this man left him scarred among our walking wounded, a fact that I slowly appreciated as I got to know him better. Still, despite everything, Wayne was passionate about the army and he seemed to possess a very old soul. He spent countless hours of his own time organizing a non-profit organization to support our ill and wounded men and women that would grow to touch thousands of veterans at the worst time of their lives. Not an insignificant contribution. He knew the ropes of the Army Reserve in Toronto and nothing could distract or fluster him. I, on the other hand, was easily flustered — especially when it came to how to incite and direct this particular pair of seasoned Reservists — Johnson and Wiesenfeld. They did not respond or move at all like their Regular Force counterparts. The buttons and levers I had used so well in my full-time career were useless with this veteran pair.

I did learn a lot from the two of them, however; they ended up showing me the ropes. I slowly learned to navigate this strange new geography and appreciate the campy world of the Canadian Army Reserve — its close ties to the old wars and the brand new one. Inside the Reserve community, for instance, Panjawaii stands side by side with Passchendaele on a regiment's altar. The old guard were cherished and not forgotten. The descendants of the horrible Battle of Walcheren Causeway in 1944 enjoy a glass of Merlot at a regimental dinner with a section commander from Camp Nathan Smith. Funerals for former COs, RSMs, and Honoraries were commonplace. All of this poses a much different paradigm from the full-time Regular Force that is posted around the country on quick two- and three-year rotations for senior soldiers.[5] The permanent force, by virtue of expectations and size, spawns a "what have you done for me lately?" culture. The Army Reserve has deep roots with deep purchase in the history of their communities. It is more organic and earthy, a distant cousin to the Regular Force I had grown up in.

During those worst days with my PTSD, I found myself believing far too many of the things Mike Wiesenfeld told me about his influence with senior officers. I had no doubt he enjoyed Dave Fraser's trust, however. It was through Mike that I first learned that there might be a chance that I could be appointed to a prized senior officer's course at Canadian Forces College. Normally this level of course is loaded off the Ottawa merit lists under the steady eye of military career managers. There were other ways and means to influence these sorts of things, he assured me; ways around the system. I liked the idea of the course. It was the last level of education for senior officers in the Canadian Forces and, in those days, was a rare level of qualification for the Army Reserve. The potential to move over to the Canadian Forces College near Toronto as a student on this scarce opportunity seemed possible. Mike assured me that General Fraser thought it was doable and although it seemed unlikely I began to believe in the possibility. None of it really added up — even then. And yet I believed. When the call came from Dave Fraser I was in the middle of a planning session for our town's fall fair.

"I am sorry, folks," I announced, "I have to take this. It's my workplace but this won't be a minute." I stepped outside into a soft summer day.

"Hello, sir. It's good to hear from you."

"Yes, well, you too, John. What can I do for you?"

"Well, I understand that I might be able to get on the DP (developmental period) Four course starting later this month as a Reservist."

"Who is picking up your Class B salary, presuming we could make a space for you? Central Area Headquarters? I doubt they would pay for it."

I was somewhat confused by his salary question. Central Area Headquarters was my employer, my Class B contract was with them but they would not spend money on this opportunity. I was so single-minded about getting on that course and showing up the stupid bastards that had betrayed me that I had not considered even the most fundamental of questions. Class B contracts come out of local budgets, unlike the centralized pay system of the Regular Force — like a casual hire. Dave Erickson was not going to pay for me to go to school. Class B soldiers are hired to do a specific job; they are contractors in uniform.

"I cannot get you on the course, but let's explore getting you over to the college and then we will see what can be done. This would be easier if you were under my command here."

I was too stunned to make much sense.

"I guess so, sir. Sure." I was disappointed, embarrassed: I felt ridiculously foolish, like a checkers player suddenly realizing he has been sitting at a chess set.

One would think a person as experienced as I would be more knowledgeable and curious on the finer points involving a career move, but I had flippantly gambled away whatever credibility I may have established in nearly twenty-five years of service. I did not care. I could not muster the energy to even begin to care.

I left Colonel Erickson in the lurch and lined up once again with David Fraser, my Kandahar boss, and moved to the CFC in January of 2008. Along with my inability to focus and a complete lack of interest in steady work, I had become reckless. I had quit the Regular Force in April of 2007, had spent less than one year with my new boss, and summarily gave notice that I was breaking the three-year contract in favour of a better situation with General Fraser. This was not the way I had been taught to treat people and not part of my character — and it certainly was not how I handled serious decisions. Colonel Erickson had been incredibly supportive of me when I left the Regular Force. He had gone to bat for me to keep my position in Toronto. He had done me a huge favour. And how had I repaid him? I dumped him at the earliest opportunity for what I impulsively decided was a better situation at the Staff College. I am ashamed of how shabbily I treated him and his generosity.

As I bounced between my various Class B jobs, I flirted with the idea of returning to the Regular Force. I was dogged with paranoia and low self-esteem and I carried an overwhelming thirst to be vindicated. I waited for someone to reach out. A few superb senior officers did ask me what happened. Generals looked in on my case, honestly open to the idea of having me back. Each time, however, I saw not generosity and opportunity but treachery and deceit. It wasn't a genuine offer, I scoffed; other times I rebuffed the offer for not being "good enough." I was wrong, of course; I see that now. But then? No way. It was too dark to see anything — except the darkness. I recall a new army chief of logistics offered me a good job at the Dennison Armoury in Toronto — where I had started my Reserve service less than a year earlier. And I would not even have to relocate my family. I turned it down flat.

No surprise, the chief of logistics was incredulous. "You are turning this down? I have moved mountains to get you this billet. I thought you were dealing in good faith!"

"Can you guarantee that I will be put back in succession, sir?"

"You know I can't make that kind of guarantee. You have to perform, obviously, but I am quite confident that things will take care of themselves, right? You have to trust us."

"Exactly. No thanks."

Another life-saving bridge reduced to smoldering embers.

My perverse behaviour was a classic example of what is known as "problem definition issues." I was solving a problem ... but the *wrong* problem. It was not a promotion or opportunities to stay competitive that was the issue for me. My issue was my mental health. *I am the problem.* I wanted something that they could not give: tranquility, peace of mind, sanctuary from my demons, release from my nightmares and the crushing sense of failure I felt as I logged my hours at work.

Sometimes it's a train; other times it's a ship that is about to disembark or a plane at a terminal. I have only a few minutes to cover an impossible distance with my suitcase in hand. For instance, I have just arrived at Frankfurt or some other impossibly enormous international airport and my connecting flight is at the farthest point from my arrival. I never know why the connection is so crucial but I know that making the flight is absolutely imperative: a matter of life and death. The race is on. Faces flash past, strangers who give my desperation no notice. Frequent glances at my wristwatch. The dream never reaches its conclusion. I never know if I make it. I wake up, my heart racing, quite resolved that I missed my flight or my train, and know for a fact that something very bad will soon follow.

The first time I experienced the doppelgänger effect in Kingston (shortly after coming home), I was deeply unsettled. I was like a person who finds an odd lump, or experiences a weird sensation in his chest. I could not make sense of it — a feeling that I could observe myself in the third person and watch myself lose control. These episodes started off like any conversation but would take a dramatic turn south. I could feel switches being thrown at certain parts of a conversation that set it off. I could feel one part of my mind working sideways to feed on large morsels of paranoia and fear.

I launched myself on self-diagnosis, a dear old friend. The sensation associated with the doppelgänger was no big thing. *I am fine. There are a ton of reasons for this separation of the mind. I am just overtired through a lack of sleep. I am not getting enough exercise. I am stressed by the numerous assholes around me in the Staff College.* On and on I worked up other reasons for the ailment. It was a battle every day to pack these different emotions down and go to work.

In 2008 the Canadian Forces College (CFC) was an institution in full-growth mode. When I accepted the offer to reunite with Dave Fraser I had no idea how dynamic an institution it had become. The war in Afghanistan had generated a renewed interest in our military from a number of civilian organizations and individuals ranging from universities to captains of industry, think tanks, and various centres of strategic study. Like a lantern to moths, the CFC was the natural portal to receive their homage. Even highly successful private companies were showing interest in the venerable war college on Toronto's north end. Space for staff was at a premium and I shared the equivalent of one long office with four other officers. Our workspace was marked off in modern cubicle dividers.

My workspace at CFC was small but heavily decorated with souvenirs from my tours. It was mostly war junk, little bits and pieces, reminders of seven months spent on an alien planet: field message books from orders groups, a large hunk of amethyst that I had purchased at a market in Kandahar, presentation coins, and plaques. The amethyst I prized most of all. I had read on a trip to the north shore of Lake Superior how the knights of the Middle Ages would wear pieces of amethyst beneath their chain mail to prevent sudden death, and it seemed like a good idea to put a large chunk in the G-Wagon during that Taliban summer. To the casual observer these souvenirs would have amounted to junk. But not to me. Not back then. I could see story and structure inside the disarray. I looked at the tactile bits and I felt recognized and more secure. These remnants of my time at war told me that I had once been something and that I had once had some relevance.

One day I came back from lunch and my cubicle was stripped bare. Absolutely every sheet of paper and pen had been removed. Gone were all of my wartime ephemera, the book Ian Hope had given me on General Ulysses S. Grant, U.S. Army paper coins from my Green Beans change, the amethyst and plaques that commemorated the tour, even the generic sticky notes, paper, pens — everything. I could see out of the corner of my eye that my office mates were busy poring over their lesson plans and computer screens. They worked on as if nothing was out of the ordinary. I felt my heartbeat double at the beginning of panic.

"What the hell?" I exclaimed.

Silence from my colleagues. George, the one naval officer among us, looked up at me with an expression perfectly mixed with boredom and annoyance.

"Guys, what the hell did you do with my stuff?" I asked too loudly. "Where is everything?"

"What are you talking about, John?" George asked, adding a dash more annoyance to his look. "Is something wrong?'

"Yes, you are fucking right something is wrong! My entire cubicle looks like it has been cleaned out."

I began quietly looking into the metal drawers of the file cabinet and desk to see if materials had been simply brushed into those open spaces. They too were bare. I could feel a choking emotion crawling higher in my gut. The notes and trinkets had been organized in a very deliberate way; some of my souvenirs were small and fragile. I fought to appear normal, even nonchalant about the disappearance of the worthless objects while at the same time being desperate to recover them.

Lieutenant Colonel Bob Chaloux leaned over the top of his cubicle wall and offered me some clues. "Yeah, Johnny, it's really weird, eh? Some guys came up here on the chief of staff's bidding to package your stuff."

I had known Bob for two decades. We had done a tour in the former Yugoslavia together and had been friends for many years. His father, Moe, had become terminally ill during that tour and it had been a terrible burden on Bob during his time in the Balkans.

"What? No. That's not right."

"They would not tell us anything," Bob continued. "Are you being moved to Tech Services?"

"I am not being moved! No one has said bugger all to me," I snapped. I chewed on his words and contemplated a couple of negative possibilities. Bob was credible. Perhaps I was being moved?

You're fired. Get out.

My knowledge of Class B Reserve contracts was thin at this point. I understood, however, that they could be terminated easily and early and that the Canadian Armed Forces held all the cards.

"Geez, John, what did you do?" asked Lieutenant Colonel Ed Haverstock, a workspace colleague.

"Nothing. I … " It was at that point that I tore away from reason and took flight. I had the sensation of being apart from myself and looking down on the entire office scene.

"I have had enough of this, you fucking assholes. Where is my goddamned stuff?" I yelled.

Silence from the room. Stunned surprise on the face of the naval officer; his bored annoyance was gone. My emotion was primitive and primal. I felt like I was watching someone else and already I was embarrassed for that person.

"Where is it, goddamn it? You guys have no right to touch my stuff!"

As their silence hardened and the sympathetic looks deepened, I became more and more unhinged, to the point where I could not form words. It became a horrible display of emotion and desperation. My doppelgänger was in full flight, much worse than experiences in Kingston, and I seemed to be looking down on the whole mess from a very great height. I could see myself manically ransacking filing cabinets, yanking open one drawer after another, and barging into neighbouring cubicles, demanding to have my property returned. Despite their embarrassed and pitying looks I was pretty sure this was their idea of a joke. With every passing second, however, my anxiety spiralled. What if it wasn't a prank? No, it's not them. *It's him.* I was in a full-fledged paranoid rage.

You should never have trusted Dave Fraser. He does not want you here.
How will you tell your family?
How will you pay the mortgage?

I finally spun on my heel and lumbered out of the office to make my way outside. I could not think clearly, let alone control my emotions.

After what seemed like an eternity of wandering the grounds of the college I came back to the office. Indeed, it had been a prank and it was supposed to have lasted a couple of days. George, the naval officer whom I knew the least, decided to break ranks on the gag. My unexpected and terrifyingly over-the-top reaction to the joke had obviously unsettled him to the point where he had no choice but to pull the plug on the prank. Even the doppelgänger had seen it. He showed me a cabinet in the far end of the large office that had escaped my attention in the emotional explosion. Inside it was where all of my work files, papers, and various war souvenirs had been thrown. The prevailing emotion I felt was deep embarrassment, not relief. They were material things, after all. Things. I was ashamed and struggled for something to say.

"Thank you, George," I said. I could not meet his eyes. I was so embarrassed I felt sick to my stomach.

"Yeah, you bet," he muttered.

He was still very uncomfortable and unsettled by my reaction. Not only hadn't it been the expected response, but it violated the ethos of the tribe; freaking out like a lunatic is not how the military rolls. I had been very unsportsmanlike — not very "officer-like" at all. A soldier needs to take a joke and bear it with élan.

I could not talk to any of them about it, even my friend Ed Haverstock of twenty-five years. Haverstock was an infantry officer with the PPCLI. He and I had fought, bled, and drunk our way through numerous rugby games together earlier in our career at Royal Roads Military College in Victoria. I suspected that the prank had probably been Haverstock's brainchild. I have not been able to connect with him since. The bubbly Bob Chaloux was the most communicative member of the office chamber. He pulled me aside one day at coffee break to tell me how much I had scared him with my reaction.

"John, you are different — I mean unhealthy, spooky different. You should get help. I mean it, Johnny. That was really bad up there." Chaloux cocked his head toward our office building.

I felt a combination of a burning shame and anger; I agreed. But I hated him for suggesting that I might be mentally unwell.

How fucking dare you? You bastard. What the hell do you know?

My life since Kandahar had become one long and sustained combat. Who needed friends like this? That was just it. These were competitors, not friends. *I would be fine if all of you shitheads would leave me alone.*

"All right, Bob," was all I said.

142

The Rays of Sunshine Everywhere volunteers (less formally ROSE or Roses) had grown out of another outfit known as the Bell Telephone Volunteers. This organization had begun a supportive campaign sending Tim Hortons coffee and eventually coffee cards over to the troops in Afghanistan during my time there. One of the determined leaders of the volunteer group was Mary Taylor, a former operator with Bell. With a heart as big as Lake Ontario, Mary and her husband, Barry, were very kind, patriotic Canadians. Barry's dad had been recruited into the Canadian Army at the tail end of the First World War; he was proud of the recruiting paperwork that showed his dad had stepped forward at the Canadian National Exhibition grounds in late 1918. There was nothing that the Taylors would not do to support the Canadian Forces. Mary also volunteered at the Clarington Museums and Archives in Bowmanville, Ontario, where my wife Martha was the executive director. Martha had introduced me to Mary while I was still in Kandahar. Initially the purpose was to assist Mary and the band of museum volunteers with the purchase of a new Afghan rug for the museum.

Shortly after the museum rug project was complete, Mary bulldozed on to her next passion — showing support for Canadian soldiers in Afghanistan. Mary and the Roses wanted to send coffee to the soldiers in Kandahar, and they had started by sending bulky cans and vacuum-sealed packs of coffee through the military mail system. We were quick to switch the kind effort to mailing gift dollars for soldiers to use as cash at the KAF Tim Hortons. The whole idea that the Roses had was born of love for the troops and a desire to show them that someone at home was thinking about them. A simple concept — buy a soldier a cup of coffee — became their mission statement for the entire Afghan War. After I came home and met Mary, I knew we were destined to become friends. She was so unapologetic in her love of soldiers. Every time that Mary and the Roses had another pile of coffee certificates to pass to Kandahar, I agreed to meet them and accept them on behalf of the army. I donned my uniform for the task. This was the hard part of the job. I wanted to avoid my uniform and being in public as the token soldier at these events. I soldiered on, though, because the Taylors, indeed all of the volunteers, were so positive on the Canadian Forces. Even in my wonky state I did not want to let them down.

DARRYL CASWELL, SUMMER 2007, KANDAHAR, AFGHANISTAN

Trooper Darryl Caswell sits relaxed and contemplative in the driver's compartment of his LAV fighting vehicle. The dirty browns of FOB Masum Gar continue over his shoulder well off into the photograph's vanishing point. He was a handsome kid who had proven to be good at soldiering. Darryl was tough and resilient, but also possessed a quirky sense of humour. For instance, he carried a gnome lawn ornament with him all over the planet. Photographs abounded among his family and friends — pictures of Darryl and the gnome in his quarters, on patrol, and on vacation away from theatre. There was an ingrained hilarity in the garden-gnome shtick, an inside joke that carried on well past his tragic loss in June 2007. Darryl hailed from Bowmanville, a big town pretty close to my home near Orono, and, because of this proximity, I got the opportunity to know this fine young Canadian soldier in death.

I was employed at the CFC and putting in my time, drawing the 85 percent Reserve pay. Employed but not working. At least not working in the true sense of the word: working with a sense of past accomplishments and with an optimistic sense of the future; working in the sense of setting priorities and creating ambitious career goals. I was dreaming day and night about Afghanistan and ammunition shortages. I was an Afghanistan junkie. I gobbled up any news from the war that found its way into the media. I was in a painful purgatory from leaving the Regular Force and not really integrated into the world of a true Reservist as a Class B contracted soldier. I was unmotivated to go forward or to go back. I could be productive in the short term. The heaviest work I did in this period came only in bite-sized chunks, projects or activities that did not demand research or too much focus. I supported the Roses and their Coffee to Kandahar campaign. At times this seemed like the only worthwhile job I had. The short speeches and acknowledgements that this duty demanded were about the extent of my contribution to society. One of the most rewarding things I did was to get to know Trooper Caswell and to support the family of this fallen soldier.

Darryl Caswell was born on July 31, 1981, in Bowmanville, Ontario, to Darlene and Paul. He enrolled in the Canadian Armed Forces in Oshawa in December 2004 and, having completed entry-level training, joined the Royal Canadian Dragoons in August 2005. Among the many noteworthy alumni of this storied regiment was Roger Cotton, my friend and colleague at the Army Command and Staff College in Kingston, and General Rick Hillier, our greatest chief of the defence staff of the Canadian Forces. There was a lot for young Darryl Caswell to be proud of in joining this particular regiment. After completing his armoured crewman training in Gagetown, New Brunswick, he joined the regiment in Petawawa, Ontario. His deployment to Afghanistan with the 2nd Battalion, Royal Canadian Regiment, was his first tour overseas. Darryl was supposed to come home to Canada on his twenty-sixth birthday. Instead, he was killed about forty kilometres north of Kandahar City by a roadside IED. His battle group was very active north of Kandahar in the summer of 2007. The year before, in April 2006, we had sweated and bled to hold on to the hell house that had been Gumbad in the north and scratch out our FOB Martello from among the rocks around Elbac. Now this work was being reversed. The Canadian Task Force was in the slow process of reorienting from the northern part of the province to turn the Canadian focus on Panjawaii west of Kandahar City. Darryl was lost during this reorientation effort. Two other soldiers were wounded in his armoured vehicle but they survived.

The dream is a frequent visitor.

The convoy is slowing as we enter the built-up part of Kandahar's west end. The little stalls and kiosks of street vendors are cloistered right up to the side of the road. Yellowing chickens hang in a row, motionless with the complete absence of breeze. Diesel drums affixed with little hand pumps, an ancient Ford tractor, its cowling long stripped away, sits idling in front of its handmade trailer. In the next instant there is a widening fireball, a sense of an explosion before the actual sound of it. Metal and flesh raining down on the cab of the truck brought me the good news. You are alive. You are still able to function. Out the door now to rally the troops. Let's see how bad it is, how quick we can be moving again. The first thought one has when stopped on this battlefield is, How soon can we be moving again? Everything is observed by an unseen enemy. Whispered into cellular phones. NATO convoy. Fat target.

Something is askew in this ambush. There is no one around the stricken convoy but me. Paddy Earles is not with me; in fact, none of the NSE soldiers are here. I am alone with jaundiced chickens and swarming thick flies to my left and a wide-open brown field to my right. I start forward to find shelter. Better take up a firing position. I have not gone three steps when shots ring out. A pair of bullets — a nice quick double tap on the AK — pierce my left hand. I fall hard to the dust.

I wake to find I am sweating like crazy. My wife is lost in a deep sleep, unmolested by the convoy action. I throw back the sweat-soaked bed sheets and gently steal away to the bathroom to check out my hand.

Martha and I attended Trooper Caswell's funeral service at Trinity United Church in Bowmanville on June 20, 2007, nine days following his death in Kandahar. Most of the Royal Canadian Dragoons had travelled the three hundred plus kilometres from Petawawa to Bowmanville for the service. Bowmanville is a sleepy lakeside community fifty kilometres east of Toronto. Darryl's funeral sat at the intersection of two very different worlds — the army family burying one of its own and a peacetime community awoken to the human consequence of war.

The funeral service was split between Trinity's own Reverend Joe Lafave and a military chaplain from Petawawa. The service was especially meaningful for Joe Lafave, as his son was a captain in the combat engineers slated for a Kandahar tour in the near future. It was a time overseas when there could not possibly be enough combat engineers on hand. Military engineers are versatile troops who can fight as infantry in the defence but are also experts at the handling of lethal explosive. The combat engineers had proven priceless in the defeat of Talban IEDs. The work of the engineers was dangerous, and Reverend Lafave was far too bright to waste any prayers. I imagined that they were all offered up with his son in mind.

As I stumbled around with PTSD after Kandahar I received a front-row education in what the war looked like on main-street Canada. The suffering of a family, the supporting sinews of community, and the tactical stresses that a soldier's family must endure years after the media stops talking about Afghanistan. Darryl's funeral service was a crash course on the impacts of war at home, and the images from that funeral service are indelible. It was a time when it seemed that everyone in Canada was touched by the war in some way — be it family member, friend, or neighbour. Nearly every Canadian was able to find some degree of connectivity with the wounded and the fallen. The young soldier who had brought Darryl's body home from theatre was dazed. He sat solemn in his pew, lost in his own thoughts. The recognizable faces of the community were suddenly strangely out of place in this context, the juxtaposition of two worlds. The military chaplain, Captain Lee Lambert, was a gifted speaker; his words for Darryl and the world that soldiers must live in amounted to a powerfully moving service. I was crying my eyes out by the end of his address. I could tell that my civilian neighbours were deeply moved. I think, too, they were astonished by my emotions and by the simple but heartfelt outpouring of grief from the green sea of Dragoons that encircled them in their own church. For them, the tidal wave of grief rose up seemingly from nowhere. This was the first funeral in Bowmanville for a combat death since the Second World War — a first peek back into a dimly remembered wartime for a town that had fed numerous sailors, soldiers, and airmen to the Big Wars. Bowmanville had enjoyed some level of celebrity for its role during the Second World War as a prisoner-of-war camp for the Luftwaffe and Field Marshal Rommel's Afrika Korps. People in Bowmanville knew their wartime history but it ended at a certain chapter. No one could have prepared the town for this funeral, for the present war to be unpacked and viscerally presented to them.

After the funeral, Mary Taylor, my intrepid friend from the Rose Volunteers, asked me if I could meet up with Darryl's father and stepmother for a chat. Mary was close with Marjorie Caswell, Darryl's grandmother. I was cautious about meeting Darryl's family. My guard went up. I was not in a great mental shape myself. Although I knew both his regiment and the

Petawawa Garrison well, I had never met Darryl, and I did not want to get in the way of the assisting officer (AO) who was appointed to help the family (AOs have one of the most difficult and emotionally demanding jobs in the forces, for obvious reasons). Mary persisted, however, explaining that it would mean a lot to the Caswells if I could just have a coffee with them. There would be no agenda. Reluctantly, I agreed.

The day we had selected was sun-washed, perfect for coffee at an outdoor café. Sitting in the shade of the café's porch, Panjawaii and Kandahar seemed thousands of miles away. We talked about the war. I was nervous going in but found the meeting went just fine. The Caswells were gracious and charitable. Marjorie Caswell, Darryl's grandmother, had come along and she proved to be a sharp and engaged lady, possessed of deep wisdom. Very early on, it became clear that there was no judgment — only gratitude — for my time. I had been foolish thinking it was not a good idea meeting them. Immediately I felt Darryl had a wonderful supporter in his stepmom, Christine Walsh, and that his younger brother, Logan, was still in shock over Darryl's death. His older brother had been a hero to him. Logan's wide eyes and shy comments broke my heart. I decided that I would do anything I could to support this family and carry some of their grief. Both Christine and Paul had contextual questions about Kandahar. What was it like over there politically? Are we making real progress? What are the Afghans like really? Are we making much of a difference? Did Darryl make a difference? The buttons and levers of my PTSD were being flipped and pressed throughout the conversation. Still, I answered all of their questions, doing my best to stifle the anxiety that this conversation was provoking as best I could. Christine mentioned toward the end that a couple of Dragoons from Darryl's unit overseas were coming down to Bowmanville next week to visit them.

"Any words of advice for us?" she asked me. "Anything I should not say or should avoid?"

"Absolutely not. Treat that conversation as you would any other conversation with Darryl's friends when he was alive."

"Okay," she said. I could tell she was unsure.

"The one thing you might want to be aware of going in, however, is survivor's guilt."

"What do you mean?"

"Survivor's guilt. They will almost certainly have it."

"Oh," her eyes opened slightly wider as she absorbed this.

"Look, it's pretty simple. The IED took Darryl but left both of them. They will harbour some guilt over this. This sort of mindset is prevalent for soldiers. Heck, I feel it myself when I sit here with you guys — the guilt of survival, of being home with family, that sort of thing." I could see her eyes alight now with a full understanding.

"Oh," was all Christine said.

"You can do those two soldiers a lot of good by seeing them and greeting them warmly as friends. Treat them as you would with Darryl right there by your side."

Release them.

In dealing with our fallen we have to appreciate that families are not made with cookie cutters. In the early days of the war in Afghanistan, our unit rear parties played with the old rules that better serve the simplistic nuclear family model. It took time for these approaches to catch up. The Canadian Sacrifice Medal was introduced in 2008 in recognition of a soldier who is wounded or killed as a direct result of hostile action. In late 2008, Darryl Caswell's assisting officer in Petawawa learned that Darryl was to be awarded the medal posthumously and that his mother, Darlene, would accept on her son's behalf. For whatever reason, Darryl's father was informed by representatives of the armed forces that he would *not* be part of the presentation ceremony. Paul Caswell was unsurprisingly upset about what amounted to a snub. This is how systems and processes have the unintended consequences of exacerbating wounds.

One evening I recall speaking with Paul Caswell.

"John, I know it's just a mistake. I am sure the army is not intentionally trying to hurt us. We just want to be included in the presentation of the medal for Darryl."

"Of course. You *should* feel this way. It totally sounds like a mix-up. So you impressed upon the assisting officer that you and Darlene are no longer married, but you are his blood father?" I asked.

"Yeah. He understands that, John."

"Hmmm."

I explained to Paul that I was just an instructor at the CFC in Toronto and had limited influence. He was grateful but I could hear the disappointment in his voice. I became increasingly ashamed of myself for what must have seemed to this grieving father as a limp and completely unsatisfactory explanation. I suddenly saw the tables turned. I saw Trooper Caswell sitting with my own family at a café in Bowmanville, trying to pass comfort to my grieving children. I also saw Logan Caswell setting out on the rest of his life without his big brother. No Blue Jays games in October. No best man at his wedding rehearsal party. No Darryl.

Do your goddamned job.

Some deep corner of my broken mind told me I needed to do a better job of advocating for this family that had paid the ultimate price.

"Okay. Having said all that, Paul, I will see what I can do. I will reach out to Petawawa, and if they cannot resolve it, I can send a note to the Office of the Chief of the Defence Staff — General Walter Natynczyk. You remember the general, right? He visited us here in May."

The next morning I tried communicating with the Dragoons and Darryl's assisting officer in Petawawa. This proved fruitless as I was not in the army chain of command and to be frank, I was a Reserve lieutenant colonel teaching at the CFC. To an overworked captain serving as an assisting officer in a Regular unit, I was an irritant. I might as well have been calling from Saturn, and I was blown off by the unit. I pondered what to do at this point.

General Walt Natynczyk had been in Bowmanville on May 28, 2008, as the keynote speaker at the Durham "Support Our Troops" Rally. Natynczyk was then serving as the vice chief of defence, second-in-command of the Canadian Armed Forces. This visit was prior to Natynczyk being anointed as the chief of defence staff (CDS), the top Canadian Forces general. It was clear from the way our member of Parliament, Bev Oda, talked about the general at the rally that he was probably going to get the top job soon. Bev was the minister of the Canadian International Development Agency (CIDA) and clearly a fan of Natynczyk's. As the CIDA minister, one of the big players in Canada's "whole of government" approach on the Afghanistan campaign, she would have a lot of work with the defence department and the next CDS. I had known General Natynczyk since my days at the Royal Military College where he used to help coach our varsity rugby team. The general was good with names; he remembered people. He remembered me. I felt lucky in having that connection with one of our most important and charismatic senior officers. At the Bowmanville troop rally we had a chance to exchange a few words after the ceremony. He also had the opportunity to talk with some of Trooper Caswell's family and hug Darryl Caswell's mother, Darlene Cushman. It was evident that General Walt had been moved by the Caswell story.

As I contemplated Paul Caswell's anxiety at being excluded from Darryl's imminent Sacrifice Medal presentation, I rehashed in my mind how General Natynczyk had been in our community. The new CDS already had a good sense of Bowmanville and the Caswell situation. Furthermore, he knew Bev Oda, and I reasoned that he would not need any friction from this corner. He would surely appreciate having this Sacrifice Medal oversight cleaned up. If I did it correctly, contacting his office might not be a bad last resort. I pondered how to do the right thing over lunch and then made my decision. I sent an email to the principal staff officer to the CDS, a captain (Navy),* outlining the situation. I apologized for contacting him directly and explained the situation succinctly.

"We can easily avoid doing some harm and bringing any kind of embarrassment to the military by allowing both blood parents to participate in the ceremony."

Writing the email proved a grave mistake. My world and the executive staff officer's were oceans apart. I was living the war. He was administering around it as if it behaved according to the pat peacetime rules of 2008. He did not respond or acknowledge my email. Instead he pushed it directly to the army commander with the intent of having him square away the issue. By coffee time that afternoon, I had been summoned to the commandant's office.

---

* The rank of Captain (Navy) is a senior one and equates to the army rank of colonel.

"What the hell did you do?" Dave Fraser asked me. My heart raced and I had a sickening flash of déjà vu. The spectre of our emotionally charged conversation on ammunition shortfalls in Kandahar two years before danced in my head.

"What do you mean, sir? Nothing."

"Nothing? *Nothing!* Did you, or did you not, send an email to the chief of the defence staff earlier this afternoon?"

"I sent one to his executive aide."

"What the hell for?" he barked. "Do you know how much shit we are in with General Leslie?"

General Leslie? My brain started snapping, I could not connect the dots. I would walk over glass to support General Leslie. I admired him. *Why is he angry?*

"I wanted to save the CDS and the army some embarrassment. I really thought I had his back here. And the family. The trooper that was killed in July 2007 was from my local community in Bowmanville. There is a mix-up with his Sacrifice Medal.... I told his father I would try and help ... and —"

"Stop. Just stop. Don't do it again." Fraser's tone had softened.

"Sir, believe me, I was just trying to provide the kind of representation the army deserves to the family of a fallen soldier. I could have let this sit and fester but it would have been wrong."

"Don't send emails to generals without talking to me first from now on."

I felt like crying. *Fuck.* I had the clear sense that Dave Fraser had spent the better part of the afternoon fighting for my job. Class B Reservists and their contracts can be dispatched with the stroke of a pen. He had the look of a man who had been whipped. I could not escape the sudden feeling that the bastards were after Dave Fraser as much as they were after me.

"I am sorry, sir."

"Yeah. Okay," he said, as he exhaled deeply. To his great credit he even managed a brotherly smile. "Just be careful, John, okay? Jesus."

Later that afternoon, General Fraser sent me the email that he had received from the army commander after my attempt to help the

Caswells. It was bad. It confirmed my darkest thoughts of my own self-worth and just how estranged I had become from the Canadian Army. My head swam as I read the note through three times and then deleted it. Then I emptied all of my deleted emails to ensure it was wiped clean for good at least from my computer. If I had been serious about a potential return to the Regular Army, that comeback had just evaporated. I had done myself some serious damage. What's more, I doubt that General Natynczyk ever saw the email note I sent to his executive aide. Even if he had seen it, would the results have been different?

I thought of General Walt and how great it was to receive his challenge coin in front of my community that day in May 2008 at the Bowmanville troop rally. As shitty as I was feeling, as difficult as it was for my scrambled head to be the token "army guy" in a small community, it felt good to have his support. I was just a tin whistle Reservist in a small town — General Natynczyuk was a bona fide rock star. But there is a lesson here for the institution. There is something wrong with showing up in a community, giving a great speech, hugging the family of the fallen, and then leaving the whole matter all behind you. That does not fly in wartime, not in Panjawaii nor Bowmanville. What the generals are missing is that the Reserve soldier is integrated with the community and always has been. You are the army in small-town Canada and you cannot retreat to large bases or layers of protective staff after hours.

That night I called Paul Caswell from the farm and tried to give good representation to the institution that had just kicked my teeth in. I was deeply depressed and working on many hits of blended scotch. Cheap stuff.

"Hi, John. How are you this evening?"

"Good, thanks. I sent the note to Ottawa today Paul. The matter is going to receive their full attention. Let's keep our fingers crossed, eh?" A white lie if ever there was one.

"Thanks for everything, John. I know it will work out. The army is one outfit that knows how to take care of its people. We appreciate you guys so much."

"Yeah. You bet." I looked at the receiver on the phone cradle for a long time after I hung up. I refilled my glass.

What the hell am I doing? What have I done?
I am more than ever on the outside.
I am nothing.

Trooper Karine Blais was a mere twenty years old. She was killed by a roadside IED north of Kandahar on April 13, 2009. Her death remained on my mind for weeks after her casket came home. I still have the front page of the *Toronto Star*, where her parents described her as "our little Ray of Sunshine." Karine's fate reminded me of a story Andy Singh had shared with me about an incident in early 2007. In his case the soldiers had survived a catastrophic explosion:

> Another day, another combat logistic patrol, a sixteen-ton truck driven by a trucker and accompanied by a weapon-technician passenger was catastrophically destroyed by a SVBIED in downtown Kandahar. Thankfully, even after all the shrapnel entering the cab of the vehicle, both CSS soldiers made it safely, having only sustained minor injuries.[6]

Whether one lived or died in an IED attack on a convoy was a matter of sheer chance. The factors of good equipment, good training, and courage had little bearing in the opening salvo. This randomness added to the psychological load of our soldiers. One has to accept that there is only so much that they can control in the fight.

On my commute home one evening in mid-April 2009, Highway 401 was thick with traffic. On the westbound side of the highway I noticed every overpass was crowded with civilians and personnel in uniforms of all stripes — fire, paramedic, and police units.

Karine Blais, twenty years of age, was coming home.

Eventually the long column approached us eastbound commuters. Tears welled up in my eyes; my mind filled with imagery and thoughts of my own family, my own soldiers. I saw the black hearse heading west. I recalled Karine Blais's impossibly youthful face from the *Toronto Star*.

I broke down into heavy sobs, and steered my car to the nearest exit. I sat in a fast food restaurant parking lot and cried it out. I thought about Raymond Arndt coming along this highway two years earlier; I thought about Darryl Caswell and his recent funeral. I could not understand the severity of my reaction. I could not understand the meaningless nature of my life. I could not understand why I had destroyed my Regular Force career and continued to fart around as a bottom feeder at the CFC, where I perceived myself as Class B junk. I was puzzled as to why being away from the Regular Force did not make me feel any better.

I did understand that, for me at least, this war will never end.

CHAPTER 6:
FORWARD MOMENTUM

Why some people are affected more than others has no simple answer. In Canada, it is estimated that up to 10 percent of war zone veterans — including war service veterans and peacekeeping forces — will go on to experience a chronic condition known as Post-Traumatic Stress Disorder.

— Veterans Affairs Canada, *Post-Traumatic Stress Disorder (PTSD) and War-Related Stress*[1]

There are only a few ruins and groundworks remaining to suggest the earlier war that the island once fed. However, this place too was once inside the heart of darkness — a northern Ontario Guadalcanal. Fort St. Joseph, on beautiful St. Joseph Island, Ontario, was the western frontier of Canada on the eve of the War of 1812. Captain Charles Roberts, a band of forty British regular soldiers, 150 Canadians, and some three hundred warriors from our First Nations mounted up in canoes on July 16, 1812, and set out for the American fort on Mackinac Island.[2] They paddled the long miles in the pre-dawn darkness from the southwestern tip of St. Joseph Island to launch their *coup de main* operation on the enemy. The bloodless taking of Fort Mackinac was a bounty of good news for British

North America and Major General Isaac Brock, hundreds of miles away in southern Ontario. The victory is now the stuff of legend. What is less well known is that many of Captain Roberts's 1812 commandos returned to St. Joseph Island after the war and made lives for themselves on the land. Good lives.

I discovered the island on my return from Afghanistan in late 2006 — the war I could not shake. Given my September return to Canada, we elected to pull the kids from school and take a short holiday up to our favourite Ontario park — Pancake Bay on the southeastern snout of Lake Superior. There are fewer people on this beautiful white-sand beach — particularly after the Labour Day weekend. Operation Medusa was gobbling up precious ammunition in Kandahar and I was desperate to be disconnected from the outside world. Every round expended overseas added to my anxiety levels. My dreams about ammunition holdings and my last conversation in Kandahar with Dave Fraser were constant companions.

We had been to Lake Superior on numerous camping holidays over the past six years and had become well acquainted with the causeway cut-off to St. Joseph Island and the intriguing Parks Canada sign for historic Fort St. Joseph. We had never taken the time to come and explore it. On our numerous journeys north we were either just setting out at the beginning of an eight-hour drive home or coming close to the end of one. Stopping to tour this place, as alluring as it was, would not work with the demands of being back at work in the megacity on Monday. This time we were dragging our feet on the return to the south. I felt physically ill at the thought of reporting in to my new job at the Army Command and Staff College in Kingston. My channel was stuck on one station — Kandahar — and I was having difficulty imagining myself in a different unit than the one I had been through the wringer with. This time when the sign for the fort appeared, we took the turn and crossed the causeway. The island boasts historic old buildings, gorgeous vistas of the top of Lake Huron and the Saint Mary's Channel, and a slower pace that felt good to us. By the time we left the island a day later we had fallen in love with it. Two months later we purchased a rundown stone house on the island that soon became a point of escape for both of us.

Through the course of numerous weekend escapes over the coming months, we began to work on the old stone house ourselves. The bones of the structure were sound but its striking mansard roof had been admitting the elements for years. Piece by piece, Martha and I worked on ripping out mouldy lathe and plaster, ruined cupboards and fittings. We saved what we could to preserve the charm of the historic house. We hauled our kids along on these rennovacations and at night slept like logs on the kitchen floor. The routine comprised working all day on the house, sitting bone tired on ramshackle furniture with warmed-up canned pasta off a beat-up Coleman stove or a restaurant sandwich. Later on we might watch dated movies with a grainy VCR or play board games with the kids reclaimed from Goodwill stores in nearby Sault Ste. Marie. The enterprise was illogical, earthy, and exhausting. I loved it. In organized society, far to the south, my world continued to unravel. I was drifting between dead-end Class B jobs, frequently losing my temper at work, and over-reacting to issues that seem embarrassingly trivial in retrospect. I flirted with a return to the Regular Army and an ill-defined need for vindication from the Logistics Branch. There was something about the ruined old stone house and its need for physical investment that struck a healing chord with my mental wounds. My doppelgänger flight was not possible on St. Joseph Island. I found a deep satisfaction in manual labour, and the rich military history of the island provided an overarching context to my world that I found agreeable. The war that had happened here was cured and dried. Time will heal all wounds, the island assured me.

Normally trips to St. Joe were free of interruption from the army and the shaky ground that I felt I was on at work. I remember one renovation trip where I took a call from Captain Mike Wiesenfeld, the personable public affairs officer, who had been sympathetic to my sense of betrayal and neglect from the Regular Force. Wiesenfeld was still full of advice and connections, and this phone call was no different. The call amounted to an assurance that someone was going to be tuned in and that an opportunity for me would soon be appearing. I listened intently to what he had to say, offering few words in return. I was really excited by the time I hung up the phone.

"This is crazy, Martha. Wait until General So-and-So weighs in. Then these logistics assholes will get their comeuppance. They are going to be coming to me with a much different attitude."

Through my elation I did not notice that my wife was not buying any of it.

"Wake up, John," my patient wife replied. "They are not going to reach out. This is not going to happen."

"Of course it is. I will be put back on track, things will be set right. I will be vindicated."

That really tore it.

"Arrrrrgggghhh!"

My daughter looked up from her My Little Pony set to see what was going on. Both of us were arrested by Martha's reaction.

"What is the matter?" I asked my wife.

"You are! Listen to yourself. Goddamn it! You have to get over yourself. Who cares what any of them think? To hell with the army!" She whipped her arm sharply to indicate our children sprawled across the adjacent living room. "These people, these little people need you."

"I know that," I retorted, but I was confused by the ferocity of her explosion.

"These little people are the only ones that matter," she continued, now at a more normal level. "Goddamn it. General Whatshisname is going to do this; Colonel Thanksfornothing is doing that. Christ, they are playing you. Nobody is doing anything. Can't you see that? They don't care about you. You quit the army. That was your choice."

"I quit the Regular Army, I still serve."

"You know what I mean. You walked away. They are not going to help you. You have got to stop it. Stop all of this!" Her voice threatened to rise again to the spooky level. "Get over yourself!"

Her desperation reached me. For a few moments of stillness I could see inside the insanity of this game I was playing with Mike. I had to acknowledge the impossibility of his assurances for senior intervention into my tiny career. I looked over at my daughter, back with her ponies on the floor, and felt a wave of searing shame. I recalled my ride back to Camp Nathan Smith in Kandahar after the double suicide attack that had taken Corporals Francisco Gomez and Jason Warren. I recalled looking through the armour plating at Kandahar's black streets and thinking of my children, wanting to hold them one more time. That simple act was all that mattered in my life at that point. The "just in case letter" that sat locked in my barrack box on KAF was a poor surrogate to watching them grow up. I wanted to be part of their lives. That evening-of-survival in Kandahar when, earlier in the day, I had peered in on what felt like absolute truth, my prevailing thought was to give anything — risk anything — to be able to hold them one more time. Well, here they were, I realized, all around me in this crowded eight-hundred-square-foot house. Instead of paying attention to *their* needs and *their* challenges, I was dialed in on the wrong things; I was fixated on the army and obsessed with being vindicated — obsessed with showing up the whole lot of them.

The experience really scared me. It was not okay, I realized, to keep limping along and waiting for my mental problems to fade away like a bad dream. These dark dreams had consequences. I was hurting other people as I stumbled, deluding myself that I could live these things down. I finally had to accept that my behaviour was affecting my family. I was no picnic to live with during this period. In theatre, I was forever putting emotions and thoughts into locked compartments to stay focused on my battalion. I even dreaded the weekly phone calls home when we would connect for a few minutes in the sea can telephone trailer. Tuning into home and to the voices I loved chipped away at my resolve.

Don't think about home. Don't worry about the kids. Try and focus on the job at hand.

In the months after Kandahar, the endless practice of compartmentalizing dark thoughts rapidly unspooled. Long battened down hatches of experiences and emotions crashed out of their boxes and became constant companions. I needed help. I could see it in my wife's eyes. I just did not know how to start, and more importantly, how to start without anyone knowing.

My Styrofoam coffee cup leapt into the air and spilled all over the aisle. The tremours of the aircraft have startled even the aircrew. The plane drops maybe forty metres, leaving my stomach way up in my throat. I suddenly have the imminent barfing feeling one can get on the combat approach to KAF. The nose of the aircraft suddenly drops forty degrees. Its nose is pointed down to the earth — a horribly unnatural angle. The metal coffee-and-snack cart returns doing double time. It screams past my aisle seat en route to the sagging cockpit of the craft.

Everyone around me is screaming. We are going down. I have my Kevlar helmet on — the new American-style one that we started using in the Balkans. I nod to the woman beside me and tuck my head toward my lap. The aisle is nearly perpendicular now. The scream of overstrained aluminum competes with human ones.

This is it.

In early 2011 I received word from the Regular Army in Alberta that Darcia Arndt, Ray's widow, wanted to talk to me. Darcia had travelled to KAF with the senior leadership of the Western Army and she wanted to know more about Ray's commanding officer. She had asked the military for assistance with my contact details and it was not hard to find me in my Reserve role teaching at the CFC. I was intimidated and more than a little concerned. I had never met Darcia. More to the point, the fog of PTSD so clouded my thinking that I could only reason her desire to talk with me was for a dark purpose. I was convinced Darcia Arndt was going to accuse me of a dozen different horrible offences. We exchanged email notes and arranged for a good time for a call. The day of the call I dropped my son off at a high school event and sat in a Tim Hortons in Peterborough to ring her up.

I needn't have worried. Darcia was very kind; she was mostly curious about unit-life; travelling to where Ray was stationed at the King of the FOBs had answered some questions for her, she said, but it raised so many more.

"What was a typical day like outside the wire?" she asked. It was that sort of thing. We talked and talked for the better part of half an hour. By the time the call wound down I felt like we had known each other for a long time. I told her about some of the convoys I had been on with Ray, and the conversations we had had: we talked about the waiting and the long tracts of mind-numbing boredom, less so on the punctuated minutes of pure and unspeakable terror. Talking with her I had the strangest sense that Ray was sitting right beside me.

"You can, you know."

"Can what?" I asked him.

"You can get help and keep it low."

Not long after my conversation with Sergeant Singh in the field up in Borden, I made an appointment with the mental health section of 32 Medical Support Unit. The 32 Med Unit was the part of the medical corps that was designated to provide health services for the Toronto Garrison. As the date of the appointment drew closer, I thought a lot about cancelling, including right up to the hour of my appointment.

The Med Unit was located in the architecturally challenged Denison Armoury, home to many of the Reserve units as well as functioning as the Regular Force Area Headquarters.[3] The Denison Armoury was once described as Toronto's ugliest building, which seems unfair, if you fancy a building that bears a striking resemblance to a giant shoebox. The clinic was in the same part of the building where headquarters held its sick parades and medicals. I was experiencing a mounting sense of dread, already having regrets about the appointment. I sat in the waiting area reading an old *Sports Illustrated* when — sitting across from me — I recognized one of my corporals from my current Reserve command, 32 Service Battalion. Our eyes met, he assessed the situation in a split second, then quickly averted his eyes. The motion signalled clearly that conversation would neither be necessary nor desired. I was a bit taken aback; unlike soldiers like Andy Singh and Joshua Wood, the soldier sitting across from me was not on my radar screen as one of our mentally wounded. I was surprised. This well-spoken thirty-something Torontonian had always given me the distinct impression that he was in full control of his health; in civilian life he was highly successful in his work for a busy city agency. I had recently been at a city hall ceremony in recognition of his service in Afghanistan. Meeting him by chance in the waiting area of a mental health clinic was not a moment for backslapping celebration and soldier banter. The fight or flight instinct presented itself as an option, but I fought through it. I looked down at my *Sports Illustrated* and feigned interest, as nonchalant as if we were in a dental clinic. In my head, my brain was revving with fear. *My unit will know I need help. They will know I am weak. They will know I am damaged.* Clearly, he had the same fears. I thought that if I walked out right then he might assume that I was actually at the clinic on military business; that I was there merely to check on some aspect of medical administration in my capacity as a commanding officer.

It was an excruciating wait, but finally I heard my name called. I slapped down the magazine and jumped up as buoyantly as I could and was introduced to a counsellor.

"Good evening, sir. My name is Carol." I relaxed a bit, realizing she was a civilian practitioner.

"John. Please, call me John," I mumbled. I felt embarrassed for being a lieutenant colonel and for being in the mental health office. Hell, there were plenty of our young people who needed her time. Not an old bastard like me. I should not have attempted this.

"Would you like to come in?"

"Sure. You bet. Sure," I said, looking hesitatingly at the outer door that my corporal had just walked through.

"Right this way," she indicated.

"Where do we begin?" I asked. "I honestly don't know how."

"Why don't you start by telling me something about yourself?"

"All right then." Like my first time on ice skates, I ventured short half-steps.

At first the conversation was stilted and needed her continuous but gentle priming. I told her about the tour, sticking to the context and main facts: the enormous size of the Canadian Area of Operations in Kandahar Province, the small size of our logistics battalion, the eradication of logistics in the battle group (which made the small size of my battalion even more poignant),[4] and the efforts of the Taliban in that summer of 2006. The words and thoughts came in choppy bursts. She wrote nothing down and just listened — intently — like we were having a normal conversation over a Green Beans coffee on the KAF boardwalk. I was surprised at one point to find myself crying. When I looked into her eyes through my hot tears, I saw all of the humanity and goodness of the angel medic of 2006. There was no judgment and no agenda. That first meeting with Carol was rough, really rough. It took an incredible amount of energy to tell a stranger some of my story. I left the session feeling physically exhausted.

Carol was a brilliant counsellor. Her professional approach placed her, for me at least, somewhere between little sister and trusted clinician. Whatever the reality, she began to build my confidence in the transactions we had. I grew to trust that I could actually give voice to the blackest storms inside my head: paranoia, abandoned confidence, low self-esteem, and my hatred for particular senior officers. In subsequent visits I actually found myself telling her about my flights of unchecked rage. I confessed to her my doppelgänger moments, which seemed to be present at the zenith of my emotional outbursts. I described the third-party perspective characteristic of the doppelgänger experience, checking her eyes frequently for reaction.

Holy shit. You really are nuts.

I eventually arrived at point where I stopped searching her face for judgment. It was a rare space. As we conversed over a span of a few sessions, I described some of the things I had experienced; I felt as if a large clock spring, under tension for an age, was beginning to ease. Carol's patient and empathetic demeanour never wavered. She saw a lot of our soldiers in those days. Over the years I have wondered after her. Hers was not an easy job, and I hope she is getting the support she herself needs for delivering care to the walking wounded.

Eventually we got around to discussing the sharpest memories and emotions, including the worst dreams and the double IED attack on July 22, 2006. After a half-dozen sessions with her, she referred me to a psychiatrist who confirmed my diagnosis for PTSD. I remember feeling an immense relief. I stayed in routine care with Carol right up to the time I accepted a new civilian job in Alberta.

And then I stopped treatment.

CHAPTER 7:

THE LONESOME DEATH OF CORPORAL JOSHUA WOOD

Josh was more than just a part-time soldier. He loved the army and, like most of us, lived for the army. Throughout the years within the battalion he made many close friends, and if you weren't close, you were still a friend. But friends or not, when a job had to be done there was no skylarking. It got done. He was recognized as one of the most respected soldiers within the battalion. If he had something to say, or when mentoring soldiers, they listened.

— Sergeant Andy Singh, 32 Service Battalion

Chug, chug, chug, chug, withick!

Another bale of Timothy alfalfa presents itself at the chute for piling. Hmmm. Way lighter, I think to myself as I head to the back of the wagon to store the hay bale. The southern Ontario sun hot upon my neck could be Afghanistan's; the weight of the hemp twine in my hands mimics the extraction strap of a soldier's webbing.

Chug, chug, chug, chug, withick!

The next bale has taken its place. *Yeah, way lighter as well.* This mental check will go on for three heat-soaked days, the remainder of the harvest and some twelve hundred bales. All of which are easier to lift than a priority-one casualty.

Easier to move than the dead.

Every time I lift a bale of hay on the farm I do a quick mental comparison to the weight of a soldier. It could be Captain Tony Ross, whom we lifted out of the ruined Bison LAV II and passed to the Canadian medics. It might be the dead-weight of the wounded soldier we scrambled to load onto the Blackhawk helicopter in that same ambush. Speed means everything in the life and death world of medevac: its price is high … and painful. Every ounce of effort is spent to try and achieve the golden hour between point of wounding and surgery. We ran our asses off and yet it seemed to take forever to get to the American helicopter.

Chug, chug, chug, chug, withick!

The weight of the stretcher seemed disproportionate to the four of us lifting. I thought my heart was going to explode from the effort. I was so happy to see the U.S. aviators in the bowels of the UH-60 Blackhawk. The cool efficiency of the airmen had a bracing effect. Tom Cruise-esque. Hollywood competence. Their eyes swam nearly invisible behind their tinted goggles as they relieved us of our physical burden. I am stacking hay while deep inside my brain these images replay. These day trips in the mind are more real than cinema.

The baler belching out this hay once belonged to my grandfather. The machine, like me, is a child of the sixties but it looked much older when we purchased it from my uncle in 2009. My father-in-law was skeptical, convinced that we had wasted our money. The joints and extensions of its various parts carried an air of the antique. A drive shaft like an octogenarian's forearm, a fly-wheel cast in iron so thick it could have driven one of the *Titanic's* propellers. This was my first baler — the John Deere 24T — and it was an engineering marvel. I loved pulling it apart, working on it when it broke down in protest on a hot day; being tested, measured by the situation and your ability with your hands. The machine's complicated knotter is a comfort to a splintered mind. The baroque device has not changed a lick since the early fifties. The machinery of tying bales worked so well, why change it. Its brooding precision and longevity inspires hope for a time after this. I derive a good measure of comfort knowing my father, and my father's father, worked on this puzzle.

Chug, chug, chug, chug, withick!

The next bale appears. The sun beats down on my stricken convoy at the top of the world.

Generations of Canadians bound to the land have worked to the mechanical music of the baler and its knotting assembly. Somewhere in that John Deere lullaby is the recognition of a metaphysical truth, an assurance that I am not a worthless piece of shit and that I might still have some gifts to contribute — that suicide is not the way to go. I love that tune; I even crave it. It is more soothing than classical music.

The walking wounded are alive with internal dialogue and the constant churning of images, conversations, and events. These things remain unseen by the external world, but to the veteran with PTSD they are more than real. The violent storms that rage inside my head are quelled by mindless mental exercises: comparing the weight of a hay bale to the weight of a man, or sitting alone in a bathroom stall forcing my heart rate down before an important briefing in my civilian workplace. It feels stupid really, but the drills are absolutely essential. Eight years on, the gore and sulphur of a double suicide attack can seem like it was only a moment ago. Some nights it can seem like it is happening again. If I think of myself doing a mundane physical task — if I use a set of pat drills — I can stay even at work: the thousands of words I am speaking to myself are dulled. I can talk to groups or even deliver a public address like the old days, like my head still works well.

What have I become?

Last night after the attack, I went to the NSE Command Post and made sure that everyone was safe, that the inbound recovery convoy was safely returned from outside the wire, and that the ammunition boys on the northern side of the runway were secure. Next I looked in on our Tim Hortons civilian staff, as some of the rounds had landed near their spanking-new trailers on the boardwalk. They were not too badly rattled, and after sharing a couple of jokes with them I finally stumbled past Canada House and found my own tent. Paddy was already asleep on his side of the canvas. I don't know what time it was. Late. The veneer of dust had been refreshed on the inner vestibule, and as I sealed the door of my Weatherhaven quarters I realized I was too tired to do anything more in that instant. I barely made the four steps into my bunk. I was instantly collapsed into the deepest sleep I have ever known. A breathing corpse.

Inside that sleep I descended into the most organic of dreams. I was fighting to get home through a vicious thunderstorm, an old fashioned Ontario humdinger. Flashes of lightning, brimstone in the air; the smell of electricity. The G-Wagon rocked back and forth from the buffeting of the elements. Finally I made it to a safe harbour — the old hundred-acre farm I lived on as a child in Wallace Township. My first glimpse of war had happened inside the yellow-brick farmhouse that now rose in front of me — televised body-counts from an earlier head game. I left the G-Wagon and saw my grandmother Alice on the porch of the farmhouse. Grandma Conrad had died in 1996 while I was posted to the army headquarters in Halifax. I loved her so much and by perverse contrast had seen next to nothing of her since I enlisted in the forces in 1983. She was saying something over and over again — something important — that I could not make out. I leaned in to hear the words — but to no avail. She began to hug me in an embrace that tightened to the point that I could hardly breathe. I woke up and noticed dimly that my lamp was on; I was still in my boots and full combat uniform. My loaded pistol was slouching in its shoulder holster off the side of the bed. So real was the dream that I looked through the knock-off Kashmir scarves that lined my bunk to see if she was still in the Weatherhaven. She had been here. I was filled with an overwhelming sadness and a sense of some other world. If I dared venture outside right now there would be no King of the FOBs, no Hawker Harriers waiting to pounce on a pack of Taliban, no NATO. Rather, I would be in some other worse place. A place of phantoms and lost aspirations.

This was the only dream during my entire time in Kandahar.

For most of the twelve years that we owned a fifty-acre farm near Orono, Ontario, I yearned for a yard sale. Our farm was the perfect location to hold one. The paved road that ran in front of our place was always busy with traffic. There was superb skiing at Mount Kirby, just three kilometres to the east, which drew traffic in winter. The fantastic bass fishing in Rice Lake even further east generated a steady stream of vehicles in summer time. Catherine Parr Traill first wrote about Rice Lake and its allure over a century ago. It is so strange to think of Rice Lake as one of the dark places on the edge of the civilized world. Today the lake begs for rediscovery of its charms, a rewarding find for adventurous Torontonians.

Martha finally agreed to a sale on the Saturday of the Victoria Day long weekend in 2011. I was excited about it. Work had been a bear with my Reserve command picking up. All of the soldiers of 32 Service Battalion would be looking forward to this holiday weekend because it represented one of the few free weekends we would have that summer.

My new-found Army Reserve career was going well and the unit was in the field a lot. I had begun to attend counselling sessions at the Mental Health Section in Toronto and I was feeling its early positive effects. Having the interest in a yard sale was tangible proof of my psychological improvement. Exactly one week ahead, I ran an ad in the local newspaper, which lauded the forthcoming sale on the old Stone House farm. Once the ad appeared, there was no turning back. I had crossed the point of no return and even my skeptical wife would not veto the operation. I planned and sorted merchandise for days. I loaded up my hay wagon on Friday evening with various bits of treasure and farm junk. Before the sun set, I pulled the wagon down on the front lawn with my vintage Massey Ferguson, parallel to the traffic of Concession Road 7 that would soon be going by with plenty of city folks with full wallets.

Not all of the kids were enthusiastic. They shared their mother's aversion to anything that might involve barter — except my eldest daughter, Harriet; she was all for it. She was with me Saturday morning, which was bright and crisp. The morning breeze encouraged us as we wiped away dew and organized the various bits and pieces on the hay wagon to make them appear like "finds." Suddenly Harriet disappeared up the lane that led to the house — a girl on a mission. I was curious but could not dwell on the abrupt departure. The early shoppers — the serious crowd — had already swooped in.

"You take ten dollars for this?"

"How much for the old saw?"

"If I buy the whole box of books will you give me a deal?"

The game had begun. At some point I noticed that my daughter had returned. She had in tow a small children's card table, a tea towel, and a Tupperware container full of homemade muffins. Tucked in with the muffins was a small tin for donations. She was ten years old and I was not even aware that she could bake. Her muffins were an instant hit with my customers, and she looked over with a shy smile at me as she jammed loonies and quarters into her tin cash box. I had to chuckle. My long-courted lawn sale was meeting both of our expectations. I stopped for a moment and took in the vista of my prized Massey Ferguson tractor, the emerald-pine hay wagon that my father had built with his own hands before I had left for the army, and my daughter giggling as she flogged her baking. The moment was one of sheer stillness. I looked up and took a long drink of the peerless sky and suddenly realized that I felt strangely untethered. I could not remember the last time I had been happy.

I feel good, I remember thinking. *I feel really good.*

That morning Marg Zwart, the editor and publisher of the *Orono Weekly Times*, showed up to take some photos and to pass the time.

"Clearly a slow news day in the neighbourhood, eh, Marg?" I joked.

"Yeah, right," she responded. Marg is a refreshing small-town editor who runs a newspaper the way they were originally intended — full of debate and opinion and not a repository for public and private advertising and political apple polishing — either for the current member of Parliament or members of town council. The *Orono Weekly Times* is a small newspaper with a big voice. The newspaper was forever pissing off local politicians with Marg's frank common-sense take on life. Marg had won my admiration forever when she wrote a blistering editorial after Remembrance Day, 2006, a little over a month after I came home. It was a municipal election year and the handful of veterans shivering in the crowd went nearly unnoticed in the event at the expense of the politicians who were scrounging for votes. She is one of the bravest journalists I know.

As we chatted, Marg threw a smile at someone coming up the lane. I turned and smiled too: It was Martha.

"Hey!" I yelled up the lane to her, "we should do more of these." My smile slumped when I saw her expression. She had on her "something is very wrong" look. The same hard stance in the depth of that face I have come to associate with calamity.

My gut tightened.

"Hi, Marg. You mind if I borrow this guy for a minute?" she said, smiling broadly to Marg. Martha steered me a few steps away from the sale so we could talk in private.

"Hatty, keep an eye on the sale," I called to my daughter, not pausing to see if she had heard me.

"The battalion called. Charles is still on the line. They tried your BlackBerry."

I felt the slide begin inside my head, a free fall into blackness. Whatever it was going to be, it would almost certainly be my fault. Her voice seemed to be coming to me from far away. I had made the decision to leave the BlackBerry in the house and focus on the sale. I looked down at the lawn at the edge of our lane, noticing how abruptly the line of LAV III–green met the pale packed gravel of the laneway — green camouflage paint on hardened brown mud.

"You need to talk to him; one of your soldiers is dead. He committed suicide."

The edges of the lane swam. Straight clean lines dissolved as I raced to process the information.

This is my fault.

"I should have brought my phone down here."

This is my fault. The ridiculous guilt at not having the BlackBerry when the unit needed to connect hit me like a blow to the stomach. Numerous questions began to swirl inside my brain.

"Who? Who … is it?" I asked Martha stupidly.

"I don't know. You had better get up to the house. Charles is waiting for you. I can watch your sale." I stumbled up the lane to the house, drunk inside the darkness. A rising dread clenched my heart. Over my shoulder I could hear Martha talking to Marg, shifting gears as if our quick sidebar conversation had not occurred.

My fault. *Which one? Not Andy, please God, not him.* Andy Singh had recently begun to take great strides forward with his PTSD. He was even thinking about making an application to the Regular Force, which was something he had contemplated before his Kandahar tour in 2006.

Surely not him.

I recalled our field exercise in Borden, my first with the unit where I got the opportunity to know Andy in the darkness of the bivouac. Our tours had been so closely linked in time and velocity, something about this shared experience had opened a safe space for me to talk about the tour and my mental anguish. I had told another human being about my problems for the first time. After three years of suffering in silence he had set me forward on my first steps to mental wellness. I prayed that he was okay. I could pick up that phone and learn that he was dead.

Why did this happen? Are we running too many exercises? Are we not running enough? How did we fail this soldier?

The questions raced through my skull. I blundered through the door of our living room and all I could see was the tiny military BlackBerry with its hateful red eye rapidly blinking, indicating a live call. I braced myself to hear the soldier's name from my deputy commanding officer.

"Charles, it's the CO. What happened?"

"Sir. It's Joshua Wood." My mind stopped.

"What happened, Charles?"

What happened?

We are still asking.

In a Reserve unit we become a very close family. Heck, I practically grew up at 25 Service Battalion! I was twelve years old as a cadet (2754 Royal Canadian Army Cadets) when I first paraded with them on Remembrance Day. After I left the cadets, I joined 25 Service and then stayed there until I joined the Regular Force at thirty-five years old. We have seen people enlist that can barely grow a moustache and years after laugh about trying to hide the grey hair. We lost girlfriends and boyfriends, got married, had kids, cried, laughed, disagreed, and in some cases fought together. But always looked after each other. All the qualities of a functional family. The unit and people within will always be part of my family. That is pretty much the same belief for all the soldiers within 25 Service Battalion.

— Andy Singh, September 2015

The Canadian Army commander directed the strangest thing in 2009: an optimization plan for Army Reserve logistics units. The timing of the move during the waning years of conflict was puzzling. In a nutshell, the Ottawa-centric plan cut the number of Canadian Army service battalions in half, from twenty units across the country down to ten. As far back as Brian Dickson's report, "The Special Commission on the Restructuring of the Reserves," some two decades before the Afghan War there had been some thought to adopt a brigade group structure instead of the geographically based Militia District Structure then in place. Some believed that this implied advocacy to reduce the number of logistics battalions down to one per district; however, this was not the intent of the old proposal.[1] The new optimization plan was a clear move to rationalize the numbers of battalions along these lines so that only one per brigade remained. Such a disarming word: "rationalize." Some units were dropped; others were unceremoniously renamed under new designations. There was no resistance from the Canadian Force's tepid leadership in the Logistics Branch. Indeed, there were few senior logistics officers that understood the Reserves and even fewer who would have considered challenging Lieutenant General Andrew Leslie, the commander of the army in 2009. I was just taking over my first Reserve command, 25 Service Battalion in Toronto, my first professional steps forward since 2006. 25 Service Battalion's unit designation was dropped and my battalion became overnight 32 Service Battalion — the designation number of a storied maritime unit that had been disbanded. The names and histories of these units were rebooted with the stroke of a pen. I was disappointed at the shoddy treatment of an entire military community that had contributed significantly to the war. The plan devalued us all, but it sat perfectly with my own sense of worth in 2010. This organizational change did nothing to improve army logistics other than furnish the illusion of progress. However, the impacts on veteran soldiers, where unit traditions (titles, ceremonies, designations, bits of ribbon) are concerned, were huge. In the kingdom of the mind, this is not a trivial business. Regiments and their organic histories are important to the moral health of an army at war — no less so for its Reserve component. Regiments are the altars upon which soldiers draw spiritual strength. In wartime, the regiment nurtures the raw material of memory, hope, and expectation.

The Army Reserve is a unique creature. Regiments for the Canadian Reservist are not postings, but rather community installations. Men and women join the Reserve units often for a lifetime. Andy Singh recalls starting as a green cadet before he was even shaving, in awe of the more grown-up soldiers around him in Toronto's North York Armoury. Memorial services at the passing of ancient commanding officers and regimental sergeants major long-retired out of active service are major events for the whole tribe — from the newest private recruit to the current commanding officer. I found that my Reserve soldiers resisted the new designation number and continued to refer to the battalion as 25 Service Battalion. These unit designations were not just numbers to the rank and file; they were the names of their regiments. The part-time soldier goes to the armoury after the end of his or her civilian workday. Time for courses or for field exercises are carved out of weekends and holidays. The level of energy and dedication to service that the Reservist maintains across the span of a career is impressive.

Most Regular Force leaders do not understand the Army Reserve — but they think they do.[2] Even more dangerously, the Regulars do not understand the effects of the recent war on our Reserve soldiers. An article in November 2015 in the *Globe and Mail* on veteran suicides in the post-Afghanistan army does not even touch on the Reserve community.[3] The job in assembling information on the Regular Force was hard enough. The Canadian Army could not have survived a decade in Afghanistan without staunch Reserve support. Today the army's few remaining Reserve service battalions are withering under the leadership of an institution that neither understands *nor cares to understand them*. The Canadian Army has been forever strong on the regimental system. The psychological strength maintained by a band of sisters and brothers. War is fought in greater proportion with the mind, not the body.

We should have known better.

A wave of memories is upon me when look at photos of our fallen comrade: the flood of youthful enthusiasm of my Toronto Reservists; the juxtaposition of military equipment with the megacity funk like Dundas Square; and the endless charm of Yonge Street. The battalion had a diverse ethnic flavour, a mixture of tough Indian- and Chinese-Canadian soldiers. A unit of bright young Canadians of all stripes — but Corporal Joshua Wood was among our brightest. Here is a picture of Corporal Joshua Wood standing by a light field gun. The context is work-up training, the combat uniform is green, not the tan, arid Cadpat worn in country. Furthermore, the body armour lacks its all-important ceramic plate. Joshua Wood is not yet in Afghanistan — but soon. He is not smiling but you can tell he is happy. A tight "almost" smile adorns his helmeted face. Another photograph shows him in his best uniform in downtown Toronto between tours, one of our G-Wagons in the background. My favourite is the photo of Joshua at age six or seven sitting behind the wheel of the Batmobile. This is no mock-up, his father points out to me; this is the real deal. That explains the quiet satisfaction on Joshua's face. Joshua Wood was the youngest of three children born to Bruce and Susan Wood of Elliot Lake, Ontario, in 1981. The photos have been given to me by Bruce Wood. Even now, four years after Joshua's death, Susan cannot bear to look through them. The grinning face in the campy sixties-era Batmobile punctuates nothing but promise and optimism for his future. And his future was bright. From the earliest age he had demonstrated skills for organization and sound financial management. Joshua was good with money. His father remembers how you could always go down to Joshua's room and get change for a fifty-dollar bill. He enlisted in the Canadian Army the same year as Darryl Caswell, on April 20, 2004. By the time he made corporal he owned a couple of properties, one of which he rented to his older sister, Jennifer.

When you met Corporal Joshua Wood there was the sense of motion all around him; a feeling that even while he is standing still and talking to you he was somehow making kinetic progress, completing a series of tasks beyond the full grasp of the eye. Joshua Wood was a go-to soldier, a young man who could be relied upon through thick and thin. He almost never missed an exercise with 32 Service Battalion, where he worked in the unit's quartermaster stores doling out supplies. He was all about the work at hand and getting it done efficiently, with pride of craft. His quartermaster stores were superbly organized down to the last rifle bolt or spare spark plug. There was something of my own John Deere lullaby to the meticulous order of Joshua's supply section. I suspect the mindless sorting and arranging of machinery and tools brought him as much solace as I derived from my ancient hay baler. The sergeants praised him for his suggestions. He never challenged an order he received but routinely sought clarification, to lock it down in his mind. He would often come up with suggestions and ideas that could get the job done in a more efficient manner. He had done two tours in Afghanistan, the most recent of which had been completed around Christmas 2010. My memories of him are spotty and resolve around quick conversations on our field exercises. These exchanges were mostly work-related, superficial — nothing of substance, nothing like the conversations I had with Andy Singh where we actually exchanged demons. I knew Joshua as a solid soldier, with a high level of operational experience for his age and brief service record. I looked forward to getting to learn more about his time in Afghanistan.

His first tour in southern Afghanistan was two years after my own: August 2008 to April 2009. By the time he deployed on his second tour the unit had been clumsily redesignated 32 Service Battalion under the army's optimization plan for Reserve logistics battalions. This final tour was during my time as the unit commanding officer in May 2010 through to December 2010. When I took command in September 2010, I emailed all my soldiers in Kandahar and recall getting a short but polite acknowledgement from Corporal Wood. He seemed happy enough for the contact from his home unit:

Hello, sir,

How are you? Things are going well. Time is flying by. This is my second tour and they have me out at FOB Masum Gar again. I'm getting good experience. I'm finding things are a lot more quiet out here this time, at least in this area.

I see a few of the other members of 32 occasionally roll through the FOB and they are doing good as well.

We all look forward to returning to the home unit and getting caught up with everyone.

Thanks,
Cpl Wood J.S.

When he came home at Christmas, he gave me the impression that he had returned in good form from Afghanistan. He was always there for us, solid and competent. The sort of soldier you want on your side.

Things were far from ordered behind the mask of the good soldier. Six weeks prior to Joshua Wood's suicide the unit became aware that he was struggling with his mental health. Our unit RSM, Chief Warrant Officer Keith Robb, had received some information — pieces of a story, really — that had come to the battalion from some of the soldiers. Joshua had had a particularly bad argument with his spouse. While engaged in the altercation with his new wife, he had said something to the effect that he might hurt himself. As fragmented as the account had been, the senior NCOs wasted no time in intervening. Wood's section commander, Sergeant Andy Singh, received a phone call shortly after from the battalion operations NCO. Andy was at home, his first day off in a number of weeks. His wife, Natasha, was lying next to him in bed; they both decided to sleep in.

I was informed that a vehicle was en route to my house to pick me up, that there was an issue with one of our soldiers, that I had to go get him, and accompany him back to the base. I looked over to Natasha, who obviously had overheard our conversation; she whispered, "Sounds serious — get dressed," and went back to sleep. Almost like she was accustomed to it. We arrived at Corporal Wood's house in Newmarket, Ontario. Only thing, he didn't live there. His sister and her family did. I was instructed to go to another address by Josh's nephew, not too far from where we were.

When Singh finally got to Corporal Wood's home, he was invited in by his wife, Jessica. Immediately, he could tell that things were not quite right in the house. The atmosphere of the home was infused with a latent tension. Singh took off his combat boots and sat with her. He made small talk about the regiment and how things were going at work and avoided any pointed questions. Jessica suddenly opened up and started describing in rapid order what was going on within their lives. Andy Singh said he took a slow look around as she unloaded; his eyes fell on unwashed dishes, strewn laundry, and other signs of general neglect. The house was a far cry from the immaculate quartermaster stores Joshua Wood had managed. This was not the home of the tidy and ultra-organized Supply Technician that Singh knew so well. He remembers being shocked by the contrast.

"Knowing Josh and now being at his home and seeing its state was off-putting," he told me. "This was foreign behaviour for Joshua Wood. After speaking with his wife, I called a number of people to offer professional help to her as a spouse; she was happy and intended to keep in contact with these organizations."

Singh realized Wood needed help. He was damn sure that he would see this through tonight. Andy said his wife gave him "the address of Josh's civilian work place and Corporal Cook and I proceeded there. I got to the parking lot of his work place but decided that I should call first. I didn't know how he would react, if I showed up in uniform and requested him to come along. I didn't want to create an awkward situation for either of us."

Singh called Wood on his cell phone and the two soldiers worked out a good arrangement. Wood asked Singh to meet him at his parents' home in Newmarket at the end of his shift. "I remember," he recalled to me later, "that it was getting a little late, and Josh wasn't showing up. But at the last minute I saw his vehicle pull into his mother's driveway. We gave him a few minutes to get settled and then knocked on the door."

The mood at the Wood family home was completely opposite to the tension of Joshua Wood's. Andy Singh recalls the smells of a freshly cooked dinner, and the big welcoming smile on Susan Wood's face. Bruce Wood, Joshua's father, was no less pleased to have the soldiers join them. Bruce is an intelligent and insightful man. He understood the world his son had entered when he joined the army. The senior Wood's respect for the men and women that serve the nation as first responders and soldiers is deep. I can imagine his delight in hosting some of Joshua's comrades that evening. Susan offered the young men soft drinks and tried to convince them to partake in the supper that was ready. It felt good to have Joshua's soldier friends in her home. Like all parents, it is reaffirming to see positive influences connected with our kids, a tangible endorsement that they are finding a good direction in the world, that they have good support around them — every parent's fervent hope. Susan was worried for her son and his readjustment after this second Afghanistan tour. This impromptu gathering brought a world of comfort as the family and the soldiers blended. Singh recalls Susan Wood reminded him of his own mother.

After a period of conversation and pleasantries, Singh said he looked Corporal Wood in the eye and told him point blank the reason for his visit. He explained to Joshua and his family that the unit was of course very concerned particularly since he had just returned from his second deployment from Afghanistan. He spoke for about thirty minutes about the options for support and assistance available to their son. Singh realized it must have been difficult for Joshua to hear all this — especially in front of his parents. The young man's ethos of enterprise and order would have been impossible to square up against his current state of emotional disarray. "In his heart of hearts, I think Corporal Joshua Wood knew he was wounded," Singh said. To his relief, Wood was very understanding and did not put up any resistance. In fact, he seemed willing to get some help. "I can only imagine that the meeting was even harder for Bruce and Susan Wood. In the end it seemed like terrific progress had been made."

Prior, to his leaving the house, Susan Wood looked Sergeant Andy Singh in the eyes, grabbed his hand, and asked him very softly to bring her son home please.

"He's my brother, I promise you, ma'am. He'll be good to go soon."

> Once a Class C contract ends, it cannot be reinstated so, if you have symptoms, call to be seen within thirty days of return to avoid loss of extended benefits. (Canadian Forces mental health pamphlet, 2011)

The Canadian Army Reserve, the largest component of our part-time forces, is predicated on the volunteer. Soldiers are deployed only when they put up their hand. When a Reserve soldier deploys on an overseas operation he or she is moved from part-time status of one-evening-a-week one-weekend-a-month to a full-time contract that sees him paid and supported in nearly every respect like the Regular Force. This full-time contract is called the Class C contract. Under a Class C contract, Reserve soldiers are eligible for Canadian Forces medical support for the deployment period, including mental health care: eligible but not entitled. On the surface, everything briefs well. There was a qualifier back in 2011. To be eligible for support as a Reservist, your injury had to be manifest while you were on your full-time status; it could not occur once a deployment contract (Class C) ended. In other words, a soldier had to be having the symptoms and in some stage of diagnosis for the deployment contract and attendant medical benefits to be extended. As one might suspect, these Class C contracts are designed to close off fairly quickly after a tour. They are instruments for in-theatre service. For soldiers who have not been diagnosed with PTSD, mental health benefits terminate once a Class C contract expires. In other words, *you are shit out of luck, soldier.* The obvious problem here is that in some cases it takes years for the symptoms of PTSD to surface. The other factor for Reserve soldiers is that they must put their lives back together in the shadows, away from the paternal gaze of the full-time military. If you do not want the prying attention of your platoon sergeant or regimental sergeant major you merely stay away: you call in sick or you tell your section leader that your civilian work is too much right now. The Reserve soldier can cover his absence so easily. The follow-up care for the Reserve soldier is heavily dependent on the persistence of the unit.

Joshua followed up with a visit to the mental health section in North York at 32 Health Services Clinic. Andy Singh recalls the early supports that Corporal Joshua Wood received:

> The night we met with the social worker, I stayed about fifteen minutes with them both. Josh started talking to her, and as soon as I saw him getting a bit comfortable, I left. Later on that evening, I met with Josh, the social worker, and the DCO of our unit. I was told, because his full time contract with the army was completed, he wasn't entitled to continue seeing the social worker. Josh had agreed to call if he experienced any other issues and stated that he would see someone from his civilian work place. I was disgusted. No entitlement to Mental Health. But that was the policy at the time.

Unseen by his military employer, Joshua's life became more complicated. He had separated from his wife and was focused on his health and attempting to get his life back on track. Andy Singh was keeping pretty close tabs on him and he recalls that Joshua had indeed followed up to see a social worker from his civilian employer. However, a civilian social worker starts with a distinct disadvantage to those associated with the Canadian Forces.

"I stayed in contact with Josh on a daily basis over the next six weeks," Andy told me. He mentioned the civilian therapist. "But what do they understand about combat?"

Four weeks after his separation, Joshua was on exercise in Meaford, a training outpost on Georgian Bay, when he received a phone call from a civilian hospital. Jessica had been admitted to the facility. She was doing fine but the stranger's voice told him that she had miscarried. They had lost their baby. Wood did not even know that his wife was pregnant. The thunderclap of shock must have been overwhelming. I can sense the magnified effect of this bad news on Corporal Joshua Wood, the good soldier who kept things in careful order, who made things better. I can see him striking his field gear, throwing stuff in his truck on near autopilot as he raced to get back to Toronto. I can imagine the guilt he must have felt, the choking feeling soldiers feel when their family battles and they are not there to help. Shortly after they lost the baby, the couple moved back together. Joshua's friends said he believed Jessica needed his support and that he could continue to work things out for himself. But belief can be irrational. I recall how my own belief system was crumpled, ever so briefly, for a period on Highway 1 in Kandahar. In those few nanoseconds of unvarnished brightness I found something to ponder the rest of my life.

The same Saturday as my yard sale, Sergeant Andy Singh was enjoying some well-deserved time off. He was launching his boat up near Lake Couchiching in central Ontario, and enjoying the bright sun. Singh was a little glum that Joshua Wood had not joined him. He had tried to convince the hard-working Wood to take in the Saturday with him — a chance to de-link from the complexities of the world and focus on some fishing. He was about to have an even worse day. At eight that morning, just as he was backing up his trailer to launch his boat, his military cell phone rang. The call was from the unit regimental sergeant major, Chief Warrant Officer Keith Robb.

"Sir … really … it's the long weekend. I've been working like a dog. Can't I go fishing just one day, please?" Singh begged. Usually the RSM would bark a "suck it up, soldier!" and that would be that. But the voice that came back to him was heavy and serious.

"Where are you?" Robb asked.

"Orillia."

"Get to base immediately."

"Wood?"

"Yes."

"Could I at least get some details?" Singh asked.

"I will fill you in when you get here but I need you back here right now."

Andy Singh cannot account for the time spent between getting from the lake to Toronto. He said the entire time-block is crowded with dark images, a slide show of recollection. He knew, even from the clipped conversation with Chief Warrant Officer Robb, that Joshua was dead. When he arrived at his house, there was a throng of Service Battalion soldiers waiting for him. Andy was the natural leader of the unit. They had gathered there to await his return. Without a second thought to his boat, he locked the truck and jumped into the vehicle with the soldiers.

"When we arrived to the base," he recalled, "I could just see long faces. Everyone looked dazed, disappointed, drained. Chief Warrant Officer Robb called me into his office and gave me the details."

At the unit, there were scant details about what had happened. All the soldiers knew for certain was that Corporal Wood was dead. Keith Robb briefed Singh on what facts he knew. Singh recalls asking Robb if it would be acceptable for him to put on his best uniform and offer some support to the Wood family. He remembers feeling that an edgeless guilt was alive inside him and he wanted desperately to make amends. He had a favour to ask.

"I asked [Robb] if some of the guys could accompany me. I told him I had met Josh's family before. He didn't hesitate; he sent us on our way."

Words were scarce on the drive to Newmarket. Some of the young soldiers in the car had been exposed to the sudden finality of combat and IEDs but this loss was different. For Sergeant Andy Singh the darkness was welling up inside him. Guilt and unfounded ineptitude are familiar enemies for many who suffer from PTSD. When the men, now changed into their best army tunics, arrived at Josh's house, no one was home. Singh looked through the windows and saw that Joshua's home was empty except for a couple of items lying on the floor. He remembered Joshua's other property, the house rented to his sister Jennifer. It was just down the street. He decided to see if Jennifer Wood was home. The soldiers could offer initial condolences and support to her. She would help them gauge if her parents were even up for a visit at this time. It would be a start. The desire to be there for the family was strong.

"We arrived at his sister's house," Andy recalled to me. "I knocked on the door and had no answer. However, the neighbours came out and told us that his sister was in the process of moving to Keswick and they had just left. But they should be back for another load. I ended up giving the neighbours my phone number to have Jennifer contact me when they get back for another trip."

At the same time, Singh confided that he did not believe the neighbours. He figured that because Joshua's death had been a suicide that the family was being private. Chances were that a visit from his pack of soldiers might not be welcome so soon after the incident. He contemplated his next move and decided to go to the home of Joshua's parents. He felt on edge, the move was a risky one. He wanted to respect the privacy of the Wood family but at the same time he knew it was important for Joshua's battalion to be there for him. When they arrived at the residence of the senior Woods they were thwarted once again. The doorbell was attempted and then a cautious series of knocks on the door. No answer. Singh was well past his comfort zone now. He was about to stand down the well-intended mission of condolence when a neighbour suddenly came out next door. Curious no doubt about the group of young soldiers turned out in full-dress green uniforms, the neighbour explained to Singh the family had gone up to their trailer park to spend the holiday weekend.

"I went back to the vehicle and started to get worried," Andy said. "I just couldn't understand. But at the same time, again, I was thinking that the family may have wanted this to be private."

Andy Singh recalled one of his corporals suggesting that they go to the local police station for information. "It was the police, after all, that had put the battalion in the know." The receptionist on duty at the station nodded as they entered, clearly understanding the appearance of uniformed soldiers on the evening of a holiday Saturday.

"Are you here to see Detective Thompson?"

"Yes, I am." Singh was ushered inside. Detective Thompson greeted the soldiers with an air of professional sympathy. The men spoke for a while as Thompson gently laid out in detail what had occurred. Joshua's death had been gruesome. A commuter train had left Union Station in downtown Toronto on Friday night bound for Barrie when it stopped quite suddenly on the approach to the town of Newmarket. Joshua Wood had laid himself across the tracks in direct line of the approaching train. Singh said he was stunned. Hearing it cold and direct from the police, it seemed unbelievable. "It did not seem like our friend."

Singh was devastated. Somehow he could not equate the cold facts that he had from RSM Robb and the desperate loneliness of the act itself. Singh beat himself up over his "failures." *How could he have allowed this to happen?*

"Why didn't I take him fishing!" he recalled thinking. "I'm such a piss-poor leader. This was my fucking fault!" His own PTSD showered him with guilt and ineptitude.

"Do you know where the family is?" Singh asked the detective. "We would like to go pay them a visit."

"Huh? Are you kidding? I was hoping that you guys knew where they were."

The realization hit home like a rocket-propelled grenade. The police had not yet made contact with Joshua's family. The party of soldiers had been trying hard all day to console a family that had no idea of their loss. The police had found Joshua's dog tags on his body and contacted the military. Our unit was under the impression that the next of kin had been notified and we were trying to offer support.

Singh said he immediately asked his corporal to get RSM Robb on the phone. "Josh's family had not been notified. They had no idea that their son was gone! Oh my God!" The information was already getting out to everyone through social media, he realized. The dog tags had been the only piece of identification on the body. "The only thing that I was thinking is that my friend and brother is in the morgue all mangled from the train and his family doesn't have a clue … and about that promise I made his mother."

By this time, the battalion chaplain, Captain Phil Ralph, had joined up with the group of soldiers at the police station. Sergeant Singh was feeling helpless. His soldiers were leaning on him to rectify the matter.

"I had a number of corporals with me that were very close to Josh," he remembers, "and now we can't find the family. I decided to go back to his parents' house and ask the neighbour if they had a contact number. I explained that it was an emergency."

Casualty notification is a nightmare job. Most of us carry the image of the 1950s nuclear family when we consider the job of notifying next of kin. The "mom and pop" model: Coca-Colas in the fridge, maybe a roast of beef and potatoes in the oven for dinner. Perhaps mom is hanging out the last of the day's laundry on the line, waiting for the family to gather for supper. It's a powerful image: the good old folks at home. Unfortunately, this is not the reality of family notification in our time. It was now getting close to 8:00 p.m. Sergeant Singh and his soldiers were all waiting in the parking lot at the police station for Detective Thompson to return from another call. The Woods' contact number burned hot in Singh's hand. When the detective finally returned he explained to the soldiers that he would have to dispatch an officer to deliver the notification message. As they were about to cut ties with Detective Thompson, Andy Singh's phone rang. Looking at the incoming number, he felt some relief. *Thank God! It's Jennifer Wood.*

"Hi Andy! It's Jennifer!"

"Have you returned for another load?"

"Uh … yes. I am in Newmarket." Jennifer responded, slightly perplexed.

"We will be there soon," Singh told her.

"Who is we? and … why?"

"We will explain when we get there."

They arrived at the house a few minutes later. Detective Thompson, Chaplain Ralph, and Andy Singh entered the house. Detective Thompson broke the news to Jennifer Wood. Singh recalls his reaction to the moment: "Watching Jennifer curl up in a ball was worse than being in contact with the enemy." Bruce and Susan Wood would have to be informed, and Singh told Jennifer that he and his soldiers would accompany her to meet with her parents at the campsite.

"We got there in darkness," Andy said. "You could tell that the fire was just doused; they were about to go to bed. We knocked on the door and Josh's father came out. We were all dressed in DEUs (distinctive environmental uniforms)." He remembers Joshua's mother coming out and seeing them in their dress uniforms and knowing the news was bad.

"I never want to deliver a message like that ever again."

Colonel Tom Endicott and RSM Serge Froment came down to Toronto for Joshua's funeral from 2 Area Support Group Headquarters in Petawawa. I was deeply impressed with Tom, my army boss. He had done a ton for our little battalion. We were, after all, an earthy little Reserve unit in his large Regular force organization and he was hopelessly time-impoverished. This is the way of the contemporary senior army officers, who tend to be too busy for anything but the upper edges of PowerPoint briefings. Their trip to Toronto was a testament to their leadership and sincere commitment. Endicott was an excellent officer, from the Royal Canadian Electrical and Mechanical Engineers. Tom was a balanced family man despite an enormous work ethos. No one outworked Tom Endicott — ever; and yet he was insightful enough to appreciate how heavy a blow Wood's death delivered to our Reserve community. His presence at the funeral meant a lot to all of us, and especially to me. Andy Singh was in a black place. He was too angry to be impressed. He had been the one most tightly connected to Joshua; who had made him promise to come in for help. He had even attended the first counselling session with him until Joshua was comfortable.

> But in my mind it was too late for good gestures. What most of us wanted was an explanation on why Josh was not entitled to mental help. I'm the one that personally brought him to the social worker … my entire chain of command knew about what was going on with Josh. They tried their best to get him help. But in the end, "policy" failed Josh, his family, his friends, and the Canadian Forces. All because he was a Reservist. That is what I truly believe. It was a sad day; it was the saddest day of my life! The Canadian Forces that we love so much, and would do anything for, anything! Broke our strong proud hearts into a billion pieces. And then left us with no answers.

I saw Carol, my counsellor from 32 Mental Health Clinic, at the funeral. Of course Carol should be here, yet I had not considered the possibility. I had been through a number of sessions with her by this point but I found myself unseated by Joshua's death. I was struggling. I wanted to keep her at the opposite side of the room. I was waiting for Joshua's parents, Bruce and Susan, to be ushered into the pastor's chambers for a quiet chat before the service. Carol met my eyes and I gave her a smile.

You stay away from me, please.

I was firmly in role. I was in my dress uniform with medals and badges. Our best order of dress for the business world. I could have been a tier 3 actor on a Hollywood set. My wonky head was not going to add to the suffering of this family. Poor Carol. She was a smart person and she knew her job at least as well as I knew mine. She kept her distance from me throughout the entire funeral and I was grateful.

When I hugged Susan Wood, I felt like never letting go. I was seized with my Kandahar notion of one last conversation, one last hug. I felt awful that the Woods were denied this.

I was a washout as an army officer. I could not even think about the right things anymore. My thoughts were with the dead. I still held the ethos of wanting to help but my capacity — my will to go on — was running on fumes.

I had to bolt from Joshua Wood's funeral service to attend a civilian work meeting in Ottawa. Part-time soldiers are constantly sprinting between two worlds for the privilege of serving their country. One of my troops was pulled aside to drive me to the Oshawa VIA station. Reserve units are less formal, earthier than their Regular Force counterparts, a quality that I found initially off-putting when I came over from the Regulars. I was used to the approach now and usually loved to hear about the civilian jobs our men and women held. The troops held no compunction about asking their commanding officer questions as well:

"Why aren't we going to Meaford more often? Borden is not a challenge, eh, sir?"

"This is kind of lame, are you happy with the exercise?"

"Do you think we are winning in Afghanistan?"

In all cases I would offer them honest assessments and answers, enjoying immensely their perspectives and the conversation. I was wishing I could stay with my battalion tribe this afternoon.

The Wood family, now carried along in a sea of dress green, was preparing to make the drive out to the cemetery. I watched Bruce and Susan from a distance as my staff car began to roll. The parking lot was jammed full with a massive turnout. Bruce had told me a few things about his son that sank into my bones, wonderful things. The naked, palpable grief of a father's loss tore at my heart. As his heavy words flowed I suddenly imagined I was talking to the fathers of Corporals Jason Warren and Francisco Gomez — soldiers who had died in my convoy on July 22, 2006. I had prized their boys right up to the last moments when they left my sight in that vertigo of noise and blood. Their lives had been cherished right up to the end. It was different to be here; to be among the family of one of my soldiers and to share what I had seen of their splendid boy. An alien space. And yet my internal conversation was rampant. I could feel my mind moving sideways even while I nodded and talked with Bruce Wood. I thought of my hay baler and the John Deere lullaby but it took every ounce of effort to maintain the face of a properly functioning officer. A real officer. I wanted to cry. I wanted to hug them both one more time.

The car rolled out a sticky sound on the pavement of early summer. There was no conversation between my young driver and me. What could I say? That funeral was one of the most difficult I have endured. Worse somehow than the fifty-odd ramp ceremonies I attended in Kandahar, worse even than Trooper Darryl Caswell's emotional funeral service in Bowmanville in 2007. One look at my driver's swollen face said it all. There was no space for small talk, about the battalion, about the weather, or anything. I sat dumb and dazed, the silence pure agony. I had fewer answers today than ever. At last we pulled into the crowded Oshawa railway station and I plopped myself down in the rail car.

You are a fraud; you are not a real officer. You have no business leading soldiers. Get out of the Reserves.

I proceeded to get drunk on the tiny flat-bottom glasses of wine the railway company pushes in its First Class car. Over and over I could hear Bruce Wood's words in my head. I could see his face and its lines of devastation carved by the weight of burying his son. The wine started to dull the conversations in my head. Somewhere around Kingston I became aware that the seat next to me was filled. I sat cradling my wine cup, the original meal tray and utensils long gone. Through the large passenger window a town that looked a lot like Gananoque, Ontario, was melting from view. I thought for a second on my military college days a million years ago in this vicinity — the Thousand Islands. A green, stupid kid in the early eighties, my largest concerns back then were getting Springsteen tickets for the "Born in the U.S.A." tour, playing rugby, and meeting pretty girls at Queen's University in Kingston. It was a time of life when I was strong — more ignorant but more alive.

"You're pretty quiet there," the man next to me said. I was startled out of a blissful numbness. Bruce Wood was long gone from my alcoholic pondering.

"Yes, I suppose so," I replied with what I hoped was a nonchalant smile.

"You're in the Forces, I see."

"Yes, the army, twenty-six years."

"You over there?" he asked, leaning toward me as he said it, as if we were sharing a secret.

"Yes. Bosnia, and Cambodia too. Kandahar really took the cake, though."

"Pretty tough situation. Pretty tough," he said, moving back away from my red wine cloud.

"I can't get back," I muttered at him in the darkening car. My own words startled me.

"How's that? Sorry?" He leaned in again and I turned to the aisle, avoiding eye contact.

"I can't get back and I can't move on. I am stuck… I am lost."

The man went quiet. Poor bastard. He did not deserve that. He was only trying to be polite and supportive.

"Hey, man, I am sorry, sir, really sorry. It's just … it's been a rough day. We had to bury one of our very best." I hold up the now empty VIA glass as if it might help explain.

"Forget it," he said. "Forget it."

I wrote a letter to the train engineer through their corporate head office. I expressed the army's concern for the mental health of their engineer and I hoped he or she would be all right. I took great pains to tell them a little bit about our young man and what a superb soldier he was. I told them that Joshua would not have wanted the engineer or anyone to suffer; that he was the sort of soldier who endlessly fixed things, who made bad things better — a Canadian soldier. I will always remember Joshua as our "go-to" guy on exercises, the Cadpat-clad driver of the Batmobile, a casualty of the war in Afghanistan.

The soldier I will always want by my side when the going gets tough.

Andy Singh, now a warrant officer in the Regular Army, remains haunted by the promise he made to Susan Wood that April evening in 2011 while leaving the warm confines of the family home:

"I promise you, ma'am, he will be good to go soon."

"How can I make a promise like that, I'm so ashamed of myself," he confided to me in 2015. His PTSD still robs him of the big picture. Such is the irony of the walking wounded and the tunnel-visioning characteristics of PTSD. Warrant Officer Andy Singh is one of my personal heroes, and yet he is so clouded by his sense of duty, his own inherent goodness, that he cannot tell that he is among the very best of us.

CHAPTER 8:

THE SUN ALSO RISES

It's funny. I was looking at some pictures today at work and a few with you in it and I realized that I never had the opportunity to see you before I left Kandahar and never saw you on your return to Edmonton for the brief reunion. My return home was a little rough for a while as it sure took some time to shut that situational aware-ness switch off and get on with my life, but things are now going well.... Anyways, I will be in Kingston sometime in February for a week on a Convoy operations workshop ... it would sure be nice to have a coffee with you.

— letter from one of my Kandahar sergeants,
December 2006

Spending time as a Reserve officer not only placed me in proximity to some of our wounded but it also gave me a unique perspective denied to the Regular Force. The quirky U.S. Civil War–earthiness of the Canadian Army Reserve puts you into situations where you are exposed to the connective tissue of our cities, communities, and large corpor-ations. The Reservist hears things that a Regular Force soldier cannot.

One of the most valuable traits is that the Reservist can look back on a cherished institution with the eye of the outsider.

This is what made Colonel Tom Endicott so special — he could see immediately the advantages to Regular and Reserve integration in the accomplishment of the army mission. His approach was dead simple: Tom Endicott treated his Reserve troops like any other soldier in his formation. He had been commissioned out of the Royal Military College in 1986 and served his whole career with the Regular Force. I left Class B Reserve service in 2010. I wanted to get out of the contract-to-contract angst that dogs the Class B Reservist. Further, it did not take a genius to see that the Class B ship was sinking. The war was over and the Canadian Armed Forces was dramatically reducing the numbers of Class B soldiers in an effort to tighten the purse strings. I took a civilian job with the Ontario government and became a part-time officer as the commanding officer of 32 Service Battalion in Toronto.[1] Tom was my boss for the time I commanded 32 Service Battalion, my first Reserve command. Tom contributed a lot to my initial recovery because of his essential goodness; he was a rare example of a very senior officer who cared. He took the time to have real conversations and he treated me like a valued battalion commander, indistinguishable from his Regular Force charges. The level of trust and support he gave me assuaged my feelings of paranoia and incompetency.

Like most organizations, the military has an annual review process to go over the performance of its soldiers. The reports are called Personnel Evaluation Reports (PERs), and no small amount of institutional effort is spared on their creation. These documents amount to a one-page combination of words and dots more difficult to interpret than chicken entrails. They are used to determine promotions, training, and education opportunities and, of course, future jobs. I was dreading my annual PER debrief from Colonel Endicott despite the good feeling I had working with him. I remained uninterested in all the old processes. They still seemed meaningless and rhetorical to me. The night he had set down for my PER debrief I had driven to Peterborough to pick up my oldest son from a high school event. The rain pelted the window and the first wave of pellets jumped on my nerves. They made little progress on the bug meal and grease of early summer. I was glad of the dark, for without it I would have been hard pressed to make out our path through the downpour. At least in the lighted darkness I could see the road and still concentrate on Endicott's words.

"Good evening, sir. It's John. I have you on speakerphone here. I also have my son in the truck. We are on our way home."

"That's fine." He suggested we get right to it. Great, I thought. "It's been incredible, John. You have had such an immediate, positive impact on the unit." Across from me in the blackened cab my son wrestled noisily with his hamburger wrapper and fries. I was pretty sure he was oblivious to my telephone conversation, nestled securely in the music of his iPod.

"Thanks, sir. Thanks a lot." I was grateful for the warm tone of the commander. Any words I would give back would fall short of conveying my thoughts and how deep their impact was on my wonky head.

"It's a pleasure, John. You are rated as our number one lieutenant colonel in the area and I have pushed hard for you to be the next commander of the brigade. And why not?"

"Wow. That's great," I said.

"I gotta tell you, John, that you had a lot of friends in the room. I know you have suffered, but the generals … they don't exactly hate you. It's going to happen, John. You will be promoted and I am proud of what you have accomplished." He went on to explain that they were going to give me command of 32 Brigade in Toronto, one of the largest Reserve brigades of the ten in the Canadian Army. Colonel Tom Endicott was a full-timer and one of the busiest senior officers in Ontario. And yet, somehow he knew. I had never discussed PTSD with him at any point. He had read my book about Kandahar, which came out in 2009, but beyond the texture and detail of that account of the war in Afghanistan, there was no direct communication on the subject of mental health. I had never shared with him that I was getting therapy in Toronto, and my diagnosis of PTSD was confidential. That I shared with no one. At Joshua Wood's funeral, which he had attended, I had gone to great lengths to avoid contact with my counsellor. He could not have made the connection through Carol. The rhythmic sound of the windshield wipers filled the quiet while I searched for some words.

Thwick, thwick, thwick.

"Uhh. I cannot tell you what a pleasure it has been to serve with you once again, Colonel Endicott." I meant it.

"The pleasure is mine. Now any questions about the written assessment before I let you go?"

"No. Are you kidding? None, sir. Thank you again."

"Okay, then. I will see you up in Pet for the O Group then? Both you and RSM Robb, right?"

"Right."

"Hey, John. Congratulations, man. I really mean it," he said and rang off.

As I grew through the weeks of recovery with Carol's sessions I had come to the realization that there would be no declarative vindication, no childish deus ex machina that would set my world back the way it had been. A return to yesteryear was impossible and even if it was a possibility, there was no call for vindication. Yet in that exact moment I felt a warm stillness in my soul, the leading edges of happiness. The BlackBerry had gone silent and I was suddenly left with the symphony of wiper blades and my french fry–munching teenager.

Thwick, thwick, thwick.

"Hey, Dad," my son piped up, crumpling his hamburger bag and slurping hard on a towering soda. "Way to go."

I was grateful for the dark. Behind the pelted windshield the tears were flowing down my face faster than the rain.

In late 2011 I accepted a civilian job and moved back to Alberta as a director with the Alberta government. I was excited about the opportunity but, more important, I relished the feeling of curiosity and energy — of wanting work again. My time at the clinic in Toronto had helped me enormously. I left my last session with Carol with a number to call for additional Operational Stress Injury (OSI) support in Alberta. At this point, I had more knowledge of my PTSD and more tactics to manage it. I wanted to believe I was better. I wanted to believe the crack was fixed, that I could go on without additional issues — that I was whole again.

I had not looked into bookings at the Alberta-based OSI clinics. What was the point? I had been diagnosed; I knew what I was. I had received treatment and now I have moved on. I felt better in the fall of 2011 than I had since late 2006. It was a foolish approach.

Summer 2013 for many people in southern Alberta will always be the summer of the rains. The ensuing flood spawned the worst disaster in the province's history up to that point.[2] There were decisions to be presented to government decision makers, planning teams to organize, and a thousand different duties that large-scale public emergencies demand. I slept at the office, near the province's Emergency Operations Centre (EOC) for the first five days of the disaster. I recall one of my provincial government colleagues, Colin Blair, helping us through some of the worst times of the flood response. Colin stayed with me on the evening of my son's graduation from high school. We worked on a re-entry plan for the town of High River, which had been forced to evacuate its entire population. Colin had been in the army with me for over twenty years. He had been an officer with a lot of overseas experience. We worked well together and we finished the plan around 4:30 in the morning, and once the plan was set I showed him a corner of my office where he could crash on the floor. I quickly dropped and lay down on the broadloom, forging a pillow with my sports jacket.

"Don't do that, John. Don't sleep on the floor. There is no need."

"Too late," I replied. I was down and nearly asleep beside my desk, craving every minute of rest available. We had to be back up and presentable for 0630. Colin disappeared noiselessly into the basement of the aging operations centre building. He might have been gone for an eternity, or a few minutes. I have no idea. All I know is that he reappeared in my office with two fold-out cots.

"I'm too tired, Colin. Can't be bothered to set that thing up. Thanks, though."

"I've got it," he said softly. Inside of half a minute he had both cots set up and he helped drag me up onto the one intended for me. "No need to sleep on the floor."

"Thanks again," I half mumbled before I descended immediately back to sleep. It was a deep dive, reminiscent of the rock of ages sleeps in the Weatherhaven tent at KAF where silent concrete framed the tents and protected our sleeping bones. For ninety minutes the world was gone and there were no dreams, no expectations.

In my role with the Alberta public service, I was responsible for coordinating response and recovery for the province. In the latter capacity, I had the Disaster Recovery Program (DRP) team in my business unit. People were angry and scared, and the provincial government pushed us hard to assuage the grief and loss as much as we could with the DRP. The DRP team was a small one, some seven full-time provincial staff including the management team. The task that faced my DRP crew in the summer and fall of 2013 in addressing thousands of loss claims was unprecedented. There were thousands of cries for help, people who had lost entire businesses, lost their homes and belongings. Each application was full of legitimate grief. The small size of the team and the daunting task DRP faced was all too similar to the fate of my NSE in Kandahar in 2006. My Kandahar dreams had returned in earnest by mid-July.

NIGHT MEETING IN EXSHAW, ALBERTA

The little town of Exshaw is nestled between the foothills and the mountains just a few kilometres south of Canmore. Exshaw and County of Bighorn had been hit early and hard by the torrential rains of late June 2013. There were unprecedented damages and losses all across the municipality. I was locked into a routine of two to three of these town halls per week across southern Alberta. My life became an endless conversation with stricken homeowners on subjects ranging from destroyed homes to ruined basements to replacement of essential appliances. Most of these conversations were emotional and difficult. Many of them demanded my full capacity to deliver the heart-breaking news that one hates to deliver to another human being. Public programs only go so far to mitigate loss, and many people were angry about the amount of financial support they were getting. Until one was done fighting with the DRP, one did not have to accept the finality of true losses. This meant that none of my work files in this crisis was either straightforward or easy. It also meant that I had to approach each one with a full heart and complete attention. I put everything I had into the job.

The evening in Exshaw was particularly long. Tons of people attended the town hall meeting. There were numerous problems to be resolved for individual land owners from silt contamination along the Bow River through to complex erosion issues at Lac des Arcs where vintage homes were placed in peril and irrecoverable as living spaces. Over the course of the evening, dealing with each person in turn I experienced a carnival of emotion. At times I was berated and insulted. At other points I tried to offer comfort as clients sobbed over the hard realities of flood damage and the painful decisions they now faced. Finally, the last family packed up and trundled out of the school. The Exshaw town hall was over. After a quick meeting with my staff I headed out as well. It was late. I had more DRP meetings in the morning that demanded preparation. I drove the long windy road to Canmore that night. The rain and darkness engulfed the truck. I had the sensation that emotionally I had arrived at the very bottom and my doppelgänger was riding along beside me.

Hey, it's been a while! Good to see you again. You must be tired. Let me drive.

I was feeling a deep depression that I could not shed; a heavy worthlessness. It was approaching midnight and there were a dozen flood issues that I really should be working on. I could feel that my capacity was unstitching. The anxiety of imminent failure haunted the road to Canmore and the temptation to crank the truck tires hard to the left and escape a thousand problems in one fell swoop was powerful. I felt the sharp edge of the mountain road calling me, reassuring me that it would be better. I stopped for a six-pack of beer in a late-night liquor store in Canmore and checked into a hotel. I ignored the several notes on my BlackBerry and email returns that I owed and began to dampen the words inside my head with the beers. I would have to leave for Calgary and a series of tricky meetings with individual homeowners in the premier's riding in a few hours. But for now, I was safe and, other than the doppelgänger, alone.

It was still pouring rain as I approached Calgary the next morning. I had packed down the effects of the Exshaw meeting into a tight bundle in my mind. I approached the address I had and noted the war zone feel to the neighbourhood. A major battle had been played out only days before. The destructive power of flood water is unfathmomable. I found a place to park between two huge dumpsters and a line of hastily deployed porta-potties and I made out at a fast walk for the address. My brand new suit, bought on sale that fall, was soaked within seconds of leaving my truck.

My first meeting this morning was with a homeowner named Rosa. Rosa was in her mid-sixties. She motioned to me from her half-open door. Her house along the gorgeous Elbow River looked small and unassuming from the street. Once inside, however, it opened up to a beautiful and large series of spaces. Terra cotta floor tiles and wonderful oak accents gave the open-concept living room the semblance of a medieval great hall. There was warmth in here once. Today, with the never-ending rain still pounding and the electricity cut, the place had the damp feel of a tomb. Standing in wet clothing, I found the cold and damp magnified. I drew a tissue from my pocket to dry my glasses but it had dissolved into a ball of white muck.

Her husband had died a month or so before the flood disaster of June 2013. She was grief personified, and I could see the lines of stress that marked her beautiful face. She was dressed very smartly for the meeting and she bore the expensive clothing with grace. Rosa was currently staying in the city with her daughter and son-in-law. Her home was dead now — as cold and dark as a mausoleum. Rosa had only returned to the house this morning to meet with me: the government representative. She was in pain and I felt the energy marshalling inside me to help her any way I could.

"I am not going to leave today until you are happy or at least happier," I assured her. I liked this dignified person immediately. Rosa and her late husband were avid world travellers. They had amassed quite an art collection. She invited me to look at how their paintings were being stored. The more valuable ones had already been removed and the rest were stacked in the master bedroom upstairs. It was freezing cold in that bedroom, like one of those ridiculously open Balkan houses so common in Yugoslavia. Grief was heavy in that clammy space. The feeling of a military operation was upon me and I fought to suppress the memory slide show and to stay in the moment. I knew I had been admitted to a deeply private part of her world. I treaded very lightly out of respect and a deep desire to make things better for Rosa and her family.

Out in her backyard was a gorgeous sitting area that led to the lip of the Elbow River. The home could have been in the heart of Budapest or Paris. It was Calgary as I had never seen it. It would have been an engaging sitting area to have one's morning coffee under normal circumstances. However, at present the Elbow River was a bloated anaconda that would no longer lie tame at the lip of Rosa's stone patio. Rather, the river had become a menacing stranger threatening to engulf the entire space. We retreated indoors and sat in her freezing kitchen for our final deliberations. Rosa told me her story, how she had lost her husband and how she was ready to leave Calgary. She was going to move to Vancouver with the money from the DRP. The rain continued its mockery on the roof of the dead mansion.

"So much confusion about the home sale program, I have heard this and then I read something completely different that contradicts what I heard."

"Let me alleviate at least the burden of uncertainty around the sale of your house. I represent the province of Alberta. I am telling you here and now that our word is our bond. We are buying your magnificent house if you still wish to sell." I could see her visibly lighten. Her colour seemed to brighten.

"Thank you, John. Thank you."

"Believe me, Rosa, the province is doing all it can and it is truly my pleasure to be the messenger for your family. I am delighted to have met you, Rosa, and I am so sorry it had to be under these circumstances." I shook Rosa's hand.

"Oh, thank you so much," she whispered. She pressed my hand again and I could tell that I had done something good for a change. So many times in 2013, I had been the bearer of bad news. Rosa gave me a quick set of directions to my next house and with one last gracious wave she closed the door. I had some twenty minutes to spare before my next appointment further along the Elbow River. I walked back to the truck oblivious to the endless rain. I fumbled with the key fob, plunked down behind the wheel and came apart. I sobbed and gasped for about ten minutes, heavy tears. The intensity of the emotion caught me by surprise. My mind filled with the faces of Raymond Arndt, Joshua Wood, and Darryl Caswell — fallen warriors and their loved ones who needed advocacy. I grabbed some tissues and dried my eyes and then my glasses. I adjusted my tie in the rear-view and stepped out again for my next appointment with calamity.

Rosa was one of hundreds of people I met on that battlefield that comprised the 2013 flooding in southern Alberta. A dignified figure from a world of privilege — a lifestyle that I had only glimpsed in my travels. She is a reminder to me that all of us suffer loss — the very wealthy, the average, and the poor. Disaster is the great equalizer.

CANADIAN HEADQUARTERS, KANDAHAR AIRFIELD, JUNE 2006

"Hey, sir. What's going on?" A large sergeant with helmet and full battle rattle lumbers into my sea container office on KAF.

"Jonesy. Hello there, come on in!" I almost shout, surprised to see the dust-encrusted fighting order of Sergeant Pat Jones darken my office door on KAF. In all my memories of Jones going back to the Balkans and the peacekeeping era before that, none of them are indoors. He is perpetually of the field. It's almost off-putting to see him in an office, even a shitty little tin one like mine. His body armour and Velcro webbing makes robotic creaks as he enters.

"You off for a drive today?" I ask, jerking my head toward the convoy form-up area just up from the HQ at the battle group TOC.

"Yeah, sir. A short one. Nathan Smith and back. Nice little circuit around No Drug." No Drug Mountain was the distinctive feature that separated the King of the FOBs from Kandahar City. Its name was suggestive of the interdiction activities that went on here in the earlier iteration of Operation Enduring Freedom. In our time the soldiers had begun to call

the feature the Three Sisters, a more fitting Canadian label for No Drug Mountain. Our ticket naming was slightly softer but replete with irony.

"That's good. You need some shorter runs."

"You're pushin' paper, I see," Sergeant Jones commented, quickly turning the conversation in a different direction.

"Yep. Desk jockey CO, a regular Martin Sheen, I suppose."

"What's this?" He suddenly blurts, picking up the clear purple hunk of amethyst off my desk. His query is full of wonder, surprisingly animated for Pat Jones.

"Amethyst."

"How's that?"

"Amethyst. Medieval warriors believed that it protected them from sudden death on the battlefield. I figured the battalion could use the biggest piece I could find." He held it for a full set of seconds. Contemplating its weight, its warmth on his hand. He eventually sets it down gingerly.

"Fuck," was all he could muster, but a half smile on his face betrayed a glimmer of belief in the notion. Why not?

"Take care today. See you when you're back."

"Yes, sir. You too. No paper cuts."

He was already creaking and clicking his way through the doorway.

I gave the brief at my old Edmonton-based battalion in 2008. I never came back to this place after Kandahar. I never returned to its stink of diesel and grease from weekly stables — the care and feeding of machinery and weapons. The drum of activity in the mornings as soldiers returned from physical training and off to their various assignments of the day. Bent on purpose. Somewhere to be. Part of this business trip had been set aside as a quasi-official reunion of the 2006 gang. I had been asked to say a few words.

War heroes do not necessarily fall into the Hollywood stereotype. The chiselled chests and square jaw good looks of the rich and famous. Lieutenant Douglas Thorlakson who saved his entire column and all of our recovery equipment with his quick action to shoot a vehicle-borne suicide bomber would pass unnoticed through a sparse crowd with his unassuming quicksilver grin. Thorlakson was pulling metal shards out of his forearm and elbow long after the tour was over. Doug Thorlakson was not in attendance. If he were to enter the room you would never look twice. Maybe a hunter? Truck driver? Nor did Sergeant Pat Jones attend this little reunion. Pat Jones, one of the greatest soldiers I have ever served with, was a workhorse for our battered battalion in Kandahar. He took off his uniform for good when he touched down back in Canada. He gave you the impression of a man who had been cooked at high temperatures from the inside out. The high duty of his weather-beaten skin was to contain the black demons and nightmares that writhed within. Sergeant Jones's last words to me in Kandahar haunt me still. Pat Earles and I had caught up with him moments before he boarded the Hercules to take him south.

"I am just … just tired of seeing dead people, sir." The words have stayed with me but what burns more than this is the memory of his face as he said them — the vacant hundred-mile stare.

Master Corporal Randy Potts, a giant of a man who did our radio repairs in Kandahar was there. Potts was such a study in contrasts. He was a virtual man-mountain, physically dominating, yet he fixed the tiniest and most sophisticated of our electronic equipment. He pulled me aside after my short speech. His eyes met mine and seemed to pierce me, like he knew something about me that I did not. I found myself looking away.

"Leave it alone, sir."

"What? Excuse me?"

"Leave all that shit alone. Walk around it. It's only good things now," Potts amplified.

"Ugh … yes, yes. I agree," I said awkwardly remembering him hunched over the tactical communication sets, radio gear, complicated monitors, and test equipment. His radio repair shop amounted to a pint-sized Frankenstein laboratory in the dust — high-tech sci-fi stuff wrapped under canvas like a vendor at the corner of the airfield workshop.

"Just good things now," my master corporal reiterated.

Who said anything about bad things? I thought to myself. I was still struggling with anger and depression, locked inside the throes of PTSD denial but my mask was firmly in place, or so I thought.

What can you see? What are you looking at?

"Just good things, Master Corporal. You bet." The reunion was brief. It was over inside of ninety minutes but I walked away unsettled by Master Corporal Potts and his quixotic comments. I found the accuracy of his aim upsetting but could not put my finger on why.

As the 2013 Alberta Flood crisis moved into the early fall, I became a train wreck in a tie. The stressors of the flood disaster soon wore through my mental health and I found myself awash in my old PTSD symptoms. My civilian team responsible for the DRP recovery claims had crumbled under the volume of work and the merciless hours demanded by the crisis. The management team was gone, fallen to extended medical leave, and I was doing hands-on work all across southern Alberta as a senior bureaucrat. I strove to rehire DRP staff while personally inspecting the basements of disgruntled homeowners with an engineer and a flashlight. There were a thousand important issues in play that needed close attention: interviewing new staff that might be able to step in; reorganizing basic DRP services in rented infrastructure.

My worst Kandahar nightmares started to come back to me at night with new Alberta Flood twists.

At work I frequently found my mouth in gear with intense emotion. I felt my mind going sideways when old, familiar stuck-points were hit. I would pipe up with more volume or more anger than was warranted or than I intended, shocking my new colleagues in the process. I tried to coach myself around the wound. I wrote reminders to myself on my government notebook and my desk blotter. Things like:

Remember it's not personal.
It's not as bad as 2006.
You do not always have to say something.
You don't have to talk.
Some people do like you.

These simple inscriptions helped a little bit at the start but they could not keep me afloat. I was struggling to stay effective and keep my doppelgänger at bay, my emotions even. The energy needed to look calm and exude some level of confidence had pushed me to the limits of my capacity. Even though my PTSD had been long diagnosed I had not been into a clinic in almost two years. It had taken so much effort to bond with my counsellor Carol in Toronto. The thought of starting over again in Alberta with a strange counsellor was a serious impediment. I did not have enough time to keep up with my job let alone take more time to find an OSI clinic here. Besides, I wanted the entire mental health issue to be in my past; to be whole again without flaws. A fool's notion.

Out of the blue one day in October, a package arrived at my civilian office in the emergency operations facility in Edmonton. It was from Master Corporal Randy Potts, the soothsayer genius of my Kandahar workshop in 2006. I ripped the package a bit awkwardly and something dark and hard hit my desk with a clunk. Polished black granite. I saw the familiar black and grey colour of the stone and knew immediately what it was. Tears instantly welled up in my eyes. Potts had recently been back to Kandahar, now as a sergeant, to close out the Canadian Afghanistan mission for good. The monument to our fallen on KAF was being dismantled and repatriated to Canada. He had kept a piece of the monument's base that was unsalvageable, a square piece of black granite. The portion in this package he had carefully severed for me.

The short note inside said it all.

"Just good things now, sir."

My mind suddenly closed to the contemporary crisis and my thoughts returned to that earlier one; that period of quiet desperation across Kandahar and Helmand Provinces with my combat logistics battalion. I could feel the presence of hundreds of soldiers around me in that stressful space. I stood motionless in my civilian office and held the black granite in my palm for a long time.

I was committed in that moment to get some additional help. I was not going to slide back to where I had been in 2007. Not too long after the flood disaster in southern Alberta I made contact with the Operational Stress Injury Clinic in Edmonton and returned to regular care.

The HLVW tractor is suspended in the air, its mammoth over-engine cab jacked forward while the soldier drivers grease its joints, change its oil. It is suffocating hot and the heavy metal sinews of the army truck can vaporize beads of sweat instantly.

The young corporal is well muscled with the looks of a professional athlete. He is bent over, inspecting the plating on the truck cab. With his Gerber knife he is patiently prying Taliban bullets out of the armoured skin of the beast. His face when he shows me the bullets is off-putting. The splayed grin is too wide to convey happiness or bravery convincingly. Rather, his face is filled with question marks, like he wants a deeper explanation of what all of this means. When is one of these slugs going to find me? Will it be a red badge of courage or the full enchilada? He shakes his head at my silence and turns back to the task as if to say, "Fucked if I am going to waste any more time on you." There are no answers to questions like these, just as there is no winning in a war like this.

Inside of this shared version of hell there is only the steady unearthing of new questions.

MEETING WITH CORPORAL JEFF CARPENTER, OTTAWA, SEPTEMBER 2015

"Hey, sir! Colonel Conrad!"

A large voice booms over the cacophony of race contestants preparing for the Army Run — the celebrated annual half marathon comprising soldiers and civilians. Ottawa's Elgin Street is filled with runners, and the autumn air is electric with anticipation and nerves of fifteen thousand runners. At first I do not recognize him. His bushy beard dominates and distracts, but in the next instant the eyes give him away. Corporal Jeff Carpenter is a bit thicker, somehow less solid, less put together than when I last saw him. He is also a lot older around the eyes. Carpenter, hailing from a proud military family, is one of my soldiers from 2006, a convoy driver who had suffered on the long lines of supply in that Taliban summer.

Standing in the middle of Elgin Street in September 2015, Carpenter related to me the struggles he had experienced. He had been hard at the bar scene, drinking nearly all the time. He told me he had bedded dozens of women. He had been a good-looking young soldier in 2006, brandishing the bullets pulled from the truck armour with his Gerber knife. A muscular V-shaped body and thick, cropped blond hair. The hair today is long and flowing, tucked under a "Soldier On" ball cap. His body is now wracked with an internal ailment. He was not the powerful young man of the 2006 tour. He had been diagnosed with PTSD in 2007 but somehow the diagnosis did not reach him. He was currently embroiled in a fight with Veterans Affairs Canada over a different claim.

"I got sent over on Lamarre's close-down tour. Smitty got hurt, they needed an immediate replacement."

"I see."

"I hit the gym every day, I quit the beer, I applied myself like hell 'cause I just wanted it back so bad. I had no idea I had the PTSD. After a few weeks back in theatre it became clear. I really lost it when I came home, had enough of the army crap. The first week back from Afghanistan, they were on my ass about going on the rifle range. I wanted time to settle, I was tired. Christ, going on the range. Don't you know where I have just come from? Send someone else. I am not in need of shooting practice. 'What the fuck is the matter with you, Sergeant Major!' Geez. No more fucking army for me." He is searching my eyes for reaction, for condemnation. There is no condemnation here. I see elements of my own wounds in his emotional narrative.

"You were a hell of a soldier. And you are still," I tell him.

As I started to rejoin my friends and find my start point among the sea of nerves and running shorts, he blurted out, "I love you, sir."

"I love you too, Jeff. Take care of yourself. Have a good run."

"Why do we make it so difficult for veterans to access entitlements?" asks a VAC employee in Fred Doucette's *Better Off Dead.*

Jeff Carpenter's ongoing battle with Veterans Affairs is not unusual. I think it's important for Canadians to understand the contemporary approach to veterans' issues being half-heartedly attempted by our government in the immediate aftermath of the Afghanistan War. While the military has made at least some improvement in dealing with mental wounds, Veterans Affairs Canada seems to subscribe to the adage "If it ain't broke, don't fix it." The organization has an off-putting culture that casts the veteran as a grabber. Further, VAC is run like a truculent insurance company with many dated forms and form letters surrounded by confusing instructions. A veteran needs an interpreter to help decipher how to approach the department for services. The Royal Canadian Legion has carved out a niche role in offering help to veterans navigate VAC's complex administration. This is madness. Why don't we fix the source problem? It remains to be seen if the new Liberal government's approach will be any different.

TYPICAL VETERANS AFFAIRS CANADA CONVERSATIONS

"Mister Conrad, a decision has been taken on your file," the voice of a VAC official said.

"Oh my God! Finally! That is great. What does it say?"

"I cannot tell you," she responds. "You should receive our letter in one to two weeks."

"You're kidding, right?"

The application was already late — over two weeks beyond the stated norm of sixteen weeks.

"After all this time and an additional delay you want me to wait for a letter when you have it in front of you? Why don't you scan it for me?"

"That's not allowed under our policy. Sorry."

I am fighting to keep my emotions in check. Anger and frustration will not help this absurd situation. After all this delay the thought of waiting another two weeks when the decision is in her hands was torturous.

"Well, can you at least tell me if I will be able to get the orthotics or not?"

My clinician had recommended that I get inserts for my shoes to mitigate a chronic back problem.

"Can you tell me at least if I am covered for those? I can get started perhaps with my chiropractor."

"What makes you think you need orthotics, Mr. Conrad?"

"What makes me …?" A flash of anger but I know now how to hold onto it. "Well … the fact that I have not been able to stand up straight for two years, for starters. Also the fact that the pain in my back is constant." I pause. "Have you ever had to live with a pain that never yields, never goes away?"

She does not respond.

"Also, the fact that my practitioner tells me the orthotics would help reduce my pain. That is what makes me think I need them."

"Keep an eye out for the letter, Mr. Conrad."

It arrived only a week and a bit later, a form letter with an unrecognizable signature block. Another employee had signed over the signature block of the official. The entitlement for additional care on a service-related back injury was denied.

Another curiosity of Veterans Affairs is as fundamental as calling the organization. It is not a simple case of picking up the phone and calling the office of one of the staff. To reach someone in the organization a veteran has to go through a one-eight-hundred switchboard. Direct calls are not permitted.

"Can I give you a call tomorrow on this?" I asked the young woman on the other end of the line. Like most of the junior staff at VAC, she has been positive and helpful.

"Sure. That would be great, Mr. Conrad."

"What's your number?"

"Just call the one-eight-hundred switchboard; they will patch you through. If I am not in, they will leave me a message and I will call you back."

"Well, I am in meetings most of tomorrow with only a couple of windows to talk. Wouldn't it be easier for both of us if I just had your office number? I could call you at 10:15 sharp."

"Well … umm, no. We cannot give those out."

"I won't paste it up at the subway. You can trust me, I am a Canadian soldier."

"Just call the switchboard, sir."

This whole business of Veterans Affairs Canada is sticky. Soldiers are tough, with the default to carry on as best they can under all circumstances. Furthermore, our soldiers hate to ask for things, even when they are hurting for them. These men and women have a propensity to avoid complaint and suck it up. This ethos is played to advantage by the senior officials who run the department. The senior bureaucrats of VAC seem impervious to change while the focus of their political masters is elsewhere. As I write this, the Liberal government is sending troops to Latvia. Canada and its armed forces are on the move. Yet very little seems to be occurring inside of VAC, despite the public mandate letter the minister has received.

WAINWRIGHT, ALBERTA, OCTOBER 2014

I had read about it: the modern training facility the army had constructed in the Wainwright Training Area to mimic the King of the FOBs. The imagination and industry in this fake Kandahar are uncanny. Here, in the middle of a wind-blown Alberta landscape, are the remembrances of an empire of plywood and two-by-four lumber. The angles and details of the battle group TOC in front of me are ding on. Further on is a maintenance compound; concrete pads for sleeping quarters and even ablution areas are laid out in near-perfect replication. The dining hall, or DFAC as they were called in KAF, looked like it could serve up the infamous U.S. Army grits with the best of them. My driver rests in the G-Wagon and fumbles with iTunes on his gadget. It's not the typical fifty-plus degrees Celsius of Afghanistan but rather an eight-degree bluster that hints at freezing.

I know you.

There is no reassuring elixir of raw sewage to blanket one's dreams, no colourful mood ring sewage lagoon altering the intensity of its green and brown nuances with the heat of the day. But the likeness of this Alberta FOB to KAF is very, very good. Too good. I wander deep into the empty war village and enter the TOC, lost in thought. The cold helps to keep me grounded, and a good thing too. Inside the large plywood TOC there are many ghosts.

I can hear Colonel Kevin Owens barking. Owens was the American commander of the 173rd Airborne Brigade, the formation that our Canadian-led brigade was replacing. He was lean, muscular, and just this side of forty years old. Owens was wizened with combat command experience, having been heavily embroiled in the fight in 2005.

"Hey, who the fuck took my chocolate cake!"

I had taken it. I had thought Owens, a fitness-worshipping sky soldier, had hacked off only half of the piece for himself at the end of the briefing.

"I took it, sir," I almost say again out loud. I explain all over again to Owens that I thought he had only intended on half of the remaining piece of cake, finding the whole piece too much of a calorie hit. My face was red with the apology. Right there in that fake TOC I relived the mortification I felt when I realized that I had taken the morsel from a seasoned combat leader. But Kevin Owens had only exploded in laughter and comradeship.

"Oh, hell, that's good. I really didn't need it. Jesus, you saved me, John."

I could hear Owens's voice over the Wainwright wind and its cease-less buffeting of the sprung shelter canvas of this faux Kandahar. I fought down a sense of vertigo. The hair on the back of my neck was standing up; I was on high emotional alert. One of the work stations held a dust-covered notepad. A remainder from the thorough scrubdown of the facility by the previous training group. Folded and jammed into the corner of the desk was a fake Afghan banknote. It had been made on a colour photocopier and was fully blank on one side. The banknote was the final remaining clue pointing to the last task force validated here.

I know you. I remember.

I am okay among these ghosts now. I was back in routine care with the Edmonton OSI clinic and had built a new confidence with an Alberta-based counsellor. I have come to terms with the fact that occasional counselling sessions are necessary for PTSD. And that is okay. It is merely part of taking care of your health. I was unwise to treat PTSD as something in my past, something that could be left with 32 Health Service Unit in Ontario. With the support I have received, I have even more tools in the approach to an old wound. Embracing the wound was crucial for me. It is part of who I am now, part of who I will always be.

This is where we could begin institutionally — with a fundamental shift in our acceptance of wounds to the mind. At the speed our information-obsessed society moves, the hard lessons about mental health injuries have not been internalized. The Canadian Armed Forces' approach to PTSD is not much advanced beyond the depth of a PowerPoint slide. There are many things that the Canadian Armed Forces and Veterans Affairs Canada could do better tomorrow to alleviate the wounds to our soldiers, and to Reservists in particular. Where mental health and PTSD are concerned, there have been only baby steps forward and then numerous stumbles backward as we lived through the Afghanistan conflict. The fact is, in most cases the walking wounded can be healed. As chronicled by Doucette in *Better Off Dead*, a former Canadian Armed Forces psychiatrist goes even further:

> It's sort of interesting because I have done a lot of work over the years with people with PTSD. If you asked me who I would take on tour with me, who would I trust to do the job, it would be most of the patients I have dealt with. I know they can do the job. PTSD doesn't keep you necessarily from doing your job as a soldier. Some of these guys are the best soldiers you will ever see. What PTSD does, though, is it exacts such a cost when you come home to your family, to your friends and [try] to be a Canadian again. That's the problem. I have been a soldier for almost twenty-two years and almost all of my service has been with the army. I have been around a lot of soldiers. There are a lot of people I have respect for. But the people I truly trust are some of the people I have treated, some of the people within the PTSD group, because I know they would do the job. I know they would take care of me. But it would be such

a cost when we came back home that I would never ask that from them.

Despite current circumstances there is a way forward through the institutional stuck-points on mental health wounds, if we want to take them. We have to stop declaring the PTSD problem solved and pointing to our well-worn pamphlet "The Road To Mental Readiness" as the complete solution. This pamphlet is not enough. At best it is a good start. We have not gone the full distance where mental health wounds are concerned. A pamphlet is no cure for bias and deeply ingrained prejudice. We need to pick up the pace and get serious about our soldiers and our veterans' well-being. Until we address the fundamental culture and stigma around mental health wounds in the Canadian military, we are only dabbling in it.

Treatments for the walking wounded and their families who suffer from PTSD are effective. Many of these men and women can recover. This treatment is expensive, but are our soldiers, the best heart's blood of our nation, not worth it?

EPILOGUE

It is a clear February day, the road is screaming past us and we are making good time. Despite the wound that is draining my strength, I have to admit that this convoy is going well. Today we are not driving down the centre of the road. I dimly think to myself that this is risky. We glide along in our lane, easier pickings for a roadside IED.

Move over to the centre! Drive fast, Be aggressive! Speed saves lives.

Stupid Kandahar thoughts surround me even in the middle of my heart attack. The pain in my jaw and in my chest is a growing heat that I suspect will consume me before we can get to the hospital. I am not talking to my wife, but I see her hands pounding on the steering wheel of the truck. She keeps looking over at me and asks me how I am doing. I cannot raise the energy to comfort her, to sweep it all behind the mask of composure. And I want to so badly. I want to tell her I am fine, don't worry. I am fine. Instead I continue to lose my grip on the pain; something unseen is pulling me down into the centre of myself and I want to save my strength to hold on. It suddenly occurs to me that there will be no further words. Everything I was ever going to say has been said. Then the back right tire of our truck gives out. I can process the ragged image of the tire in the passenger-side mirror and think to myself, *I need to check that out.*

I cannot move.

I cannot even hear my wife call in the nine liner medevac. She is onto 911 immediately.

EPILOGUE

Now my toes are dragging on the Yellowhead Highway east of Edmonton and thirty minutes from an emergency cardiac unit. Two angels of the Lord in Alberta Health Services uniforms are lifting/dragging me toward their ambulance. I can dimly make out the sound of UH-60 Blackhawk rotors and the smell of torn flesh and gunpowder from a distant smashed convoy. Time past is present in time future. Is this what death is like?

Fuck, I am dying. It is happening too quickly.

I am afraid.

I had that similar sensation to the one I had in 2006 during the double IED attack. I could see beyond reality into a bright, shining truth. My whole existence was distilled down to this very moment. The most distressing part of the realization was that I had wasted my time and left so many words unsaid, to my wife, my family, everyone. I regretted in that instance not talking more about Kandahar and what had happened to us since. I never really did describe what my problem was. How ashamed I had felt those past ten years. Martha had never wanted me to leave the Regular Force. She felt it was a bad move but had trusted my emotional decision — thinking I knew what was best. I never really apologized for what I had exposed our family to, what I had put them through. In those lost years after Kandahar there were enemy in the wire all the time. They were all around us. If only you could have seen the things that I have seen, dreamed my dreams.

I wanted to tell you.

Now I will not have that chance. It ends here.

I was cold with acceptance and sadness as the paramedics pull me from the truck and drag-walk me to the ambulance. Like the counter-insurgency in Afghanistan, you only get so much time.

Tick, tick, tick, tick, tick …

After all the struggles to beat back depression and PTSD a blood clot in my heart is going to bring things to an abrupt halt.

My doppelgänger is disgusted with me. *"You can't even die well."*

There is an air of close-quarter fighting for the heart attack victim. The same well-loved faces I saw the night of the double suicide attack west of Kandahar City all appeared to me. My children. My parents. The same thought that I might not survive this thing to tell anyone about it. The same sense that I have had a good run, a rich life. If this is it, so be it. However, if I am spared, I would like to try and talk about how that place changed me and changed many soldiers of my generation.

As it turned out, our freaky exploded snow tire saved my life.

I spent four years after Kandahar behaving erratically, even immaturely. I abused alcohol recklessly, taking comfort in the numbness that drink brings — a quelling of reflection, a quieting of the mind. I smashed my Regular Force career; I destroyed numerous friendships and my network of colleagues. In a hundred ways I am embarrassed and ashamed of that period. I can count the number of senior officers in the army on one hand that knew about my struggles or ever asked about what the heck was up.

Two, exactly.

It struck me as odd that in an organization that prides itself on caring for its people one could collapse so enormously — behave so differently — and never draw more than a couple of casual observations. In fairness to the army, I never told anybody I was struggling and that I had been seeking psychiatric help. In fact, I did my best to hide the fact that I was wounded. Although there was a lot of literature, training, and awareness on PTSD issues and on mental health in general, as late as 2003 the army was still quite infantile as practitioners. It is one thing to study a subject and quite another to work with it proficiently. Additionally, there was a stigma in the Canadian Armed Forces about mental health disorders, a sense that soldiers with them were weak, or faking it to get away from the heavy lifting. The institution has made some progress on this stigma, most notably with its Road to Mental Readiness program; however, the prejudice and stigma still exist today in 2017. The senior leaders of the military are quick to declare success on the eradication of prejudice and stigma, but as an institution we take our eye off the ball too soon. We have not accomplished true cultural change with mental health injuries. Not yet. Attitudes and conviction are among the hardest elements to change in any organization.

I bought into the stigma. I blame myself more than anyone; I wanted to hide the wound. I had been the commanding officer of a logistics battalion, one of the neglected corps of the Canadian Armed Forces. I did not want to invite more judgment. When I look back now on notes and letters from friends and senior officers it is like poring over the papers of a dead relative. Each has a familiar look but the content is fresh. In 2006, the words attacked, criticized, even wounded. With the benefit of years I can see how far from wrong I was. It is like reading the notes for the first time.

> This is just a quick note to offer you my personal support. No one can claim to fully understand your challenges on this mission. While others have perhaps occupied the same chair, only you can understand your professional concerns and the impact that the loss of soldiers had on your unit. During these challenging times, the men and women of the National Support Element depend on your strength and fortitude, and for good reason. Your experience and demonstrated leadership have resulted in the respect that you enjoy within your team and the trust of those you serve.... I want to offer you all of my support and to personally wish you, as the commanding officer of the NSE, all of the best soldier's luck for the remainder of your appointment — commanding troops in an active theatre. If you need anything, please call.

How could anyone read conspiracy in this letter? How could I have been enraged over this note from a senior logistics colonel? Why did I not call for the help he offered? The author of this letter ended up as another burned bridge, someone I no longer trusted and pushed away. I have a fistful of other letters and email notes. Rereading them today is like awaking from a dream and seeing the correspondence for the first time. The effect is startling. Where the hell have I been? Who was I when I read this for the last time?

> "I don't care what anybody says, I just don't like it."
> "I hear you. I feel the same way."

"He told me he has PTSD. I just don't know how he is going to react. It gives me the creeps. I don't want to be alone with him."

I wondered in silence as I absorbed this street-side conversation, Just how many others feel this way about us? How many others?

For the longest time I debated writing a book that involved my mental health challenges. I was aware of the stigma in our society on wounds of the mind — tier 2 injuries, though no one in the institution would ever refer to them as such. I was afraid of what people around me might think and, to a lesser extent, the potential drying up of Reserve contracts that might result if my superiors knew. Besides all of these concerns, what good could come of such a personal bloodletting? After all, the damage to relationships and lost time are deep in the past now. Self-loathing and self-confidence, as I came to appreciate, are key hallmarks to my PTSD and I remain, even as I write this, somewhat afraid of judgment. I used to think it would be far easier to just fade away with these demons and live them down as much as possible than to risk humiliation. I lost a lot of friends when I came out of Kandahar and drifted away from the Regular Army. Some were not really friends, as it turns out, merely colleagues or associates as so many of us have in our lives. People like this drop away as soon as you stumble. However, some of the men and women I lost contact with were people I deeply cared about. In a few cases, ever so slowly over the past four years I have made progress in reconnecting. I remain stunned at how quickly I fell from the ranks and was left behind. Stumbling backwards into a career with the Army Reserves while the rest of the institution moved ahead. I was bitter at first, one more emotion balled up with the others in that post-tour stress. Over time, as I grew in recovery, I began to appreciate that I might be able to help. My heart attack on February 5, 2014, convinced me that I needed to get going.

I feel better for writing my experiences down. Post-traumatic stress disorder has meant being adrift in a tidal wash of worthlessness, unable to stem the flow of self-loathing, paranoia, and dread. I was lucky. I stumbled into a conversation with Sergeant Singh that assisted me with some forward momentum toward recovery. There are many hundreds of Canadian soldiers who have had experiences of war through the peacekeeping era and Afghanistan far worse than my own. I hope that in adding another voice to the PTSD conversation and trying to articulate its internal manifestations, this book will help another person. After all, it was through something as simple as a conversation that I began to find help. Writing about my meandering path and hopefully making it easier for some of my fellow soldiers makes me feel a little more worthwhile.

As for Trooper Caswell, a street in Bowmanville was named in his honour. The community has rallied around his family and they are currently fundraising to have one of the worn-out LAV III fighting vehicles put on display in the town with Darryl's name attached to the monument. I still wince a bit when I think about Darryl and the damage I incurred over his Sacrifice Medal charade. Should a mere lieutenant colonel have emailed the personal staff of Canada's top soldier? Was my judgment so badly impaired? It occurred to me years after that the better move, if I had wanted to send a signal to the top, would have been to email the army commander's executive aide, preferably through Dave Fraser's office. I can appreciate in hindsight how my well-intended email was unfair to General Leslie. It easily could be viewed as "airing dirty army laundry" to the Chief of Defence Staff. That was certainly not the intent. When you wade into the political waters of the senior generals there is always risk. I am glad, however, that I found the courage to take a shot at helping the Caswells, poorly aimed though it was. An officer who sits on his hands when the chips are down is not worth a fistful of phony Afghan notes. As a country, we asked Trooper Caswell to do some pretty extraordinary things for us, and he paid with his life. If I was humiliated trying to represent his father and stepmom, well, that is something I can live with. There is no room for inauthenticity in times of war. But my blood runs cold when I think back on the damage I received in my weakened state of mental health and the black days that followed the engagement.

Darcia Arndt still makes an annual pilgrimage to her husband Ray's graveside. She aims every year for early August because it was the same time as his death on that stretch of Afghan highway leading to Pakistan. Friends and family are always welcome. Nowadays, Darcia hosts an annual Run For Ray event that is well attended by those who knew and loved him. The invitation is widely shared through social media. Suffice it to say that Ray Arndt is well remembered in the Edmonton garrison and the Loyal Edmonton Regiment in particular.

North of Toronto, the tight ring of current and former 32 Service Battalion soldiers gathers for Remembrance Day at the graveside of their fallen comrade Corporal Joshua Wood. The soldiers of 32 Service Battalion understand that Joshua was taken by the war, not a holiday weekend commuter train. His is but one of a number of Reserves suicides that do not factor in to the wider army or VAC statistics. The war took Joshua. Some of the soldiers have joined the Regulars now and are moving up in rank. Occasionally their full-time duties preclude their attendance at Joshua's side on November 11. Regardless of where they are, their thoughts are never far from Joshua on the eleventh hour of the eleventh day of November. Corporal Joshua Wood is always on my mind. His mother, Susan, who was very supportive of telling Joshua's story in this book, passed away unexpectedly in August 2016. Susan died as a result of wounds she received from an automobile accident. I know she still suffered daily from the loss of her son. Looking back on the events of 2011 and the final weeks of Joshua Wood, I can see that only questions remain. This will always be the case. I ask myself often if I could not have done more for Joshua. There are a thousand things I can think of after the fact. I could have checked in more often on his civilian mental health care, I could have rallied harder against the lack of entitlement for military care for him after his overseas contract had expired. His loss raised a cloud in my heart that will never truly dissipate. In the end, all I can do is honour his memory and his abundant gifts. For me the Reserve Force was the safe space where I could escape the velocity of my war and get healthy. Losing this fine Reserve soldier put me into a psychological speed wobble for a long time. I like to think on how Joshua and his mother are together once more in the great beyond. They shall not grow old as we who are left grow old.

EPILOGUE

It has been somewhat of a muddled journey coming to grips with PTSD and depression. All through that horrible period, senior leaders thought I was being arrogant, a prima donna of sorts. Meanwhile, I thought I was worthless. The suffering that could have been avoided for want of a meaningful conversation, if either party had raised their hand, is considerable. You never really know what dragons are being held in check behind the face of another person or what private hell they retreat to at night. When I deployed to Kandahar I was forty-one and very sure of my unit and my abilities. I aspired to retire as a senior colonel or perhaps even a brigadier general in Canada's army. When I came home something was different about me, subtle at first but different. It's not that it is hard to tell your loved ones and friends that in your heart's core, you are not the same. Of course that is hard. This kind of conversation does not generally get started as it has no handles, no means to pick it up. What's more, my own family, my wife and children, were suffering effects in their own ways from our shared experience of the war in Afghanistan. Family suffering is an undiscovered country for our military families. I had no desire to extend their suffering.

As for Veterans Affairs Canada, I am not very tolerant or optimistic. I know first-hand that there are scores of dedicated public servants inside VAC, but there is a bureaucratic rot at the top of that department that consistently escapes scrutiny. I do not have the credentials to stab at this department like the former Veterans Affairs ombudsman Colonel (Retired) Pat Stogran, but I do encourage the many good people inside the organization to push back against their superiors. Canada's treatment of veterans is not exemplary, it is not right, and it has not been right for a very long time. We can do so much better by our nation's soldiers in terms of the federal government's relationship with veterans. The truth behind the current organization of this federal department needs to be laid bare.

"Canada's Afghanistan mission," wrote reporter Renata D'Aliesio in a story titled "The Unremembered" in the *Globe and Mail*, October 31, 2015, "may have officially ended. But in reality it is far from over. The consequences of our nation's longest war are still reverberating through Gagetown and other military communities across the country."

Our wounded veterans cannot move on; they are grounded in their pain, grounded in their own memories. Senses are evocative, and the veteran can never entirely leave that hill, that crossroad, or that market place. A tune on the radio, a movie trailer, or the smell in the supermarket meat department has the power to send you back to 1974, 1992, or 2006. Fixing the situation unfortunately remains mired in partisan politics. The political issue of the day means little to an individual who fights to get though the day without a drink, who is jerked around by their senses and at times betrayed by their own mind. The walking wounded can never entirely move on without our help. In many cases, we have to go back for them.

What is taking us so long?

Somewhere along the way the idea of Canada has become congruent with a bean-counting Treasury Board–driven culture. Inside this culture, government officials and politicians are not even remotely on the same page as the men and women they are abandoning. Veterans are not insurance clients. For many veterans the fight to survive is constant — a struggle every day, to look the part and to appear as outwardly normal as you can for your children, your wife, or your boss. The brave men and women of our armed forces answered the call when we needed them. They embraced unlimited liability and gave their service to Canada without looking back, without any reservations.

Now they need *us*.

Corporal Joshua Wood during his time as a member of 32 Service Battalion in Toronto. Joshua did two tours in Afghanistan before his death by suicide in May 2011.

Corporal Joshua Wood, shown in battle gear, during the work-up training for one of his tours in Afghanistan.

NOTES

INTRODUCTION

1. Similar to those automobiles used at the Canadian Camp Mirage in the United Arab Emirates outfitted with internal governors that prevented the vehicles from going over eighty kilometres per hour. The vehicles were shielded from speeding. Unlike Kandahar, you could not speed in Dubai even if you wanted to. I understand that this aspect of traumatic memory loss is very complex and the focus of a lot of contemporary research.
2. Veterans Affairs Canada, "Post-Traumatic Stress Disorder (PTSD) and War-Related Stress," www.veterans.gc.ca/pdf/mental-health/ptsd_warstress_e.pdf.
3. Logistics has its own uphill battle in the tiny cap-badge–obsessed Canadian Armed Forces, where the interests of individual corps, regiments, and environments (army/navy/air force) often outweigh the interests and needs of the wider enterprise.
4. Bruce Campion-Smith and Allan Woods, "Canadian Casualties Drop in Afghanistan," *Toronto Star*, January 12, 2011.
5. Renata D'Aliesio, "The Unremembered," *Globe and Mail*, October 31, 2015.

6. A second NSE came in with 1 RCR after our tour. It was commanded by Lieutenant Colonel Doug Labrie. Staff-trained in India and widely read, Doug was one of the best logistics officers in the field army of the 1990s. We were lucky to have his experience in Afghanistan during the fall of 2006 and Operation Medusa. Labrie's NSE was expanded by the army as a result of our experiences and lessons from February to August 2006. Over the course of the war, NSE strength would grow to four hundred; all ranks and a contracting capability would also be added to strengthen the capacity of theatre logistics.

7. I remember senior generals complaining to us in Kandahar about using the term "war" in official correspondence in the early days of the 2006 mission. This slowly changed as those at home began to make the acquaintance of the counter-insurgency fight.

8. This sub-par understanding by the Regular Force leads to poor decisions with regard to the handling of the Army Reserve, intentionally or otherwise, by the full-time cadre. It is hard to accept that the two components do not integrate better in 2017 given our scarce resources, our demographic trend in Canada, and the need for heightened civil-military co-operation on the contemporary battlefield. The lack of knowledge of the Reserves becomes particularly harmful when it comes to the medical treatment and follow-up for injured Reservists. This is one area that needs to be improved for keeping track of mental health injuries among our Reserve veterans.

9. D'Aliesio, "The Unremembered."

10. Fred Doucette, *Better Off Dead: Post-Traumatic Stress Disorder and the Canadian Armed Forces* (Halifax: Nimbus, 2015).

11. Civilian workplace coffee break chat, Edmonton, 2012.

CHAPTER 2: REMNANTS

1. DFAC became a word unto itself in Afghanistan. The acronym amounts to a very cumbersome description of a field kitchen. There were a number of these large DFACs on KAF, all of them staffed by KBR. Grits are older than the U.S. Army but have been a deep

component of its operations from the Niagara campaign forward. Grits is essentially cornmeal boiled and heated to be served with just about anything. Our Canadian troops wondered aloud (and often) if we really needed them at "every breakfast." I think we did. Grits, even if not eaten, massages the senses — and there is a host of psychological comfort inside of tradition.

2. KBR was the logistics mother ship on KAF in our time. A lot of the services the Canadian Task Force derived were provided for a fee by KBR. The thousands of men and women who worked for this superbly capable global company were as much a part of the war as any of us.

3. This attack was the earliest double-suicide ambush experienced by Canadian Forces in southern Afghanistan. The matter seems so clinical and clean in the wording of this official document. I believe this to be a cautionary tale for the military historian: war diaries have to be read aloud and slowly to understand their full meaning.

4. I learned a few years after Kandahar from Colonel Tim Bishop, the Brigade's G3 (Operations), that sending Apache gunships to assist with convoy ambush extraction had been put into place as a drill by the Brigade headquarters at some point earlier in the tour. He had overseen the implementation of this drill but he was not in the Brigade TOC on July 22, 2006. I fell in love with that menacing Apache helicopter while I looked up at it along with our enemies. To this day, I keep a small model of the fierce little gunship on my desk at work.

5. The Romanian Battalion originally was assigned security for the inner perimeter at KAF. Later in the tour, Romania was assigned its own PRT responsibility. The battalion used Soviet-era BTR infantry carriers, which — given their use by the Russians in the Soviet-Afghan war of 1979–89 — no doubt turned more than a few Afghan heads.

CHAPTER 3: THE WIDENING GYRE

1. I often wonder if staying in Edmonton with my unit for an additional period might have saved my Regular Force career, as well as the careers of some excellent non-commissioned officers and soldiers.

I have also always wondered about the posting of senior soldiers and officers every three years simply for a change in geography. Some postings are absolutely essential for development of a career path, or to bring someone out of a tougher posting location. Not the whole pack of annual postings, however. Postings are extraordinarily expensive and a large drain on the personnel budget of the Department of National Defence. Frequent posting brings its own challenge to the mental health of a soldier's family.

CHAPTER 4: ANDY'S SONG

1. Master Corporal Andy Singh in an interview with the author, February 2015.
2. This and the following quoted passages in the body of this chapter are the words of Master Corporal Andy Singh in an interview with the author in February 2015.

CHAPTER 5: A FUNERAL FOR TROOPER CASWELL

1. According to *The Norton Anthology of English Literature*, 8th ed., eds. Stephen Greenblatt et al. (New York: W.W. Norton, 2006), "Ozymandias" is the Greek name for the Egyptian pharaoh Ramses II (thirteenth century B.C.), who is said to have erected a huge statue of himself as tribute to a military strength that had created an empire and would survive the march of time. It didn't.
2. I was always more impressed with the names that the Coalition assigned to the major roads through and around Kandahar City. For convenience's sake, they were all named after popular brands of beer: Route Coors, Route Fosters, and so on. The alcoholic ticket names in an Islamic republic furnished boatloads of irony. A small inside joke that never got old.
3. By 2014, the Regular Army had already begun to unstitch itself from the Army Reserve that delivered it during ten long years in Afghanistan,

in terms of meaningful integration and addressing an appropriate role and attendant equipment for the Reserves. It takes money, energy, and imagination to maintain a credible role for the Reserves.

4. D'Aliesio, "The Unremembered."

5. I still receive the quarterly newsletter from my Reserve Service Battalion in Toronto. It shows up dutifully in my Alberta mailbox and brings tidings of the latest details right down to expenditure decisions on the unit's private funds. Regular Force battalions cannot maintain this level of communication/involvement with unit alumni. Regimental-Level Associations do approximate this practice in the Regular Force, but there again the level of detail and involvement offered to alumni in the Reserve community is altogether different.

6. The vehicle Andy described was a sixteen-ton Austrian-designed Stehr truck; it was a beast to look at. Fielded by the army in Calgary in the fall of 1990, it was a massive logistics wagon designed for the Cold War. It's disturbing to think of it crumpled in the counter-insurgency game with the Taliban. The HLVW was not the perfect tool for the job at hand in 2006, but it was what we had.

CHAPTER 6: FORWARD MOMENTUM

1. *Post-Traumatic Stress Disorder (PTSD) and War-Related Stress* (Ottawa: Queen's Printer, 2001), 1.

2. *The Fort St. Joseph Walking Tour*, Environment Canada and the Canadian Parks Service, Supply and Services Canada (1987). If you are interested in the military history of Canada, Great Britain, and the United States and have not been to Fort St. Joseph, you have a wonderful treat to look forward to.

3. Central Area Headquarters was renamed 4 Canadian Division Headquarters in 2014, along with the other large area commands across Canada. The welcome renaming of these large force–generation formations of the Canadian Army was another piece of connective tissue with previous iterations of the army.

4. In an effort to economize on logistics when the Canadian Task Force deployed to Kabul in 2003, the Canadian Armed Forces decided to eliminate the organic logistics company of the infantry (known as Administration Company) and pool its essential elements with the Task Force Logistics Battalion — the 2003 National Support Element. This concept, which came to be known as the Kabul Model, worked well enough in the Kabul Area of Operations, which comprised some four hundred square kilometres. The Kabul Model afforded a hub and spoke logistics concept. Unfortunately, in Kandahar the model was not sufficient with the extended lines of communication of the 2006 Battle Group — some 225,000 square kilometres. Using the Kabul Model in 2006 meant too few logistics soldiers for the tactical supply chain.

CHAPTER 7: THE LONESOME DEATH OF CORPORAL JOSHUA WOOD

1. Paul E. Belliveau and J. Darrach Murray, *To Kill a Battalion* (Charlottetown: self-published, 2010), 187.
2. The time available to the Regular senior officer is tight, and a deep education in the workings and culture of the part-time army demands patience and time. I know because I was one of them.
3. D'Aliesio, "The Unremembered."

CHAPTER 8: THE SUN ALSO RISES

1. This type of true part-time soldiering is called Class A service. It is the most common engagement relationship for the Army Reserve — the standard model of military duty: one evening per week, one weekend per month, and approximately two weeks in the summer for training and field concentrations.
2. Sadly, this widespread disaster was superseded, at least in terms of material loss, by the Fort McMurray wildfire of May–June 2016.

IMAGE CREDITS

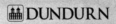